THE PSYCHOPHYSIOLOGY OF MENTAL IMAGERY

Theory, Research and Application

Editors: Robert G. Kunzendorf and Anees A. Sheikh

Imagery and Human Development Series
Series Editor: Anees A. Sheikh

Baywood Publishing Company, Inc.
AMITYVILLE, NY

To our wives

Elizabeth Ritvo and Katharina Sheikh

ISBN Number: 0-89503-062-4 (Paper)
ISBN Number: 0-89503-063-2 (Cloth)

Library of Congress Cataloging-in-Publication Data

The Psychophysiology of mental imagery: theory, research, and
application / editors, Robert G. Kunzendorf and Anees A. Sheikh.
p. cm. – (Imagery and human development series; 3)
Includes bibliographical references.
ISBN 0-89503-063-2. – ISBN 0-89503-062-4 (pbk.)
1. Imagery (Psychology) 2. Mind and body. 3. Psychophysiology.
I. Kunzendorf, Robert G. II. Sheikh, Anees A. III. Series.
BF367.P79 1990
153.3′2–dc20 90-31586
CIP

Table of Contents

Preface

In this day and age of 'dissociation' between physiological psychologists and other psychologists, between cognitive scientists and mentalists, between researchers and practitioners, mental imagery and its psychophysiology pose some intellectually 'sticky' problems—and some promising resolutions—that should bind together differing disciplines within psychology. Whereas physiological psychologists can study learning from a limited neuro*behavioral* standpoint, they must approach imagery from an expanded *psycho*physiological perspective. And whereas cognitive scientists can use computer programs and computer metaphors to model the physiological process of imaging, they must employ more subjective models to capture the mental experience of imaging. Finally, whereas practitioners have no real need for research on such topics as short-term memory, they have much to gain from research on the psychosomatic effects of imaging and on the psychophysiological differences between imaging and hallucinating.

The chapters of this book, both collectively and individually, serve to bridge the growing gap between differing approaches to psychology. The book's first part, emphasizing *theory*, contains two chapters that link together traditional mind-body philosophy and modern psychophysiology: The first chapter explores materialistic foundations for the psychophysiology of conscious imagery; The second explores dualistic foundations. Without a philosophically compelling linkage between mind and brain, empirical relationships between mental imaging and physiological change are likely to be rejected by researchers and neglected by practitioners.

In Part II, which emphasizes *research*, each chapter describes the empirical connection between mental images of a particular type—normal images, creative images, dreams, or hallucinations—and physiological changes originating in the brain. Collectively, the five chapters in this section bring out not only the psychophysiological similarities among various types of imagery, but also some very important differences. In addition, these chapters describe physiological distinctions corresponding to individual differences in imagery and, thereby, provide some of the most compelling evidence yet for the subjective presence and objective efficacy of the mental image.

In Part III, emphasizing *application*, three chapters explore the use of mental imagery in controlling three different psychophysiological reactions–mood-related performance, psychosomatic illness, and immune responsiveness. Backed up by both theory and research, these health-related applications of imaging are gaining wide acceptance among clinical psychologists and health psychologists.

We wish to thank all of our contributors, whose talents, interests and efforts have made this volume possible. Also, we wish to thank Norm Cohen, President of Baywood Publishing Company, for his encouragement and support.

Robert G. Kunzendorf, Ph.D.
Anees A. Sheikh, Ph.D.

PART I

Theories of the Psychophysiological Relation: Dualistic and Materialistic Approaches

CHAPTER 1

Mind-Brain Identity Theory: A Materialistic Foundation for the Psychophysiology of Mental Imagery

ROBERT G. KUNZENDORF

As a materialistic theory of consciousness, mind-brain identity theory provides both a philosophic and a scientific foundation for understanding the relationship between mental imagery's psychological aspects and its physiological aspects. According to identity theory, the mind is a 'bundle' of conscious sensations and sensationless thoughts, which are the *subjective qualities* of objectively distinguishable structures and functions in the nervous system. Following an introduction to mind-brain identity theory, as it defines both the difference between mental and neural events and the identity of such events, the current chapter applies identity theory to the psychophysiology of mental imagery. Specifically, it is proposed that the *sensory qualities of images* are subjective qualities of objectively distinguishable *'structures' in the peripheral nervous system*, and that the *sensationless qualities of images* are subjective qualities of objectively observable *'functions' in the central nervous system.*

THE DIFFERENCE BETWEEN MIND AND BRAIN

For mind-brain identity theorists, defining the difference between a mental event and a physical event is neither easy nor trivial, inasmuch as philosophical psychologists have tended to reduce one event to the other. On one hand, mentalistic psychologists like the introspectionists have focused scientific attention on the *self's* subjectively experienced sensations, and have reduced every physical object (like the brain) to a subset of those 'mental' sensations. On the other hand, materialistic psychologists like the behaviorists have focused scientific attention on the *other organism's* objectively observed responses, and have reduced every mental experience to a privately observed response within the causal chain of 'physical' responses. The difference between *mind* and *brain* emerges, according to identity theory, whenever the *'subjective' perspective* of introspectionism and the *'objective' perspective* of behaviorism are jointly considered. Moreover, as soon as these perspectives are jointly considered, the interdependence of mind and brain becomes apparent, and both the purely introspective study of mind–independent of cerebral matter–and the purely behavioral study of brain–independent of consciousness–become inadequate.

Introspectionism

According to the philosopher David Hume and the psychologist Wilhelm Wundt, introspective knowledge of oneself as conscious sensations is immediate, direct, and positive, whereas knowledge of oneself as brain events is mediated by sensations, is indirect at best, and is reducible to mind. Indeed, the philosopher Hume went so far as to question the existence of all introspectively unconfirmed aspects of the self, including all physical aspects of the self [1]:

> [Our minds and selves] are nothing but a bundle or collection of different perceptions [sensations], which succeed each other with an inconceivable rapidity, and are in a perpetual flux and movement. . . . They are the successive perceptions only, that constitute the mind; nor have we the most distant notion of the place where these scenes are represented, or of the materials of which it is composed [1, p. 60]. I never can catch *myself* at any time without a perception, and never can observe anything but the perception. When my perceptions are removed for any time, as by sound sleep, so long am I insensible of *myself*, and may truly be said not to exist [1, p. 59].

In contrast, the psychologist Wundt introspectively studied the process of inferring physical entities from immediate sensations, while arguing for the primacy and superiority of sensory data over physical inferences [2]. Through such study and argumentation, Wundt convinced the scientific establishment not only that the scientific study of psychological data was possible, but also that the scientific study of psychology was necessary in order to conduct studies of less immediate, physical data [3].

The introspectionism of Wundt and Hume had important implications for the mental image–especially in relation to the percept, which could be introspectively analyzed into immediate sensations but could not be positively attributed to physical stimulation. When Wundt introspectively analyzed similar images and percepts, he found only similar sensations and no introspectively distinguishing characteristics [2, p. 14]:

> The terminology adopted in many Psychologies, according to which the images of memory and fancy are alone designated "ideas," while the direct effects of sense-impression are termed exclusively

> "perceptions," we must judge to be unjustifiable and misleading. It lends colour to the view that there is some essential psychological difference between these two kinds of mental processes, whereas such a difference is nowhere discoverable.

Hume likewise observed that, although perceptual sensations and imaginal sensations usually differ in their degree of vividness, they do not necessarily differ in such a *quantitative* manner and do not otherwise differ in any *qualitative* manner [1]. From the introspective perspective of Hume and Wundt, the psychophysics of perceptual sensations was not possible, much less the psychophysiology of perceptual and imaginal sensations.

Behaviorism

In opposition to introspectionism and its 'subjective' method of studying the self, behaviorism prefers the 'objective' method of studying the other person or the other animal. Indeed, the early behaviorist Meyer referred to methodological behaviorism as the "psychology of the other one" [4]. In such a psychology, scientific knowledge of *the other one* as a physical entity is more direct, more certain, and less inferential than knowledge of *the other one* as a conscious mind.

Going beyond methodological behaviorism, radical behaviorism attempts to apply this "psychology of the other one" to the self and to reduce the self's sensations to physical stimuli. Accordingly, the behavioristic psychologist Skinner has described *the self* as a 'bundle' of objectively known stimuli–not as a bundle of subjectively known sensations, and not as a bundle that can be known both objectively and subjectively [5, pp. 16-17]:

> .... It [radical behaviorism] does not insist upon truth by agreement and can therefore consider events taking place in the private world within the skin. It does not call these events unobservable, and it does not dismiss them as subjective. It simply questions the nature of the object observed and the reliability of the observations.
>
> The position can be stated as follows: what is felt or introspectively observed is not some nonphysical world of consciousness, mind, or mental life but the observer's own body.

This radical assertion that objects of knowledge are always physical stimuli, never mental sensations, has forced the radical behaviorist to argue that *mental* images are not objects of knowledge. For example, the behavioristic philosopher Ryle argues that "imaging occurs, but images are not seen" [6, p. 427]. Similarly, Skinner asserts that imaging "is perceptual *behavior*, [which] does not require a thing seen" [5, pp. 85-86] and that "all that can be seen introspectively is the *act* of seeing, [which] is what [the imager] reports" [5, p. 86].

In making these assertions, Ryle and Skinner revert to the objective perspective of methodological behaviorism, and merely describe *the other's* imageless behavior of "imag*ing*." Ryle and Skinner cannot reduce *the self's* "introspectively observed" *images* to "the observer's own body" because, if they did, they would also have to reduce "introspectively observed" *percepts* to "the observer's own body." And then, the self's bodily mediated *percepts* would not necessarily be distinguishable from similarly mediated *images*, as Ryle noted in denying the sensory nature of images [6, pp. 249-250]:

> Hume notoriously thought that there exist both 'impressions' and 'ideas,' that is, both sensations and images; and he looked in vain for a clear boundary between the two sorts of 'perceptions.' Ideas, he thought, tend to be fainter than impressions. . . . Yet he recognized that impressions can be of any degree of faintness. . . . So, on Hume's showing, simple inspection cannot decide whether a perception is an impression or an idea. Yet the crucial difference remains between what is heard in conversation and what is 'heard' in daydreams. . . . When I fancy I am hearing a very loud noise, I am not really hearing either a loud or a faint noise; I am not having a mild auditory sensation, as I am not having an auditory sensation at all, though I am fancying that I am having an intense one.[1]

Hence, the radical behaviorist denies the existence of mentally imaged sensations, whereas the methodological behaviorist finds no objective evidence for imaged sensations and ignores the subjective evidence. In contrast, the mind-brain identity theorist distinguishes mentally imaged sensations from physically perceived sensations.

Mind-Brain Identity Theory

Mind-brain identity theory recognizes that, from a subjective or 'mental' perspective, *the self* is a "bundle" of sensations–plus a collection of sensationless relationships among those sensations. Also, identity theory recognizes that, from an objective or 'physical' perspective, *the other person* is a bundle of neural and bodily events–plus a collection of functional relationships among those events.

However, mind-brain identity theory takes issue with introspectionism's assumption that, because *the self's* brain is subjectively reducible to its mental experience, *the self's* mind is independent of a brain. If *the self* observes its own brain in a mirror following surgical removal of some skull, introspection informs us that this 'physical' brain is still reducible to a subjectively experienced "bundle" of visual sensations. But if *the self* looks in a mirror following surgical removal of optic nerves as well as skull, psychophysiological research informs us that no "bundle" of visual sensations remains [7]. The *self's* mind is not independent of its brain, in other words.

[1] From *The Concept of Mind* [6], reprinted with permission of the publisher, Harper and Row.

Identity theory also takes issue with behaviorism's assumption that, because *the other person's* conscious mental processes are objectively reducible to his brain and behavior, *the other person's* behavior is independent of consciousness. Psychophysiological research shows not only that *the other person* can control autonomic processes through the behavioral act of *imaging*, but also that *the other person* whose *images* are consciously more vivid sensations can better control his autonomic processes [8].

Thus, from a subjective perspective on psychophysiological research, the mind of *the self* is affected by a subjectively unknown brain and, from an objective perspective on psychophysiological research, the autonomic nerves and bodily responses of *the other* are affected by objectively unknown images. Mind-brain identity theory reconciles these two perspectives, by assuming (1) that *the self* has a physical brain similar to the objectively known brain of *the other* and (2) that *the other* has a conscious mind similar to the subjectively known mind of *the self*.

To the extent that brain and mind exist both in the 'physical' realm of *the other* and in the 'mental' realm of *the self*, the difference between *the 'physical'* and *the 'mental'* should be manifested not only as a difference between realms but also, indirectly, as a difference within each realm or perspective. In this regard, Becker argues that the subjectively known difference between *physical otherness* and *mental selfness* is derived from the subjective difference between *physically stimulated percepts* and *mentally generated images* [9]. Moreover, recent research confirms that the latter difference is manifested not only within the subjective experience of *the self's* mind, but also within the objective response of *the other's* brain.

First, within subjective experience, a qualitative difference between *percepts* and *images* is apparent, when that experience is subjected to phenomenological analysis rather than introspective examination. As noted earlier in this chapter, Hume's [1] and Wundt's [2] introspective examinations of their own sensations showed that *perceived sensations* are not qualitatively different from *imaged sensations*. Going beyond introspected sensations, however, Sartre's phenomenological analysis showed that the sensationless thoughts accompanying *perceived sensations* are immediately and qualitatively different from the sensationless thoughts accompanying *imaged sensations* [10, p. 3]:

> There have been psychologists, no doubt, who maintained that a vivid image could not be distinguished from a faint perception. Titchener [one of Wundt's students] even cites some experiments in support of this view. But we shall see further on that such claims rest on an error. In fact, the confusion is impossible; what has come to be known as an "image" occurs immediately as such to reflection.

Based on further phenemonological analysis and some experimental testing, Kunzendorf showed that a particular reflection—the sensationless thought *that one is making an 'effort' to image one's sensations*—accompanies those sensations so long as the mind is wakeful [11]. More specifically, in accord with Kunzendorf's phenomenological analysis that a greater amount of sensationless 'effort' accompanies more vividly imaged sensations, Kunzendorf experimentally found that wakeful subjects discriminate percepts more quickly from vivid images than from faint images. This finding refutes Hume's and Wundt's claim that percepts and vivid images are not subjectively distinguishable. In Kunzendorf's experiment, Hume's and Wundt's claim was true only for deeply hypnotized subjects, who discriminated hypnotic percepts less quickly from vivid hypnotic hallucinations than from faint hypnotic hallucinations.

Second, within the objective response of the brain, a qualitative difference between *imaged sensations* and *perceived sensations* is also apparent, along with many neurophysiological similarities between these sensations. This difference will be fully described in this chapter's final section on "the sensationless qualities of images." In brief, Kunzendorf and Hoyle found that, although percepts and vivid images exhibit identical effects in the early *sensory components* of their evoked potentials, only images evoke a late *cognitive component* that seems to neurally monitor the 'effort' of imaging sensations [12].

Given that both the mind and the brain distinguish between *the mental* and *the physical*, between the mentally generated *image* and the physically stimulated *percept*, questions arise as to the relationship between the mind as subjective experience and the brain as physical object. Mind-brain identity theory asserts that the subjectively known mind and the objectively known brain are metaphysically identical to each other, even though they are epistemologically different from one another.

THE IDENTITY OF MIND AND BRAIN

Prior to the development of mind-brain identity theory, dualistic theories treated the brain as a physical 'object of consciousness' and the mind as a *nonphysical 'subject of consciousness'*—henceforth referred to as an *homunculus*. One dualistic theory, interactionism, assumed that bodily responses could be caused either by the brain or by the homunculus. Another dualistic theory, epiphenomenalism, assumed that bodily responses could be caused only by the brain. Opposed to both versions of dualism, mind-brain identity theory rejects their metaphysical distinction between subject and object. According to identity theory, *the mind is a 'bundle' of conscious sensations and sensationless thoughts, which are the subjective qualities of objectively distinguishable neural structures and neural functions*. The metaphysical identity of certain brain events and certain conscious qualities implies that both those brain events and those conscious qualities are *necessary causes* of any bodily responses. That is, contrary to the assumptions of interactionism, consciousness alone is not sufficient to cause a bodily response, and contrary to the assumptions of epiphenomenalism, brain alone is not sufficient to cause all bodily responses. This implication of mind-brain identity theory, albeit metaphysical, is fundamental to the psychophysiology of mental imagery, and is presently developed through a critical comparison of dualistic theories and identity theory.

Dualism: Interactionism and Epiphenomenalism

In postulating the duality of mind and brain, both interactionism and epiphenomenalism reject introspectionism's assertions that the mind *is* a bundle of sensations and that the brain can be experienced only as a subset of those sensations and not as a physical object. Instead, these dualistic theories assert that a physical brain is an 'object of consciousness,' that an immaterial mind or homunculus is the self-conscious 'subject of consciousness,' and that "the subject of which we are conscious is a subject which in some sense *has*, not *is*, its different experiences" [13, p. 81]. The dualist Popper is most explicit about this [14, p. 488]:

> One might be tempted, under the indirect influence of Hume, to think of the self as the sum total of its experiences. But it seems to me that this theory is directly refuted by the memory experiences to which I have referred. At the actual moment at which the memory delivers something to us, neither the delivering memory nor the object that it delivers to us is part of our selves; rather, they are outside of our selves, and we look at them as spectators.

One problem with this dualistic definition of mind—as the self-conscious 'subject of consciousness'—is that such a definition does not account for the difference between wakeful imaging and unself-conscious dreaming. According to dualism, the homunculus self-consciously *looks at* all 'objects of consciousness,' including all dreamed objects, and "in some sense *has*" them. But subjectively, the dreamer is not self-conscious *that he is 'having' a dream* [15-18]. And later, as an objective consequence, he is unable memorially to discriminate his own dreams from other people's dreams (which he also did not 'have') [19].

Unlike dualism, mind-brain identity theory readily accounts for the difference between a wakeful image of blue sky and an unself-conscious dream of blue sky. Identity theory, which will soon be developed in detail, maintains that the sensation of blueness and the tacit self-awareness of '*having* such a sensation' are subjectively independent qualities of different brain states [17-18]. Thus, the mind of the self-conscious imager *is* both the activated set of brain states with a subjective quality of blueness and the activated set of brain states with a sensationless quality of self-consciousness. In contrast, the mind of the unself-conscious dreamer *is* simply the activated set of brain states with a sensory quality of blueness.

Even though dualism's description of how *the brain* affects *the mind* provides an inadequate account of the dream image, dualistic descriptions of how *the mind* affects *the brain* have important implications for imagery and its psychophysiology. Indeed, both interactionism and epiphenomenalism offer important, yet different, accounts of the mind's effect on the brain. Interactionism maintains that the homunculus, being a self-willed 'agent' as well as a self-conscious 'subject,' is *sufficient* to cause physical responses in the brain. At the same time, interactionism acknowledges that physical events within the brain are also *sufficient* to cause brain responses.

Unlike interactionism, epiphenomenalism maintains that the homunculus is only a self-conscious 'subject' and is *not sufficient* to cause brain responses. Accordingly, epiphenomenalism implies that antecedent brain events are *necessary and sufficient* to cause all brain responses. Moreover, given this implication, some materialists have uncritically adopted an epiphenomenalist approach to mental imagery. For example, in defending the materialistic proposition that human cognition is essentially like computer cognition, Pylyshyn asserts that the human being's "experience of imaging has no causal role" and is merely an epiphenomenon of computer-like neural processes [20, p. 22]. But as Creel points out, if the conscious experience of imaging cannot be a cause of bodily responses, then the conscious experience must not be physical at all [21].

These dualistic implications of Pylyshyn's epiphenomenalist argument are repudiated by mind-brain identity theory. According to identity theory, both the conscious experience of imaging and the neural process of imaging are *necessary* to cause particular bodily responses, because neither the imaging experience nor the imaging process can exist without the other.

Materialism: Mind-Brain Identity Theory

According to the most general version of mind-brain identity theory [22-24], the mind is a 'bundle' of *conscious sensations* and *sensationless thoughts,* which are the *subjective qualities* of objectively observable events in the nervous system. Thus, inside of the human brain, there is no immaterial *subject*, no homunculus who is "conscious of" sensory *objects*. There is never any "consciousness of" anything else. Rather, each conscious sensation is the subjective quality of a particular set of nerves in their excited state, and the entire 'stream of consciousness' in the mind changes as the whole pattern of excitation in the nervous system changes. Hence, I am not "conscious of" my sensations; I am my sensations, from a 'subjective' standpoint, and I am my nervous system, from an 'objective' standpoint.

Moreover, according to the specific version of identity theory suggested by Block [25] and adopted in this chapter, conscious sensations are the *inherent qualities* of objectively distinguishable *neural structures*, and sensationless thoughts are the *emergent qualities* of objectively observable *neural functions*. Thus, contrary to the assumptions of *functional state identity theory* [26, 27], particular sensations do not emerge from particular brain functions. Only "propositional attitudes" [25, p. 288] and sensationless meanings emerge from neural functions or schemata.

One reason for supposing that conscious sensations are the *inherent qualities of structural states*, rather than the *emergent qualities of functional states*, is that the concept of *emergent sensations* transcends physical principles. According to Sperry's functionalist version of identity theory [26], every sensory quality 'emerges' from a functionally identifiable combination of unconscious brain states–just as liquid water 'emerges' from the combination of two gaseous elements, hydrogen and oxygen, and just as magnetic fields 'emerge' from the interaction of certain metallic substances. But as the Gestalt psychologist and field theorist Kohler notes, the emergence of liquid *quantities* and the emergence of magnetic *quantities* reflect physical laws, whereas the emergence of sensory *qualities* transcends such laws [28]. That is, *quantities* of liquid water can physically 'emerge' only because water molecules have greater numbers of chemical bonds and (hence) higher boiling points than uncombined elements of hydrogen or oxygen have. Likewise, *quantities* of magnetic force can physically 'emerge' within a given field only because sufficient numbers of electrons are exchanged across that field. However, a particular *sensory quality* cannot magically 'emerge' within a brain–or a computer or any other physical entity–just because physical states have been combined to perform a particular sensory function. All that can consciously 'emerge' from any neural function or sensory-motor schema is the schema's meaning: that is, its tacit relationship to antecedent and consequent sensations.

The other reason for supposing that conscious sensations are the *inherent qualities of neural structures* is that the *emergent qualities of neural functions* have no causal efficacy. For example, according to Putnam's functionalist version of identity theory [27], the causal efficacy of the mental phenomenon *pain* is due only to the underlying neural function and not to any *painful quality* per se:

> We *can* specify the functional state with which we propose to identify pain. . . . [as a] state of receiving sensory inputs which play a certain role in the Functional Organization of the organism. This role is characterized, at least partially, by the fact that the sense organs responsible for the inputs in question are organs whose function is to detect damage to the body, or dangerous extremes of temperature, pressure, etc., and by the fact that the "inputs" themselves, whatever their physical realization, represent a condition that the organism assigns a high disvalue to. . . . This does *not* mean that the Machine will always *avoid* being in the condition in question ("pain"); it only means that the condition will be avoided unless not avoiding it is necessary to the attainment of some more highly valued goal.[2]

[2] From Art, Mind, and Religion [27, p. 46], reprinted by permission of the publisher University of Pittsburgh Press.

According to the structuralist version of identity theory, however, a machine with damage-detecting, damage-disvaluing, and damage-avoiding functions could not have painful sensations, *unless the machine's architecture embodied neural structures with painful qualities*. Conversely, a brain could embody neural structures with *pain*ful qualities, *even if it had no damage-disvaluing and damage-avoiding functions*. Moreover, a brain with *pain*ful qualities but without *pain*-avoiding functions would be 'subjectively reinforced' if it randomly innervated *pain*-avoiding behaviors and thereby evolved *pain*-avoiding functions, as the identity theorist Matson has noted [29]. In contrast, a machine lacking neural states with *pain*ful qualities would never be 'motivated' to develop any damage-avoiding functions that the machine was not preprogrammed to develop.

Thus, according to the present version of mind-brain identity theory, sensations like 'pain' are sometimes *necessary* to cause bodily responses. The objective neural structures that are identical with those subjective sensations are also *necessary* to cause such responses. But as the above discussion shows, without subjective qualities, objective neural structures would not always be *sufficient* to cause certain behaviors. Only when objective brain structures and their subjective qualities are taken together is their a *sufficient cause* of every behavior.

In this regard, the subjective ability to image vivid sensations and the objective ability to control underlying neural states, taken together, are a sufficient cause of the ability to control certain autonomic nerves and certain somatic nerves. Research on autonomic control indicates that better imagers have better control of heart rate [30, 31], neuroimmune activation [32, 33], vasodilation [34], and electrodermal activity [35, 36]. Similarly, research on somatic control indicates that better imagers are more skillful and more competitive as skiers [37], as gymnasts [38, 39], and as racquetball players [40]. According to identity theory [8], better imagers are more proficient at innervating neural locations with *sensory qualities* and, therefore, are more proficient at controlling autonomic and somatic nerves that are innervated in the same location or in the same manner. As the next section of this chapter shows, one of the main tasks confronting identity theorists at present is to identify the particular neural states that possess the sensory qualities of images.

THE SENSORY QUALITIES OF IMAGES

The thesis presently to be developed and defended is that particular sensations, both imaginal and perceptual, are the subjective qualities of particular *structures in the peripheral nervous system (PNS)*. Prior to consideration of this thesis, especially as it compares with attempts to identify sensations with *structures in the central nervous system (CNS)*, *sensory qualities* must be distinguished from *sensationless qualities*.

The *sensory qualities* that have been studied in recent research on imaged sensations include the *redness* of visually imaged sensations [41, 42], the *tonality* of auditorily imaged sensations [12], and the *'raw feel'* of tactually imaged sensations [24, 34]. In contrast, the "tacit" qualities [43, 44] or *sensationless qualities* that have been studied in recent imagery research include the tacitly known *size* of an imagined object of vision [45, 46], the tacitly known *location* of an imagined source of sound [47, 48], and the tacitly known *unreality* of an imagined object of touch [24]. The current section of this chapter discusses scientific attempts to identify *redness, tonality*, and *raw feels* with particular neural structures—central structures and peripheral structures.

The Identification of Sensory Qualities with CNS Structures

As the mind-brain identity theorist Pepper notes [49], scientists ought to be able to look at an exposed brain and to distinguish those brain states with sensory qualities from those with sensationless qualities, those brain states with visual sensations from those with auditory sensations, those brain states with the subjective quality of redness from those with the subjective quality of greenness. Although exposed brain structures with the subjective quality of redness need not reflect 650-nanometer light waves and, therefore, need not produce a red quality in the brain of the scientist objectively observing the exposed brain, some structural characteristic unique to brain states with the subjective quality of redness ought to be objectively discernible by the scientist.

However, as critics of identity theory point out, the central states of the brain cannot be structurally differentiated from one another, much less structurally identified with particular sensory qualities. The functionalist Sperry points this out, in his critique of 'central state' identity theory [26, p. 166].

> I was unable to find in . . . identity theory anything to distinguish the conscious from the many unconscious properties that seem to comprise the subsystems of any given neural event, nor did I find a distinction between neural events that involve consciousness and those that lack consciousness, as in the cerebellum or spinal cord.

The interactionist Burt [50] makes the same point in his criticism of identity theory [50, pp. 65-66]:

> We have now briefly reviewed what is known about the physical structure, chemical composition, and various activities of the cell body, the cell fibre, and the cell junction. In each of them and in all three respects there are, as Eccles has repeatedly emphasized, no essential differences between the parts of the nervous system which, like the spinal cord, are invariably unconscious and those which, like the cortex, are at times accompanied by consciousness. Accordingly, *it would seem impossible to suppose*, as so many physiologists used to do when all this was still wrapped in mystery, *that these very ordinary chemical processes can 'generate' anything like conscious experience.*

Implicit in Sperry's and Burt's critiques is the assumption that sensations reflect *something* cortical–if not cortical *structures*, then cortical *functions* or cortical *interactions*. Moreover, such an assumption would appear to be justified by empirical evidence that damage to the visual cortex and damage to the auditory cortex are correlated, respectively, with visual deficits and auditory deficits. Indeed, it is through such correlations, and not through any structurally unique cells in either cortex, that scientists distinguish visual cortex from auditory cortex. However, these empirical correlations do not necessarily justify the assumption that conscious sensations involve cortex, for two reasons.

First, as Luria has argued [51, p. 11], "the disturbance of a psychological activity by a local brain lesion does not necessarily mean that the corresponding 'function' is localized in the destroyed area." In accord with Luria's argument, research by Denny-Brown revealed that visually guided placing, lost after ablation of the post-central gyrus in one hemisphere, returned after ablation of the post-central gyrus in the other hemisphere [52]. Similarly, research by Woolsey and Bard revealed that proprioceptive placing, lost after removal of one parietal cortex, returned after removal of the other [53]. Thus, any disturbance of visual sensations by a cortical lesion would justify the conclusion that such a lesion *interfered* with those sensations, but not the conclusion that such a lesion *destroyed* brain states with visual *qualities*.

Second, it is possible that most lesions in the visual cortex do not interfere with visual sensations anyway, but instead interfere with the tacit self-awareness *that one is 'seing' one's visual sensations*. Certainly, this possibility is consistent with Weiskrantz's description of a man who, following a lesion in his right calcarine fissure, experienced left-hemifield 'blindness' [7, p. 441]:

> We asked him to respond . . . by reaching out and touching a screen on which visual stimuli were projected in his blind field. This, at first, was a very odd task–how can you reach out for something you cannot see? Nevertheless it quickly became apparent to us that his ability was remarkable and, even when eventually his own results were shown to him at the end of several hours of testing, he was openly astonished. He thought he was just guessing. Later he described 'feelings' that there might be something there, but he consistently refused to call this 'seeing.' We went on to require him to 'guess' the orientation of lines–whether horizontal or vertical, or vertical or diagonal–and again his performance was remarkable. We also showed that he could carry out simple form discriminations, if required to guess between two alternatives. . . . And never would he acknowledge seeing, although he was very quick to acknowledge this the moment even a faint stimulus appeared on the intact edge of the good field.

Poppel, Held, and Frost describe a similar 'cortically blind' subject, who sees moving test stimuli but who has no self-awareness *that he sees them* [54].

The possibility that all subjective qualities of cortical states are 'sensationless qualities,' like the tacit self-awareness *that one is seeing* or *that one is imaging*, is considered in the last section of this chapter. The remainder of this section considers the possibility that all 'sensory qualities' are subjective qualities of peripheral states: that visual sensations are subjective qualities of retinal states, that auditory sensations are subjective qualities of cochlear states, and so on.

The Identification of Sensory Qualities with PNS Structures

As noted above, neurons in the central nervous system—in the visual cortex, the auditory cortex, the olfactory cortex (the prepyriform cortex), and the somatic sensory cortex—are structurally indistinguishable. In contrast, neurons in the peripheral nervous system—in the retina, the cochlea, the olfactory bulb, and the corpuscular system—are structurally distinguishable across sensory modalities and structurally variable within each modality. Thus, according to mind-brain identity theory, particular sensations could be the subjective qualities of particular structures in the peripheral nervous system. For example, visual sensations could be the subjective qualities of innervated retinal structures, which are objectively distinguishable from cochlear structures, and colorful sensations could be the subjective qualities of innervated cones, which are objectively distinguishable from rods. Moreover, if *sensations* should indeed be *qualities* of the sensory transmitters, then imaged *sensations* must be centrifugally innervated *qualities* of those transmitters.

Evidence supporting the thesis that imaged sensations are centrifugally innervated qualities of the sensory transmitters is presently considered. From an anatomical perspective, this thesis presumes that corticofugal pathways to the transmitters exist. Such a presumption is supported by a large amount of anatomical and physiological evidence. The evidence for centrifugally conducting neurons in the optic nerve, the auditory nerve, the somatic sensory tracts, and the olfactory tract is reviewed, respectively, by Reperant, Vesselkin, Rio, Ermakova, Miceli, Peyrichoux, and Weidner [55], Klinke and Galley [56], Angel [57], and Broadwell and Jacobowitz [58]. Also, the evidence for efferent sympathetic nerves to the retina, the cochlea, the cutaneous receptors, and the taste buds is reviewed by Van Hasselt [59], Ross [60], Akoev [61], and Takeda [62].

The specific proposition that *retinal structures* are centrifugally innervated during *visually imaged sensations*, most notably during vividly imaged sensations, is supported by both the earliest studies of visual imagery and the latest studies of its psychophysiology. At the beginning of the nineteenth century, Darwin [63] and Gruithuisen [64] observed that a negative after-image follows a vivid image, just as it follows a visual percept. Moreover, Gruithuisen observed that the after-image of a vivid visual image—like the demonstratively *retinal* after-image of a visual percept [65-67]—maintains a *fixed location on the retina* as the eye moves. More than 100 years later, Weiskrantz [68] and Oswald [69] confirmed that the after-image of a vivid visual image also maintains a *fixed size on the retina*—the 'apparent size' of which obeys Emmerts Law and seems larger as the background for the retinal image recedes. Following up this latter effect, Kunzendorf found that imaginally induced after-images of *fixed retinal size* are experienced by only 5 percent of the college population, but by 40 percent of the elementary school population [42].

Like these behavioral studies of image-induced after-images, psychophysiological studies also show that retinal structures are centrifugally innervated during vivid visual imaging. In a study of drug-induced imagery, Krill, Wieland, and Ostfeld observed significant changes in the electroretinograms (ERGs) of human subjects who experienced hallucinatory images and no change in the retinal activity of control subjects who received either nonhallucinogenic doses or nonhallucinogenic analogues of two drugs [70]. Similarly, in a study of hallucinatory imagery in a suggestible schizophrenic with electrode implants, Guerrero-Figueroa and Heath observed larger and then smaller evoked potentials in the optic tract [71], when the evoking light was hallucinated to be brighter and then dimmer. In Pavlovian research on visual conditioning in humans, Freedman and Ronchi [72] and Bogoslovskii and Semenovskaya [73] obtained increases in both the subjective brightness and the ERG amplitude of a dim light, when the light was accompanied by a conditioned stimulus that had previously been paired with a bright light. In operant research on visual conditioning, Roger and Galand found that human subjects could voluntarily augment peripherally generated components of the visual evoked potential (VEP), and reported that most successful augmenters "associated the [evoking] flash with complex imagined sights such as bomb explosions" [74, p. 481]. Finally, in a study of color imagery in eidetic imagers and control subjects, Kunzendorf [41] obtained 1) unimodal ERGs when the eidetic and control subjects viewed green flashes, 2) bimodal ERGs when the eidetic and control subjects viewed red flashes, 3) unimodal ERGs when the eidetic subjects imagined that red flashes were vivid green flashes, and 4) bimodal ERGs when the eidetic subjects imagined that green flashes were vivid red flashes. Such evidence strongly suggests that visual sensations are the subjective qualities of retinal structures.

Going beyond the psychophysiology of visually imaged sensations, one recent study suggests that olfactively imaged sensations are centrifugally innervated qualities of the olfactory bulb. In a study of olfactory evoked potentials (OEPs) in animals, Freeman found that the olfactory-bulb OEP exhibits a particular "spatial pattern of bulbar activity" not only when a particular odor occurs, but also when a search image for the odor occurs [75].

In addition, some recent studies with humans suggest that auditorily imaged sensations are centrifugally innervated qualities of the cochlea. In a study of auditory evoked potentials (AEPs) in eidetic imagers, Kunzendorf and Hoyle found that the brain-stem AEP becomes larger and then smaller not only when the evoking tone is actually perceived to be louder and then softer, but also when the evoking tone is vividly imaged to be louder and then softer [12]. In hypnosis research on auditory hallucinating, Deehan and Robertson [76] reported that the AEP was abolished completely when negative hallucinations were hypnotically suggested [76].[3]

Thus, the available evidence suggests that different sensations are the subjective qualities of different neural states—not the structurally undifferentiated states of the central nervous system, but the structurally differentiated states of the peripheral nervous system. Accordingly, the mind-brain identity theorist can account for sensations, in general, and imaged sensations, in particular, by identifying sensory qualities with sensory transmitters.

The Function of Sensory Imaging and Perceiving

The psychophysiological identification of sensory qualities with sensory transmitters also enables the identity theorist to establish the causal efficacy of perceived sensations, and to define the function of imaged sensations. In order to establish the causal efficacy of perceived sensations, the identity theorist must resolve the conundrum of *the inverted spectrum*, which has been summarized by Fodor [83, p. 122]:

> It seems possible to imagine two observers who are alike in all relevant psychological respects except that experiences having the qualitative content of red for one observer would have the qualitative content of green for the other observer. Nothing about their behavior need reveal the difference because both of them see ripe tomatoes and flaming sunsets as being similar in color and both of them call that color "red." Moreover, the causal connection between their (qualitatively distinct) experiences and their other mental states could also be identical. Perhaps they both think of Little Red Riding Hood when they see ripe tomatoes, feel depressed when they see the color green and so on. It seems as if anything that could be packed into the notion of the causal role of their experiences could be shared by them, and yet the qualitative content of the experiences could be as different as you like.[4]

[3] Also, in auditory research on *attending* (which has historically been defined as *anticipatory imaging* [77]), attentional enhancement of brain-stem AEP components has been obtained in some subjects [78, 79] but not all subjects [80-82]. It remains for future research to determine whether the subjects who exhibit peripheral effects of auditory 'attention' are subjects who experience vivid 'anticipatory imagery'.

[4] From "The Mind-Body Problem", reprinted with permission of the publisher, Scientific American, Inc.

However, red and green qualities can be inverted only if they are qualities of cortical neurons, and not if they are qualities of the sensory transmitters themselves. If redness and greenness are qualities of cortical neurons, then 'subjectively red' and 'subjectively green' neurons can be switched without disrupting the causal chain of neural events and behavioral outcomes. But if redness is the subjective quality of retinal hardware responsive to 650 nanometer light-waves, and if greenness is the subjective quality of retinal hardware responsive to 500 nanometer light-waves, then red and green qualities cannot be inverted—because particular qualities of color are subjectively *necessary* to cause retinal responses to particular light-waves.

The question remains as to the utility of imaging visual sensations like redness and greenness, lightness and darkness, circularity and ellipticity, and so on—especially if visual sensations are retinal qualities. One possible answer, consistent with the available evidence, is that the imaging of visual sensations serves to develop *perceptual skills*— and contrary to popular belief, does not serve to enhance *visual memory*. In the latter regard, several reviews of empirical studies indicate that people with vivid sensory images do not remember more accurately, but merely *construct* more vivid images from their sensationless memory traces [84-86]. However, several empirical studies indicate that people with vivid visual images do discriminate visual differences more accurately and more quickly [87-89], and that they do exhibit greater mastery of visual rules like the rules of linear perspective [86, 90-91]. In addition, several developmental studies indicate that, after childhood, most people lose the ability to construct sensory images [92-95], including the ability to construct visual images that induce retinal after-images obeying Emmerts Law [42]. Perhaps then, the corticofugal construction of percept-like images on the retina allows young children to develop and test *optical rules for abstracting visual percepts from retinal sensations*—just as the construction of phonemic utterances (babbling) allows young children to develop and test *grammatical rules for abstracting phonemic percepts from auditory sensations* [96-98].

Moreover, to the extent that centrifugal control of a sensory transmitter like the retina facilitates centrifugal control in general, good imagers should have better centrifugal control of both their autonomic nerves and their somatic nerves. As noted before, research on autonomic control confirms that good imagers have better centrifugal control of heart rate [30, 31], neuroimmune activation [32, 33], vasodilation [34], and electrodermal activity [35, 36], and research on somatic control confirms that good imagers have better centrifugal control of athletic movements [37-40] and theatrical behaviors [99]. In addition, developmental research indicates that younger people, who have better imaginal control of retinal sensations [42], also have better corticofugal control of heart rate [100] and vasodilation [101]. Centrifugally innervated sensations, however, are not the only qualities that constitute a mental image.

THE SENSATIONLESS QUALITIES OF IMAGES

In the preceding section of this chapter, PNS structures were identified with the sensory qualities of images and percepts. In this final section, CNS functions are identified with the *sensationless qualities* of images and percepts—in particular, with the *sensationless quality of self-consciousness*, the *tacit quality of location*, and the *tacit quality of size constancy*. Taken together, these two sections imply that the image is first represented centrally as *sensationless qualities* and later represented peripherally as *sensory qualities*, whereas the percept is first represented peripherally as *sensory qualities* and later represented centrally as *sensationless qualities*. In light of this difference between images and percepts, behavioral studies comparing images and percepts tend to be misleading, and imagery theories based on such studies tend to be specious.

Self-Conscious Qualities

As noted earlier in this chapter, one's sensations are usually accompanied by the tacit self-awareness *that one is 'having' them*. However, according to mind-brain identity theory, there is no such thing as an homunculus who 'has' sensations or an immaterial *subject* who is 'conscious of' sensory *objects*. Rather, according to the identity theorist Kunzendorf, one's sensations are the sensory qualities of certain nerves (peripheral nerves), and the self-awareness *that one is 'having' sensations* is an independent tacit quality of different nerves (left-hemisphere nerves) [12, 18]. Thus, consciousness can consist of imaged sensations, plus self-consciousness *that one is 'having' those sensations*—as in most wakeful images. Alternatively, consciousness can consist just of imaged sensations, with no self-consciousness *that one is 'having' them*—as in most dream images [19].

Furthermore, according to Kunzendorf [11, 18, 102], self-consciousness is not only the general tacit quality *that one is experiencing sensations*, but also the specific sensationless quality *that one is imaging them* or *that one is perceiving them*. Thus, self-consciousness is the subjective quality of a CNS function that monitors whether sensations are centrally innervated (imaged) or peripherally innervated (perceived). As such, self-consciousness is a subjectively useful quality that serves to distinguish waking images from waking percepts. However, whenever the brain's image-monitoring *functions* and their self-conscious *qualities* are attenuated, as in hypnotic trances and other sleep-like states, self-conscious images become 'unmonitored' hallucinations, and self-conscious percepts become 'unmonitored' or 'subconscious' sensations.

Two recent studies confirm that the waking brain of the self-conscious person monitors *imaged sensations* and immediately distinguishes them from perceptually similar sensations, whereas the hypnotized person's brain does no such monitoring. In the first study [11], self-conscious (wakeful) subjects discriminated visually perceived sensations more quickly from vividly imaged sensations than from faintly imaged sensations—consistent with the assumption that more 'central innervation of sensations' is monitored during more vivid imaging. But under deep hypnosis, the same subjects discriminated visually perceived sensations more quickly from faintly imaged sensations than from vividly imaged sensations—consistent with the corollary assumption that hypnotically hallucinated sensations are '*un*monitored' and are *un*accompanied by any self-awareness *that one is imaging them*. In the second study [12], a study of auditory evoked potentials (AEPs), the brain's monitoring of the central innervation of images was evidenced during wakeful self-consciousness but not during deep hypnosis. That is, 450 to 600 milliseconds after subjects in a 'monitored' state of wakefulness began to image an evoking tone as louder or softer, their AEPs exhibited a significantly larger, negatively charged wave in the left hemisphere. However, 450 to 600 milliseconds after subjects in an 'unmonitored' state of hypnosis began to hallucinate the evoking tone as louder or softer, their left-hemisphere AEPs exhibited no change in waveform. (Nevertheless, the imaging *and* hallucinating of louder tones produced larger *sensory components* in the first 50 milliseconds of the AEP, when the underlying innervation ascends from the cochlea to the cortex. Similarly, the imaging *and* hallucinating of softer tones produced smaller *sensory components*—just as the perceiving of softer tones does.) Moreover, in psychophysiological research related to this second study, the attenuation of left-hemisphere functions has also been documented during schizophrenic hallucinating [103-106] and during unself-conscious dreaming [107].

Two other studies confirm that subconsciously perceived sensations, like hallucinated sensations, are accompanied neither by left-hemisphere monitoring nor by self-consciousness. One of these studies showed that, when 'split brain' patients simultaneously process both a left-hemisphere stimulus and a right-hemisphere stimulus, they self-consciously know *that they are perceiving the left-hemisphere stimulus* whereas they 'subconsciously' perceive the right-hemisphere stimulus [108]. The second study showed that, when subjects 'subconsciously' perceive stimuli, they are not self-conscious *that they are perceiving (or imaging) such stimuli* [102]. As a result, the subjects in this latter study could discriminate self-consciously perceived stimuli from self-consciously imaged stimuli *but not from 'subconsciously' perceived stimuli*, and they could discriminate self-consciously imaged stimuli from self-consciously perceived stimuli *but not from 'subconsciously' perceived stimuli*.

Unlike subconsciously perceived sensations and hypnotically hallucinated sensations, normal sensations are accompanied either by the tacit self-awareness *that one is perceiving them* or by the tacit self-awareness *that one is imaging them*. Given the above findings, such tacit self-awareness appears to be a subjective quality of neural functions in the left hemisphere.

Locative Qualities

The interactionist Shaffer asserts that, if a sensory event and a neural event are truly identical, then we should experience them in identical locations [109]. But in fact, we feel our tactile sensations *on our bodies* not *in our nerves*. According to mind-brain identity theory, this is because bodily location is one of our tacit *locative qualities* and because nerve location is not one of them. Indeed, according to the argument advanced in this subsection, if there were no CNS functions with locative qualities, then sensations would be phenomenally associated neither with bodily locations nor with spatial locations.

Two lines of research indicate that sensory qualities are both phenomenally independent and neurally separate from locative qualities. In tactual research on the sensationless qualities of *bodily location*, Bender [110] and Gerstmann [111] noted that cortical lesions cause both "allochiria," the tendency to mislocate tactile sensations on the opposite side of the body, and "allesthesia," the inability to locate tactile sensations. (Cronholm noted that cortical lesions of the latter type eliminate the amputee's tendency to mislocate tactile sensations in a 'phantom limb' [112]. From the standpoint of this chapter, the *'hand location' qualities* of a 'phantom hand' are the sensationless qualities of the cortex's 'body scheme,' and the *tactual qualities* of a 'phantom hand' are the sensory qualities of the stump's cutaneous receptors. Indeed, Cronholm noted further that the tactile sensations of a phantom limb can be extinguished by anesthetizing the stump or elicited by pricking the unanesthetized stump.)

In visual research on the tacit qualities of *spatial location*, Skavenski, Haddad, and Steinman found that, when the eye is voluntarily held at a fixed position and simultaneously loaded with weights on the right side, visual sensations are phenomenally associated with *spatial locations* to the left of their retinal locations [113]. Presumably, the efferent CNS schema that counterbalances the rightward pull of the weights has a *sinistral quality* or *leftward 'meaning'* relative to other spatial schemata.

As applied to imagery, the *tacit qualities of location* may serve both to distinguish eidetic images from normal images and to link normal images to the emotions. Although researchers dispute whether eidetic imagery is more vivid than normal imagery [12, 41, 42, 68, 69, 92] or whether it is not necessarily more vivid [84, 114], they agree that eidetic imagery is phenomenally represented 'out in the world' rather than 'inside the body.' Accordingly, in the visual modality, the sensory qualities of eidetic images are accompanied by *tacit qualities of spatial location 'in the visible world,'* whereas the sensory qualities of normal images are accompanied by *tacit qualities of bodily location 'inside the head.'* In the auditory modality, the sensory qualities of eidetic images (and eidetic hallucinations [115]) are accompanied by *tacit qualities of spatial location 'in the sonorous world,'* whereas the sensory qualities of other images (and other hallucinations [115]) are accompanied by *tacit qualities of bodily location 'inside the head.'* In the tactual modality, the sensory qualities of eidetic images are accompanied by *tacit qualities of spatial location 'on the skin,'* whereas the sensory qualities of normal images are accompanied by *tacit qualities of location 'inside the body.'* Moreover, inasmuch as the *sensory qualities of emotions* are also accompanied by tacit qualities of location 'inside the body' (in the heart, in the stomach muscles, in the facial muscles, etc. [116-119]), emotions can appear to be 'subjective components' of normal images, as Ahsen [120] and Jordan [121] and Singer [122] have pointed out.

Qualities of Size Constancy

Like *self-consciousness* and *spatial location, size constancy* is the sensationless quality of a CNS function. Accordingly, the *tacit quality* of size constancy and the *sensory qualities* from which it is derived are neurally and phenomenally separate—as the following example illustrates.

When the eye moves closer to an object, the reflected light from that object stimulates a larger number of cells over a greater area of the retina, and the *sensory qualities* of the object encompass a larger amount of the phenomenal field. But as a result of neurological computations with these retinal parameters, the cortex derives a closer object of 'constant size.' And as a subjective consequence of such cortical computations, the enlarging sensation is accompanied by a *tacit quality of 'size constancy.'*

It is important to note, however, that this process is reversed when objects of constant size are imaged, rather than perceived. For example, when subjects image a mouse next to a hamster, first they centrally access *sensationless qualities*, such as the 'constant size' and 'constant color' for each animal, and then they centrifugally generate *sensory qualities* for each animal. Similarly, when subjects image a mouse next to an elephant, first they access *tacit qualities* of 'size constancy' and 'shape constancy' for each animal and, then, from these perceptual constancies, they derive *sensory qualities* for each animal. Both of these examples of animal imaging come from research by Kosslyn [45-46], who claims that the size difference between the imaged mouse and the imaged hamster takes longer to "see" than the size difference between the imaged mouse and the imaged elephant, just as the size difference between a perceived mouse and a perceived hamster takes longer to see. However, as the above analysis suggests and as Kosslyn's critics argue [123-128], the sensationless proposition that a mouse is smaller than another small animal, a hamster, is *slowly* inferred from tacit qualities of 'size constancy' and from *rigorous* decision criteria—*with or without 'seeing' imaged sensations*. Thus, PNS structures and their sensory qualities, which necessarily contribute to perceptual computations and perceptual inferences about size constancy, do not contribute to imaginal inferences about size.

Furthermore, just as the similar effects of imaging and perceiving in Kosslyn's behavioral research need not be produced by similar neural processes, so also the differential effects of imaging and perceiving in Finke's behavioral research need not be produced at different "levels of the visual system" [129, p. 113]. Indeed, the only definitive way to determine whether particular qualities of images are represented at particular levels of the nervous system, the CNS or the PNS, is to examine evidence from psychophysiological studies not behavioral studies. But before even psychophysiological evidence can be examined, mind-brain identity theory demands that the *sensory qualities* of images be distinguished from the *tacit qualities* of images. In pursuing such a distinction, the current chapter has reviewed psychophysiological evidence suggesting 1) that the *sensory qualities* of mental images are subjective qualities of objectively distinguishable structures in the peripheral nervous system and 2) that the *sensationless qualities* of mental images are emergent qualities of objectively observable functions in the central nervous system.

ACKNOWLEDGMENTS

The author wishes to thank Theodore Barber, Mitchell Brigell, James Deese, Robert Innis, Neal Peachey, Elizabeth Ritvo, Arthur I. Schulman, Anees Sheikh, and Jerome L. Singer for their help in formulating the present theoretical approach.

REFERENCES

1. D. Hume, *A Treatise of Human Nature* (reprint of the 1739 edition), L. A. Selby-Bigge (ed.), Oxford University Press, London, 1888.
2. W. Wundt, *Lectures on Human and Animal Psychology* (J. E. Creighton and E. B. Titchener, trans.), Swan Sonnenschein, London, 1896.
3. R. G. Kunzendorf, Consciousness, in *Encyclopedia of Science and Technology* (5th Edition), McGraw-Hill, New York, pp. 558-560, 1982.
4. M. F. Meyer, *Psychology of the Other One*, Missouri Books, Columbus, 1922.
5. B. F. Skinner, *About Behaviorism*, Alfred A. Knopf, New York, 1974.
6. G. Ryle, *The Concept of Mind*, Barnes and Noble, New York, 1949.
7. L. Weiskrantz, Trying to Bridge Some Neuropsychological Gaps between Monkey and Man, *British Journal of Psychology, 68*, pp. 431-445, 1977.
8. A. A. Sheikh and R. G. Kunzendorf, Imagery, Physiology, and Psychosomatic Illness, *International Review of Mental Imagery, 1*, pp. 95-138, 1984.
9. E. Becker, *The Structure of Evil*, George Braziller, New York, pp. 123-124, 1968.
10. J.-P. Sartre, *The Psychology of Imagination* (translated from French), Citadel Press, Secaucus, New Jersey, 1980.
11. R. G. Kunzendorf, Hypnotic Hallucinations as "Unmonitored" Images: An Empirical Study, *Imagination, Cognition, and Personality, 5*, pp. 255-270, 1985-86.

12. R. G. Kunzendorf and D. Hoyle, *Auditory Percepts, Mental Images, and Hypnotic Hallucinations: Similarities and Differences in Auditory Evoked Potentials*, Manuscript submitted for publication, 1988.
13. C. A. Campbell, *On Selfhood and Godhood*, Macmillan, New York, 1957.
14. K. R. Popper and J. C. Eccles, *The Self and Its Brain*, Springer-Verlag, Berlin and New York, 1977.
15. M. Prince, Awareness, Consciousness, Co-consciousness and Animal Intelligence from the Point of View of Abnormal Psychology, *Pedagogical Seminary, 32*, pp. 166–188, 1925.
16. D. M. Armstrong, The Nature of Mind, in *The Mind-Brain Identity Theory*, C. V. Borst (ed.), Macmillan, London, 1970.
17. D. A. Oakley and L. C. Eames, The Plurality of Consciousness, in *Brain and Mind*, D. A. Oakley (ed.), Methuen and Co., London, pp. 217–251, 1985.
18. R. G. Kunzendorf, Self-Consciousness as the Monitoring of Cognitive States: A Theoretical Perspective, *Imagination, Cognition, and Personality, 7*, pp. 3–22, 1987–88.
19. M. K. Johnson, T. L. Kahan, and C. L. Raye, Dreams and Reality Monitoring, *Journal of Experimental Psychology: General, 113*, pp. 329–344, 1984.
20. Z. W. Pylyshyn, What the Mind's Eye Tells the Mind's Brain: A Critique of Mental Imagery, *Psychological Bulletin, 80*, pp. 1–24, 1973.
21. R. Creel, Radical Epiphenomenalism: B. F. Skinner's Account of Private Events, *Behaviorism, 8*, pp. 31–53, 1980.
22. H. Feigl, The 'Mental' and the 'Physical', *Minnesota Studies in the Philosophy of Science, 2*, pp. 370–497, 1958.
23. H. Feigl, Mind-Body, *Not* a Pseudoproblem, in *Theories of the Mind*, J. M. Scher (ed.), Free Press of Glencoe, New York, pp. 572–581, 1962.
24. R. G. Kunzendorf, Imagery and Consciousness: A Scientific Analysis of the Mind-Body Problem (Doctoral Dissertation, University of Virginia, 1979), *Dissertation Abstracts International, 40*, pp. 3448B–3449B.
25. N. Block, Troubles with Functionalism, in *Readings in Philosophy of Psychology* (vol. 1), N. Block (ed.), Harvard University Press, Cambridge, Massachusetts, pp. 268–305, 1980.
26. R. W. Sperry, Mental Phenomena as Causal Determinants in Brain Function, in *Consciousness and the Brain*, G. G. Globus, G. Maxwell, and I. Savodnik (eds.), Plenum, New York, pp. 161–177, 1976.
27. H. Putnam, Psychological Predicates, in *Art, Mind, and Religion*, W. H. Capitan and D. D. Merrill (eds.), University of Pittsburgh Press, Pittsburgh, Pennsylvania, pp. 37–48, 1967.
28. W. Kohler, The Mind-Body Problem, in *Dimensions of Mind*, S. Hook (ed.), Collier Books, New York, pp. 15-32, 1960.
29. W. I. Matson, *Sentience*, University of California Press, Berkeley, California, 1976.
30. R. Hirschman and L. Favaro, Individual Differences in Imagery Vividness and Voluntary Heart Rate Control, *Personality and Individual Differences, 1*, pp. 129–133, 1980.

31. D. Carroll, J. Baker, and M. Preston, Individual Differences in Visual Imaging and the Voluntary Control of Heart Rate, *British Journal of Psychology, 70*, pp. 39–49, 1979.
32. J. Achterberg, G. F. Lawlis, O. C. Simonton, and S. Matthews-Simonton, Psychological Factors and Blood Chemistries as Disease Outcome Predictors for Cancer Patients, *Multivariate Experimental Clinical Research, 3*, pp. 107-122, 1977.
33. H. Hall, Imagery and Cancer, in *Imagination and Healing*, A. A. Sheikh (ed.), Baywood Publishing Company, Farmingdale, New York, pp. 159-169, 1984.
34. R. G. Kunzendorf, Individual Differences in Imagery and Autonomic Control, *Journal of Mental Imagery, 5*, pp. 47–60, 1981.
35. Y. Ikeda and H. Hirai, Voluntary Control of Electrodermal Activity in Relation to Imagery and Internal Perception Scores, *Psychophysiology, 13*, pp. 330–333, 1976.
36. R. G. Kunzendorf and J. L. Bradbury, Better Liars Have Better Imaginations, *Psychological Reports, 52*, p. 634, 1983.
37. R. M. Suinn, Imagery and Sports, in *Imagery: Current Theory, Research, and Applications*, A. A. Sheikh (ed.), Wiley and Sons, New York, pp. 507-534, 1983.
38. K. Start and A. Richardson, Imagery and Mental Practice, *British Journal of Educational Psychology, 34*, pp. 280–284, 1964.
39. D. F. Marks, Imagery Paradigms and Methodology, *Journal of Mental Imagery, 9*, pp. 93–105, 1985.
40. A. W. Meyers, C. J. Cooke, J. Cullen, and L. Liles, Psychological Aspects of Athletic Competitors: A Replication across Sports, *Cognitive Therapy and Research, 3*, pp. 361-366, 1979.
41. R. G. Kunzendorf, Centrifugal Effects of Eidetic Imaging on Flash ERGs and Autonomic Responses, *Journal of Mental Imagery, 8*, pp. 67–76, 1984.
42. R. G. Kunzendorf, After-Images of Eidetic Images: A Developmental Study, *Journal of Mental Imagery, 13*, pp. 55–62, 1989.
43. M. Polanyi, Understanding Ourselves, in *The Nature of Human Consciousness*, R. E. Ornstein (ed.), W. H. Freeman, San Francisco, pp. 23–26, 1973.
44. M. T. Turvey, Constructive Theory, Perceptual Systems, and Tacit Knowledge, in *Cognition and the Symbolic Processes*, W. B. Weimer and D. S. Palermo (eds.), Erlbaum, Hillsdale, New Jersey, pp. 163–180, 1974.
45. S. M. Kosslyn, Information Representation in Visual Images, *Cognitive Psychology, 7*, pp. 341–370, 1975.
46. S. M. Kosslyn, *Image and Mind*, Harvard University Press, Cambridge, Massachusetts, 1980.
47. J. Jaynes, *The Origin of Consciousness in the Breakdown of the Bicameral Mind*, Houghton Mifflin, Boston, 1976.
48. A. B. Heilbrun, N. Blum, and M. Haas, Cognitive Vulnerability to Auditory Hallucination: Preferred Imagery Mode and Spatial Location of Sounds, *British Journal of Psychiatry, 143*, pp. 294–299, 1983.
49. S. C. Pepper, A Neural-Identity Theory of Mind, in *Dimensions of Mind*, S. Hook (ed.), Collier Books, New York, pp. 45–61, 1960.

50. C. Burt, Brain and Consciousness, *British Journal of Psychology, 59*, pp. 55-69, 1968.
51. A. R. Luria, The Human Brain and Conscious Activity, in *Consciousness and Self-Regulation* (vol. 2), G. E. Schwartz and D. Shapiro (eds.), Plenum, New York, pp. 1-35, 1978.
52. D. Denny-Brown, *The Cerebral Control of Movement*, Liverpool University Press, Liverpool, 1966.
53. C. N. Woolsey and P. Bard, Cortical Control of Placing and Hopping Reactions in Macaca Mulatta, *American Journal of Physiology, 116*, p. 165, 1936.
54. E. Poppel, R. Held, and D. Frost, Residual Visual Functions after Brain Wounds involving the Central Visual Pathways in Man, *Nature, 243*, pp. 295–296, 1973.
55. J. Reperant, N. P. Vesselkin, J. P. Rio, T. V. Ermakova, D. Miceli, J. Peyrichoux, and C. Weidner, La Voie Visuelle Centrifuge N'Existe-T-Elle Que Chez les Oiseaux?, *Revue Canadienne de Biologie, 40*, pp. 29–46, 1981.
56. R. Klinke and N. Galley, Efferent Innervation of Vestibular and Auditory Receptors, *Physiological Reviews, 54*, pp. 316-357, 1974.
57. A. Angel, Processing of Sensory Information, *Progress in Neurobiology, 9*, pp. 1-122, 1977.
58. R. D. Broadwell and D. M. Jacobowitz, Olfactory Relationships of the Telencephalon and Diencephalon in the Rabbit: III. The Ipsilateral Centrifugal Fibers to the Olfactory Bulbar and Retrobulbar Formations, *Journal of Comparative Neurology, 170*, pp. 321–346, 1976.
59. P. Van Hasselt, The Centrifugal Control of Retinal Function: A Review, *Ophthalmic Research, 4*, pp. 298-320, 1972–73.
60. M. D. Ross, Flueorescence and Electron Microscopic Observations of the General Visceral, Efferent Innervation of the Inner Ear, *Acta Oto-Laryngologica*, Supplement 286, pp. 1–18, 1971.
61. G. N. Akoev, Catecholamines, Acetylcholine and Excitability of Mechanoreceptors, *Progress in Neurobiology, 15*, pp. 269–294, 1981.
62. M. Takeda, An Electron Microscopic Study on the Innervation in the Taste Buds of the Mouse Circumvallate Papillae, *Archivum Histologicum Japonicum, 39*, pp. 257-269, 1976.
63. E. Darwin, *Zoonomia* (vol. 1), D. Carlisle, Boston, 1803.
64. F. v. P. Gruithuisen, *Beyträge zur Physiognosie und Eautognosie, für Freunde der Naturforschung auf dem Erfahrungswege*, I. J. Lentner, München, 1812.
65. J. J. Gibson, Adaptation, After-Effect and Contrast in the Perception of Curved Lines, *Journal of Experimental Psychology, 16*, pp. 1-31, 1933.
66. K. J. W. Craig, Origin of Visual After-Images, *Nature, 145*, p. 512, 1940.
67. J. M. von Wright, A Note on Interocular Transfer and the Colour of Visual After-Images, *Scandinavian Journal of Psychology, 4*, pp. 241-244, 1963.
68. L. Weiskrantz, An Unusual Case of After-Imagery Following Fixation of an "Imaginary" Visual Pattern, *Quarterly Journal of Experimental Psychology, 2*, pp. 170–175, 1950.

69. I. Oswald, After-Images from Retina and Brain, *Quarterly Journal of Experimental Psychology, 9*, pp. 88–100, 1957.
70. A. E. Krill, A. M. Wieland, and A. M. Ostfeld, The Effect of Two Hallucinogenic Agents on Human Retinal Function, *Archives of Ophthalmology, 64*, pp. 724–733, 1960.
71. R. Guerrero-Figueroa and R. G. Heath, Evoked Responses and Changes during Attentive Factors in Man, *Archives of Neurology, 10*, pp. 74–84, 1964.
72. S. J. Freedman and L. Ronchi, Adaptation and Training Effects in ERG: IV. Overview of Eight Years, *Atti della Fondazione Giorgo Ronchi, 19*, pp. 542–565, 1964.
73. A. Bogoslovskii and E. Semenovskaya, Conditioned Reflex Changes in the Human Electroretinogram, *Bulletin of Experimental Biology and Medicine* (translated from Russian), 47, pp. 265–269, 1959.
74. M. Roger and G. Galand, Operant Conditioning of Visual Evoked Potentials in Man, *Psychophysiology, 18*, 477–482.
75. W. J. Freeman, The Physiological Basis of Mental Images, *Biological Psychiatry, 18*, pp. 1107–1125, 1983.
76. C. Deehan and A. W. Robertson, Changes in Auditory Evoked Potentials Induced by Hypnotic Suggestion, in *Hypnosis in Psychotherapy and Psychosomatic Medicine*, M. Pajntar, E. Roskar, and M. Lavric (eds.), University Press, Ljubljana, pp. 93–95, 1980.
77. O. H. Mowrer, Mental Imagery: An Indispensable Psychological Concept, *Journal of Mental Imagery, 2*, pp. 303–325, 1977.
78. J. H. Lukas, Human Auditory Attention: The Olivocochlear Bundle May Function as a Peripheral Filter, *Psychophysiology, 17*, pp. 444–452, 1980.
79. R. Brix, The Influence of Attention on the Auditory Brainstem Evoked Responses, *Acta Otolaryngolica, 98*, pp. 89–92, 1984.
80. T. W. Picton, D. R. Stapells, and K. B. Campbell, Auditory Evoked Potentials from the Human Cochlea and Brainstem, *Journal of Otolaryngology, 10* (suppl. 9), pp. 1–41, 1981.
81. A. E. Davis and H. A. Beagley, Acoustic Brainstem Responses for Clinical Use: The Effect of Attention, *Clinical Otolaryngology, 10*, pp. 311-314, 1985.
82. W. Sommer, Selective Attention Differentially Affects Brainstem Auditory Evoked Potentials of Electrodermal Responders and Nonresponders, *Psychiatry Research, 16*, pp. 227–232, 1985.
83. J. A. Fodor, The Mind-Body Problem, *Scientific American, 244*, pp. 114–123, 1981.
84. R. N. Haber, Twenty Years of Haunting Eidetic Imagery: Where's the Ghost?, *Behavioral and Brain Sciences, 2*, pp. 583–629, 1979.
85. J. T. E. Richardson, *Mental Imagery and Human Memory*, St. Martin's Press, New York, 1980.
86. R. G. Kunzendorf, Mental Images, Appreciation of Grammatical Patterns, and Creativity, *Journal of Mental Imagery, 6*, pp. 183–202, 1982.

87. N. Carey, Factors in the Mental Processes of School Children: I. Visual and Auditory Imagery, *British Journal of Psychology, 7*, pp. 453–490, 1915.
88. C. H. Ernest and A. Paivio, Imagery and Sex Differences in Incidental Recall, *British Journal of Psychology, 62*, pp. 67–72, 1971.
89. R. Gur and E. Hilgard, Visual Imagery and the Discrimination of Differences between Altered Pictures Simultaneously and Successively Presented, *British Journal of Psychology, 66*, pp. 341–345, 1975.
90. M. S. Lindauer, Imagery from the Point of View of Psychological Aesthetics, the Arts, and Creativity, *Journal of Mental Imagery, 1*, pp. 343–362, 1977.
91. J. Bilotta and M. S. Lindauer, Artistic and Nonartistic Backgrounds as Determinants of the Cognitive Response to the Arts, *Bulletin of the Psychonomic Society, 15*, pp. 354–356, 1980.
92. H. A. Teasdale, A Quantitative Study of Eidetic Imagery, *British Journal of Educational Psychology, 4*, pp. 56–74, 1934.
93. L. Peck and R. Walling, A Preliminary Study of the Eidetic Imagery of Preschool Children, *Journal of Genetic Psychology, 47*, pp. 168–192, 1935.
94. E. F. Giray, W. M. Altkin, G. M. Vaught, and P. Roodin, The Incidence of Eidetic Imagery as a Function of Age, *Child Development, 47*, pp. 1207–1210, 1976.
95. E. F. Giray, P. Roodin, W. Altkin, P. Flagg, and G. Yoon, A Life Span Approach to the Study of Eidetic Imagery, *Journal of Mental Imagery, 9*, pp. 21–32, 1985.
96. A. M. Liberman, F. S. Cooper, K. S. Harris, and P. F. MacNeilage, Motor Theory of Speech Perception, *Journal of the Acoustical Society of America, 35*, p. 1114, 1963.
97. A. M. Liberman, F. S. Cooper, D. P. Shankweiler, and M. Studdert-Kennedy, Perception of the Speech Code, *Psychological Review, 74*, pp. 431–461, 1967.
98. A. M. Liberman, The Grammars of Speech and Language, *Cognitive Psychology, 1*, pp. 301–323, 1970.
99. D. N. Uznadze, *The Psychology of Set*, B. Haigh (trans.), Consultants' Bureau, New York, 1966.
100. P. J. Lang, W. G. Troyer, C. T. Twentyman, and R. J. Gatchel, Differential Effects of Heart Rate Modification Training on College Students, Older Males, and Patients with Ischemic Heart Disease, *Psychosomatic Medicine, 37*, pp. 429–446, 1975.
101. W. C. Lynch, H. Hama, S. Kohn, and N. E. Miller, *Instrumental Control of Peripheral Vasomotor Responses in Children,* Psychophysiology, 13, pp. 219–221, 1976.
102. R. G. Kunzendorf, Subconscious Percepts as "Unmonitored" Percepts: An Empirical Study, *Imagination, Cognition, and Personality, 4*, pp. 367–375, 1984–85.
103. E. F. Bazhin, L. I. Wasserman, and I. M. Tonkonogii, Auditory Hallucinations and Left Temporal Lobe Pathology, *Neuropsychologia, 13*, pp. 481–487, 1975.

104. P. Flor-Henry, Lateralized Temporal-Limbic Dysfunction and Psychopathology, *Annals of the New York Academy of Sciences, 280*, pp. 777-795, 1976.
105. J. Gruzelier and N. Hammond, Schizophrenia: A Dominant Hemisphere Temporal-Lobe Disorder?, *Research Communications in Psychology, Psychiatry, and Behavior, 1*, pp. 33-72, 1976.
106. R. A. Roemer, C. Shagass, J. J. Straumanis, and M. Amadeo, Pattern Evoked Potential Measurements Suggesting Lateralized Hemispheric Dysfunction in Chronic Schizophrenics, *Biological Psychiatry, 13*, pp. 185-202, 1978.
107. P. Baken, Dreaming, REM Sleep and the Right Hemisphere, *Journal of Altered States of Consciousness, 3*, pp. 285-307, 1977-78.
108. R. W. Sperry, Hemisphere Deconnection and Unity of Conscious Awareness, *American Psychologist, 23*, pp. 723-733, 1968.
109. J. A. Shaffer, Recent Work on the Mind-Body Problem, *American Philosophical Quarterly, 2*, pp. 81-104, 1965.
110. M. B. Bender, *Disorders in Perception*, Charles C. Thomas, Springfield, Ilinois, 1952.
111. J. Gerstmann, Problem of Imperception of Disease and of Impaired Body Territories with Organic Lesions: Relation to Body Scheme and Its Disorders, *Archives of Neurology and Psychiatry, 48*, pp. 890-913, 1947.
112. B. Cronholm, *Phantom Limbs in Amputees*, R. Cameron (trans.), Ejnar Munksgaard, Copenhagen, 1951.
113. A. A. Skavenski, G. Haddad, and R. M. Steinman, The Extraretinal Signal for the Visual Perception of Direction, *Perception and Psychophysics, 11*, pp. 287-290, 1972.
114. D. Marks and P. McKellar, The Nature and Function of Eidetic Imagery, *Journal of Mental Imagery, 6*, pp. 1-124, 1982.
115. P. Flor-Henry, Schizophrenic Hallucinations in the Context of Psychophysiological Studies of Schizophrenia, in *The Psychophysiology of Mental Imagery: Theory, Research, and Application*, R. G. Kunzendorf and A. A. Sheikh (eds.), Baywood, Amityville, New York, pp. 147-164, 1990.
116. C. Darwin, *The Expression of the Emotions in Man and Animals*, John Murray, London, 1872.
117. S. S. Tomkins, *Affect, Imagery, Consciousness* (2 vols.), Springer, New York, 1962-63.
118. C. Izard, *The Face of Emotion*, Appleton Century Crofts, New York, 1971.
119. P. Ekman, R. W. Levenson, and W. V. Friesen, Autonomic Nervous System Activity Distinguishes among Emotions, *Science, 221*, pp. 1208-1210, 1983.
120. A. Ahsen, ISM: The Triple Code Model for Imagery and Psychophysiology, *Journal of Mental Imagery, 8*, pp. 15-42, 1984.
121. C. S. Jordan, Psychophysiology of Structural Imagery in Post-Traumatic Stress Disorder, *Journal of Mental Imagery, 8*, pp. 51-66, 1984.
122. J. L. Singer, *The Inner World of Daydreaming*, Harper and Row, New York, 1975.

123. J. R. Anderson, Arguments Concerning Representations for Mental Imagery, *Psychological Review, 85*, pp. 249-277, 1978.
124. A. Friedman, Memorial Comparisons without the Mind's Eye, *Journal of Verbal Learning and Verbal Behavior, 17*, pp. 427-444, 1978.
125. J. M. Keenan and R. K. Olson, The Imagery Debate [Open Peer Commentary on "On the Demystification of Mental Imagery" by S. M. Kosslyn *et al.*], *Behavioral and Brain Sciences, 2*, pp. 558-559, 1979.
126. U. Neisser, Anticipations, Images, and Introspection, *Cognition, 6*, pp. 169-174, 1978.
127. Z. Pylyshyn, The Imagery Debate: Analogue Media versus Tacit Knowledge, *Psychological Review, 88*, pp. 16-45, 1981.
128. J. C. Yuille, A Laboratory-Based Experimental Methodology Is Inappropriate for the Study of Mental Imagery, *Journal of Mental Imagery, 9*, pp. 137-150, 1985.
129. R. A. Finke, Levels of Equivalence in Imagery and Perception, *Psychological Review, 87*, pp. 113-132, 1980.

CHAPTER 2
*Psi Mediated Emergent Interactionism and the Nature of Consciousness**

CHARLES T. TART

Throughout my career I have been interested in a range of phenomena I usually group under the heading of *altered states of consciousness*–phenomena dealing with the fascinating, multitudinous changes that can take place in our mode of experiencing our mind, body, self and our world. While such changes in the manifestations of consciousness can be studied without asking any fundamental questions about the nature of consciousness itself–so avoiding dilemmas that have puzzled philosophers through the ages–I have always been curious as to the ultimate nature of consciousness. I have also been curious about those phenomena, like telepathy, termed *parapsychological*, and have found them to be of great value in pointing out important directions for understanding the ultimate nature of consciousness.

In this chapter I shall discuss the beginnings of an expanded scientific framework for understanding the basic nature of consciousness, an approach I call *Psi Mediated Emergent Interactionism*. This approach would be philosophically classified as dualistic, but it has observable, empirical consequences, and so can be classified as scientific. I do not lay any great claim to originality in this approach, as I have drawn on multitudinous sources for the basic ideas, but I hope the particular way I have put these ideas together will be useful in understanding human consciousness.

My observational base for trying to understand consciousness begins with my own experience, and this base is then expanded by my experiences with the

*This paper draws heavily on an earlier one, "An emergent-interactionist understanding of human consciousness," which appeared in *Brain/Mind and Parapsychology*, edited by Betty Shapin and Lissette Coly, and published in 1979. Much material is used here by permission of the publishers, the Parapsychology Foundation, New York, New York.

world and my observations of and communications with others. Perhaps the most striking thing about my own experience is the obviously *different* nature of my consciousness from the physical world about me. Despite difficulties in knowing precisely how to think about it or express it, it is simply a given that there is something fundamentally different about the experiences I call my "mental" processes from what I call the external world. This basic distinction has been drawn by multitudes of others, and in formal philosophy has been called a dualistic position, a formal postulation of some qualitatively different qualities of mind and matter, with the consequence that the nature of one cannot be adequately explained by or reduced to the other.

I have had no formal training in philosophy, but at times I have attempted to study philosophical literature on the nature of consciousness. I have always come away baffled and disappointed. Once the basic distinction between mind and matter is postulated, I get the feeling that most philosophers restrict themselves to dealing with purely semantic distinctions. The monistic or dualistic position that results from their logic might or might not be true; but the truth or falsity of it does not seem to have any useful experimental or experiential consequences that I can discern. I am strongly committed to the kind of scientific pragmatism that says observable consequences (whether physical or experiential) have priority over intellectual formulations.

MONISTIC VIEWS

In terms of acceptance by the contemporary intellectual community, monistic positions, which postulate that mind and matter are basically manifestations of the same thing, matter, are the accepted philosophies. Mind is believed to be totally reducible to matter. This is particularly so in orthodox science. Figure 1, taken from my *States of Consciousness* book [1], diagrams the widely accepted scientific view of consciousness, what I have called the "orthodox" or scientifically conservative view of the mind. The basic reality that is being dealt with in this diagram is physical reality, governed by immutable laws and/or random processes. As a result of these laws a particular physical system comes into existence, the brain and its associated nervous system and body.

Many aspects of this brain are fixed in their functioning: instructions for your kidneys to work, for example, are encoded in the physical structure of the brain and kidneys, and ordinarily never change. This physical structure also has many programmable capacities, so our culture, our language, memories of the various events of our personal history, and our interactions with physical reality teach us a language, a way of thinking, values and mores, patterns of acceptable behavior, etc., the "software" of the nervous system. This large computer-like physical structure then functions in a wide variety of complex (but inherently lawful) ways. At any given moment we are aware of only a small fraction of the total functioning of it, and this tiny fraction of physical functioning that we are aware is consciousness as we experience it.

In presenting this orthodox model I have added something called "pure awareness" in the upper part of it. This refers in a general way here to those experiences of mental activity which do not seem tied to obvious physical and bodily functioning, such as the basic non-physical feel of consciousness that we discussed above, or to certain meditative experiences, or to various altered states experiences. More formally, I have used the term pure awareness to mean that raw proto-experience of knowing that *something* is happening before that experience gets highly elaborated and articulated into linguistic/semantic categories where it has obviously been influenced by culture [1].

In Figure 1, I show pure awareness as "emerging" from the physical structure of the brain. This is a representation of the monistic *psychoneural identity hypothesis*, which postulates that while we might find it convenient to distinguish certain types of ostensibly mental activity from physical processes for semantic purposes, this distinction is really fictional: all experience is, in principle, completely reducible to and identical with physical activity within the brain. In practice, of course, we are a long way from being able to carry out this

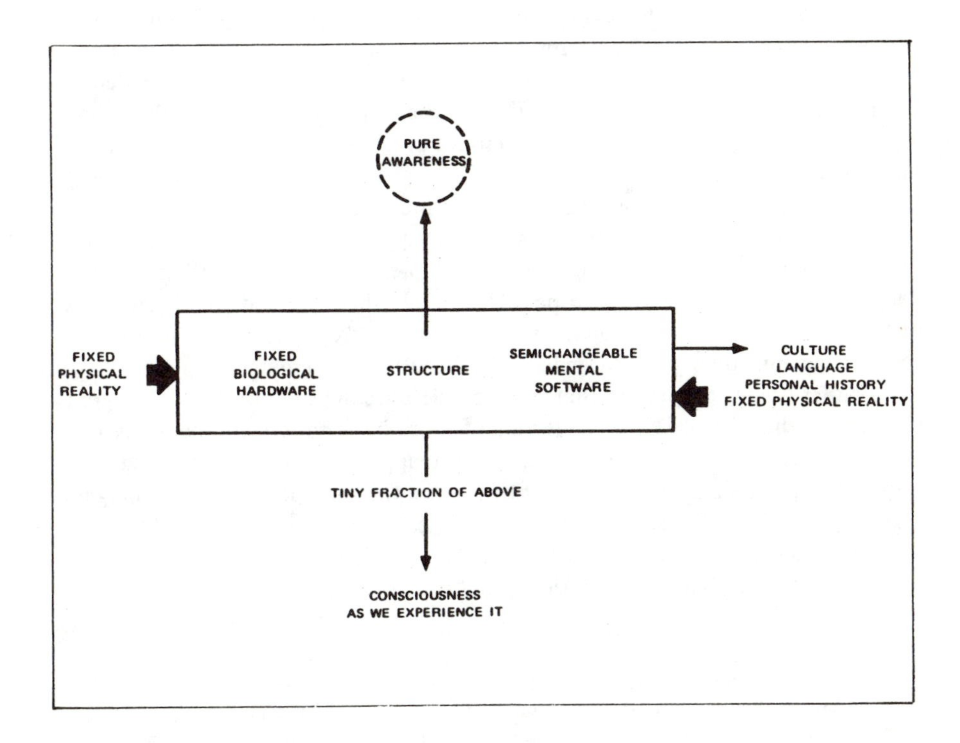

Figure 1.

reduction, due to the sheer complexity of the brain, but in principle the orthodox scientific view believes this is possible.[1]

The psychoneural identity approach is clearly a useful scientific approach, for it has observable consequences. It predicts, for example, that a physiological correlate of any and every kind of experience can ultimately be found. It further predicts that no mental functionings can occur in reality that violate the basic physical laws and system operation laws that govern the operation of the brain, although the brain may produce *illusory* experiences that seem to violate basic physical laws. I can program my computer, for example, to print out: "I have just transcended my chips and become ecstatically fused with the Great Computer in the Sky!" We do not take the content of this statement seriously, and, in monistic views of consciousness, we do not take statements about transcending physical laws or about mind being experienced as qualitatively different from matter seriously either.

Complexity

In mentioning laws governing systems operation, I am reminded of another disappointment I have always had with formal philosophical writings on the nature of consciousness. That is their typical obsession with an absolutistic understanding of *simple* mental events, when it has always been obvious to me that consciousness represents an exceptionally complex system, not a simple mechanism. My early experience in working with electronic systems—where alterations in one component can have many effects on the whole system operation, effects which are often not at all obviously predictable beforehand—sensitized me to this issue.

Modern brain science now recognizes the incredible complexity of the brain and nervous system. Starting from a simplistic approach that likened each neural junction to a relay and believing that the complexity of brain function could be handled by a simple additive operation of all these individual binary relay operations, modern understandings of the brain are increasingly looking to general systems theory to provide general laws about emergent properties of brain functioning, properties that are holistic outcomes of total system operation rather than simple linear additions of more basic subsystem elements [2]. The Psi Mediated Emergent Interactionism approach to understanding consciousness that I shall outline here tries to take this complexity, these emergent system properties of brain functioning (and, as we shall see, of mind functioning) into account, and tries also to deal with the fundamental experience of a dualistic difference between experience and the physical world.

[1] Some have succinctly characterized the conventional position as "promisory materialism." No matter how badly monistic materialsim fares in actually explaining mental events, the promise is always made that with more research in the future things will be explained.

Pragmatic Intentions

As a final introductory note, I should say that if I had to characterize my philosophical bias, it is pragmatic. As a scientist, I am committed to the proposition that our data, our experience, is *primary*, and our conceptualizations, our theories about the meaning of that data, are *secondary*. If I cannot adequately or logically express my experience, that is a shortcoming of my thought processes, language, philosophy or grammar, not an invalidation of my experience. As a psychologist I have seen too many instances where people's attachment to their theories (whether these theories are explicit or implicit) makes them ignore data that do not fit. Theories must always be adjusted to account for the data, and theories must have consequences in terms of observable data/experiences. If my theory has no testable consequences, it may be intellectually interesting, but it is not scientifically worthwhile. I do not accept the common monistic belief that physical data are inherently better than experiential data, however. I believe that the dualistic approach to and theory of consciousness I shall now present has empirically testable consequences and so forms the basis of a scientific set of theories about consciousness.

A further aspect of my pragmatism is that I do not want to get into the kind of absolutism that often characterizes formal philosophical discourse. I have no way to define concepts like mind versus matter or mind versus brain in any kind of absolutely satisfactory fashion. If I say that something is "mental" or "nonmaterial," what I am saying is that something seems to have observable properties which cannot be adequately explained in terms of our current understanding of the physical world, or reasonable extrapolations of that physical world understanding.

It is quite possible that future advances at the cutting edge of physics will drastically change our conception of what is and is not "physical" or "mental," and what can and cannot be explained within a physical explanatory system. Such possible directions have been speculated on by writers like Capra [3] and Zhukov [4]. Thus, in distinguishing mind and brain, I am doing no more than making distinctions which are pragmatically useful and necessary at present, regardless of their absolute validity. The pragmatic usefulness of making these distinctions is that we must investigate mind on its own terms *now*, not assume that someday it will be reduced to a physical explanation so we can forget about mind per se.

PARACONCEPTUAL PHENOMENA

The basic support for my dualistic approach to understanding consciousness comes from the excellent scientific evidence for the existence of certain "paranormal" phenomena, specifically telepathy, clairvoyance, precognition, and psychokinesis.

Assuming basic validity of our current understanding of the nature of the physical world, it is possible to talk about completely *isolating* or *shielding* one event or system from another so that no known, feasible form of information or energy transfer channel exists between these two isolated events or systems. If we now carry out physical observations, either of the behaviors of people or of the readings of physical instruments, which indicate that an information or energy transfer has nevertheless occurred between two isolated events, we have a so-called *paranormal* or, more appropriately, a *paraconceptual* event.

We have an observation that cannot be satisfactorily explained by our theories, that, indeed, may be forbidden by them. Since the majority of the population in America believe they have experienced some kinds of psi [5], these events are hardly para*normal*, beyond the norm, but they are certainly para*conceptual* to the orthodox, current scientific view of how the physical universe works.

While there have been many types of observations reported that *purport* to be paraconceptual events, we have only had extensive, reliable, and significant paraconceptual outcomes within four kinds of experimental paradigms. These results have led researchers to postulate the existence of four basic types of paraconceptual events, namely *telepathy, clairvoyance, precognition*, and *psychokinesis (PK)*. The first three types of perceptual events are usually referred to collectively as *extrasensory perception (ESP)*, while all four are collectively referred to as *psi* events. There are dozens to hundreds of experimental reports supporting the existence of each of these kinds of psi effects. Reviews of the literature can be found elsewhere [6-17]. This literature is regarded by some orthodox scientists as controversial or *a priori* invalid because of an *a priori* monistic materialistic rejection of the possibility of psi, but rejection of the existence of basic psi phenomena is, in my and others' observations, inversely correlated with actual knowledge of the appropriate scientific literature and often based on irrational factors ([18-20] for a discussion of such factors). This pseudo-scientific *a priori* rejection is an example of the possibility we discussed above of attachment to theory distorting scientists' judgment of data.

Psi events are defined as occurring when no known form of physical energy provides a carrier for sensory information or a channel for physical causation of the observed event. Then we further define telepathy as mind to mind communications; clairvoyance as physical matter to mind "communication," a sensing of the physical state of affairs directly with the mind; precognition as predicting a future state of events when such prediction is not possible by rational inference from knowledge of presently existing conditions; and psychokinesis as directly effecting a state of physical events simply by wishing for it.

Space considerations preclude any review of the extensive literature (probably more than 800 published experiments) on basic psi phenomena, but the basic experimental procedures, especially in the "classical" period of experimentation from the 1930s to the 1960s, which established ESP and PK, are as follows.

For telepathy, thoroughly shuffle a deck of cards and have someone designated the "agent" or "sender" look at each card for a fixed period, say one minute each, and try to "send" it. Have another person designated the "receiver" or "percipient," attempt to receive and write down what the order of the deck of target cards is. The percipient should be out of all feasible sensory contact with the target cards or sender, such as by being in another building. Then carefully check the percipient's responses against the order of the target deck and apply appropriate statistical tests to see if the number and/or pattern of correspondence is significantly different from chance.

For clairvoyance, follow the above procedure, but without anyone knowing what the order of the target cards is at the time the percipient attempts to perceive them. Having an experimenter thoroughly shuffle the cards without looking at them until after the percipient has written down his responses is the usual procedure.

For precognition, request the percipient to write down *now* what the order of a deck of target cards will be at some designated time in the future, say one hour from now. At that future time follow a prearranged procedure for randomizing the target cards (such as shuffle twenty times without looking at the cards), then compare the resultant order of the deck with the percipient's prediction list.

For PK, construct a machine to randomly throw ordinary dice. Preset a schedule for the subject trying to use PK (usually called the agent), such as the one face being the target for the first twenty-four trials, the two face for the second twenty-four trials, etc. (This regular rotation of target face is necessary to compensate for possible biases in the dice.) Have the agent, standing back from the apparatus, try to make those designated target faces come up by will alone. Use appropriate statistics to compare the obtained distribution of hits with that expected by chance.

Many variants of the above multiple-choice psi tasks have shown significant psi functioning in more modern research. Targets in ESP tasks, for example, may be actual physical locations, sounds on unplayed audio tapes, or pictures. Targets in PK tasks have been the internal state of electronic random number generators and biological processes. A good review of the range of contemporary research is provided in Wolman et al's *Handbook of Parapsychology* [6].

These conventional definitions of ESP and PK have an implicit dualism in them, but we could avoid this and still operationally distinguish the above four phenomena simply by the kinds of experimental procedures under which they have been observed. Thus telepathy becomes a matter of a percipient making a behavioral response that is supposed to relate to a stimulus presented to the agent, etc.

If these basic psi phenomena were physical in nature, we should be able to isolate the particular physical energies that carry their information and action potential and we would see lawful regularities in psi effects that paralleled these postulated physical mechanisms. If telepathy were some form of electromagnetic radiation, for example, we would expect to find a fall off in the effectiveness of telepathy with the square of the distance. Research has shown only that *psychological* distance has any appreciable effect, however: what an ESP percipient or PK agent *believes* about distance may affect an experimental outcome, but actual physical distance has little, if any, effect. Similarly, shielding which attenuates electromagnetic radiation should reduce ESP, but, if anything, it may enhance it [21]. In general research has not found physical correlates of psi or detected any known forms of energy operating in conjunction with psi: we do not have space for an adequate discussion of this here, but see [16] for reviews of the literature. Indeed, a psi phenomenon like precognition seems to violate basic physical laws.

The monistic equation of mind and matter, the psychoneural identity hypothesis, so widely accepted in orthodox science, is one result of a world view that denies the existence of psi phenomena as we experimentally know them. The existence of psi phenomena is thus a clear cut scientific demonstration that our understanding of the nature of a physical world is quite inadequate and will require major revisions. These paraconceptual psi events thus demonstrate the incompleteness of the overall conceptual system from which monism is derived.

In a general sense, then, we can argue that a psychoneural identity position is far from proven, because it rests on an incomplete and, therefore, faulty conceptual system. The existence of these paraconceptual psi phenomena provides a general basis for arguing that a dualistic view of mind and matter is a realistic and pragmatically useful view; that is, that it more adequately reflects the nature of things rather than just being a semantically convenient distinction and that it points to potentially useful research directions that would not be undertaken from a monistic position.

PSI MEDIATED EMERGENT INTERACTIONISM

My psychological studies of consciousness and altered states of consciousness, as well as my parapsychological studies, have forced me to go a step further than merely noting that a monistic view is inadequate, namely to postulate 1) that experience and high quality scientific data basically indicate that mind is of a fundamentally different nature than matter as we know it today; and 2) more specifically, that certain psi functions are the mechanisms of mind-brain interaction. Consciousness, as we experience it, is an emergent property of this mind-brain interaction. This theory is represented in simplified form in Figure 2.

The physical structure of the brain is represented on the left hand side of Figure 2. We shall not be concerned with its internal structure of inherent system properties for the moment. The dualistic factor, which I shall begin calling *mind/life*, is represented on the right hand side of the figure. I add the "life" designation to this side of the figure to point out that the "nonphysical" aspect of consciousness is not always a matter of mental experience, it includes

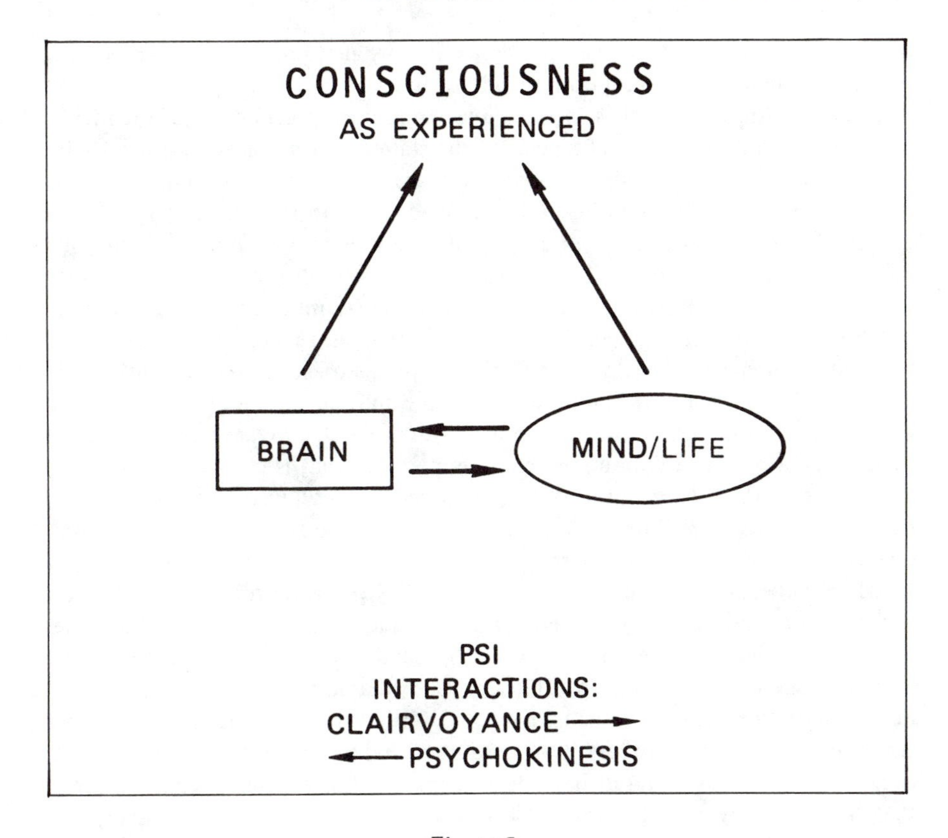

Figure 2.

a general "vitalistic" effect of mind/life that is more basic than conscious experience.

Consciousness, as we ordinarily experience it, is the higher level emergent of the psi interaction of brain and mind/life. To put it more formally, *experienced consciousness is a system property, an emergent, of the complex interaction of the subsystems of brain on the one hand and the mind/life factor on the other.*

The brain is the link between consciousness and the physical world about us. Environmental stimuli are detected through the sense organs and are represented in electrical/chemical patterns within the brain. Actions begin (at the brain level) as electrical/chemical patterns within the brain and end up as specific impulses to motor effectors that create our overt behavior. The brain is an ultra-complex and especially interesting structure. While many aspects of brain functioning seem completely determined, such as basic reflexes, many other important aspects seem to be under the control of quasi-random or fully random processes: that is, they are controlled by neurons or neural ensembles that are often almost but-not-quite, ready to fire.

My Psi Mediated Emergent Interactionism approach postulates that the mind/life factor cognizes important aspects of the state of the brain by means of clairvoyance, that is, that mind/life uses clairvoyance to "read" the brain and thus the state of the body and the body's immediate sensory world. Further, the action of the brain is influenced at critical junctures by PK from the mind/life factor. That is, in addition to self-organizational system properties of its own, there are control functions exerted over the brain by mind/life factors through psychokinetic modification of brain firing. The quasi-random processes in the brain may be specific, easily modifiable receptors for psychokinetic influence. The holistic emergent of this interaction, the mutual interaction and mutual patterning of brain and mind/life on each other via clairvoyance and PK, leads to an overall pattern of functioning and experience that is consciousness as we experience it. *Psi is here postulated as the specific, lawful mechanism of interaction between mind and brain*, a mechanism that is almost always missing from dualistic theories of consciousness.

When we examine our own experience, then, we do not ordinarily experience what brain alone is like or experience what mind alone is like; we experience the emergent of their interaction, for which I use the term "consciousness" here.

Having sketched the basic postulates of Psi Mediated Emergent Interactionism in terms of "brain," "consciousness," and "mind/life," I must now face the semantic problem that others have used these terms in wider, imprecise, and overlapping ways, as I myself have done in past writings. While I could request that from now on you interpret these terms in only the way I define them, it is not that easy to drop lifetime associative patterns, so I shall try to lessen semantic problems by adopting more neutral abbreviations for the remainder of this chapter. I shall use the term *BBNS system* to refer to those physical functions of the brain, body, and nervous system that we already understand in physical concepts or can expect to understand with straightforward extensions of current physical concepts. I shall use the term *M/L system* for those "non-physical" (given current knowledge and straightforward extensions of current physical concepts) aspects I have been calling mind/life. I shall retain "consciousness," with the reminder that I will usually restrict it to our ordinary experience of ourselves, not to more exotic experiences, and so call it *consensus consciousness*, a technical term I have introduced elsewhere [1] for everyday or ordinary consciousness.

As for the psi interactions, I shall add the prefix *auto-* to designate psi that is concerned with a person's M/L system interacting with his own BBNS system: thus *auto-psi, auto-clairvoyance* (*auto-CL* in later diagrams), and *auto-PK*. For those cases where psi reaches outside the bounds of the normal BBNS system and M/L system interrelationship, as when we ask a percipient to tell us, for example, what the order of a sealed deck of cards is, I shall add the prefix *allo-*:

thus *allo-psi* in general, or more specifically *allo-clairvoyance, allo-PK, allo-telepathy*, etc.

BBNS AND ML SYSTEM LEVELS

Figure 2 was a very general schematic of BBNS system and M/L system interaction and their emergent properties. A more realistic schematic, using present knowledge, would be of the sort shown in Figure 3. This figure brings in a number of further considerations.

First, there are various hierarchical levels of organization in the BBNS system alone, without even beginning to bring the M/L system into the picture. The lowest conventional level shown on the left hand side of the figure would be individual neurons. While these have properties we are beginning to understand fairly well, they are organized into basic neural ensembles at the next level, so this next system level has emergent properties. That is, simple neuron ensembles can have properties which are not clearly predicted from those of neurons alone. These level two neuron ensembles and these level two properties in turn influence level one functioning; thus the arrows representing interaction. Similarly, neuron ensembles are organized into more complex ensembles, etc., up to very high levels of complexity. System, emergent properties occur at all these various levels, as do numerous and complex interactions. It will not be an easy job to understand the BBNS system, especially since the brain alone, without even bringing in the M/L system, is so many orders of magnitude more complex than any well understood present day system, such as the computer.

Although we know far more about the BBNS system than the M/L system, I have assumed, on the basis of the symmetry principle [1, chapter 18], that the M/L system itself is probably a system of many hierarchical levels, and have diagramed it accordingly on the right. I have avoided putting any labeling on that part of the scheme other than distinguishing the most basic life "energies" at the lowest levels versus more "mental" levels higher up in the system hierarchy. This is a matter of being cautious and not pretending to know more than we do know, but it seems very likely that there are fundamental aspects of the M/L system that interact with each other, produce more complex, emergent system properties, and so on, as with BBNS system processes. All interaction within the M/L system is mediated by some kind of auto-psi, which might or might not be the same kind of psi auto-mediating M/L system and BBNS system interactions. Thus we have an emergence of system properties on the M/L side of the diagram as well as the BBNS system side.

Figure 3 shows auto-clairvoyance and auto-PK interactions between the BBNS and M/L systems as potentially occurring between similar hierarchical levels of BBNS and M/L subsystems, as well as potential cross level auto-psi interactions. There is probably no single locus of interaction of auto-clairvoyance and auto-PK between the BBNS and M/L systems, but a variety of interactions

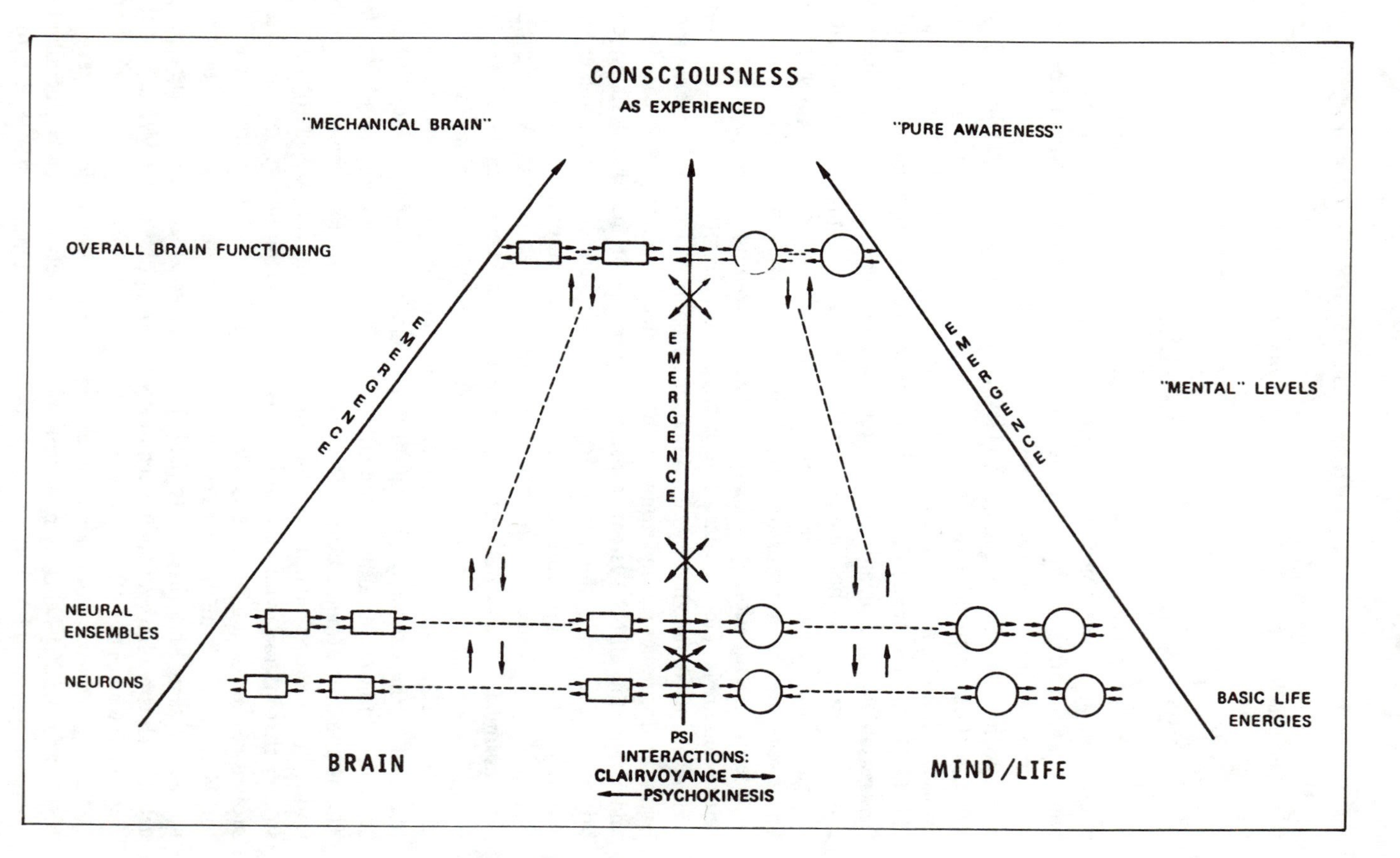
CONSCIOUSNESS
AS EXPERIENCED
"MECHANICAL BRAIN"
"PURE AWARENESS"
OVERALL BRAIN FUNCTIONING
EMERGENCE
EMERGENCE
EMERGENCE
"MENTAL" LEVELS
NEURAL
ENSEMBLES
NEURONS
BASIC LIFE
ENERGIES
BRAIN
PSI
INTERACTIONS:
CLAIRVOYANCE
PSYCHOKINESIS
MIND/LIFE

Figure 3.

occurring at different levels. Lower level auto-psi interactions between BBNS and M/L systems, then, may change the isolated properties of both neural tissue and basic life energies at those lower levels, which in turn are reflected in further interactions and system property emergence in both the BBNS and M/L system levels. I regret that this is not the simplistic kind of picture we prefer, but real systems are complex!

If we could separate out BBNS system properties alone, we might observe an emergent that I have labeled as "mechanical brain" at the top of the left hand systems hierarchy. Similarly, if we could separate out M/L system properties and functionings without any interactions with brain ones, we might observe something I have called "pure awareness" at the top of the M/L side of the diagram. I suspect that we actually have some data on both of these relatively pure cases, but not in a form we can clearly recognize and make use of. Some meditative practices, for example, or variants of out-of-the-body experiences (discussed later), lead to experiences which are usually described as "ineffable," that is, they cannot be expressed in terms of the emergent of language which deals with consensus consciousness: these may be instances of isolated M/L system operation.

This has been a basic outline of the Psi Mediated Emergent Interactionist position. Let us now consider a variety of topics from this point of view, starting with the psychological factor of automatization.

AUTOMATIZATION

An important psychological consideration to discuss from the Psi Mediated Emergent Interactionism approach is that of automatization, the habitual, automatic way that consensus consciousness seems to function a great deal of the time. Much of this automatization is conditioned and reinforced during the socialization process where various assumptions and habit patterns become implicit. Automated processes presumably have a basis in semi-permanent physical modifications in the BBNS system, "pathways" which automatically tend to guide BBNS system functioning (and some coupled M/L system interaction) along certain lines, lines which simply seem like the "natural way of doing things. I have discussed automatization at length elsewhere [1, 22].

Thus a great deal of information processing, decision making, perception and action may take place in the BBNS system without there necessarily being any auto-psi interaction with the M/L system. The BBNS system, as it were, can do a good many things "on automatic," without the M/L system being involved. We shall consider aspects of this in more detail later. For now, this point can be illustrated by considering this Psi Mediated Emergent Interactionist point of view as analogous with the operation of a "smart" computer terminal.

Computer Terminal Analogy

An ordinary, "dumb" terminal consists essentially of a keyboard and a screen or printer. Its sole function is to transmit data to and receive data from a remote computer. The remote computer does various kinds of processing of the information and sends output, "decisions" back to the dumb computer terminal, which simply displays or prints them out unaltered. The smart terminal, on the other hand, actually has a small computer of its own built into the terminal. Certain kinds of data may be input into this terminal and, rather than simply transmitting the data unaltered to the remote computer, the terminal will carry out some processing on the data right there. The resulting abstractions or transformations of the input data may then be sent to the remote computer when the remote computer is ready to accept them, and/or an output, a decision, may be made right there at the smart computer terminal and activate its output printer or control other devices.

Let the BBNS system be analogous with the smart computer terminal, and the M/L system be analogous to the remote computer. A good deal of information processing on data from both sensory input and internal, habitual concerns is carried on by the mechanical processes of the BBNS system alone and outputs (behaviors or further internal experiences) are instigated and carried out as a result of this "local" computation. For much of this, there may be no auto-psi connection with the "remote" computer, the M/L system, at all. The BBNS is a very sophisticated and capable local computer.

Sometimes the "remote computer" (M/L system) modifies the action of the BBNS system, the smart computer terminal, via auto-psi in ways which are not predictable from a knowledge of the smart computer terminal alone. The kinds of behaviors Stanford has described as *psi-mediated instrumental processes (PMIRs)* are excellent examples of this [23, 24].

Imagine a need-relevant situation where, given the sensory and stored information available to a person and the processing capacities of his BBNS system, he does not have the information necessary to reach a need-relevant decision and carry out an adaptive of action. He nevertheless behaves quite appropriately. Just luck? Sometimes. But Stanford and others have shown in laboratory studies that a subject carrying out an irrelevant laboratory task can significantly often make other wise "random" choices which match a key knowable only by ESP, and which then reward the percipient with a pleasant, need-relevant condition in the second part of the experiment. The subject can not know by ordinary means that there is a "hidden agenda" of this sort, yet he responds appropriately. The M/L system has used allo-psi to scan the environment, gather the needed information and then has influenced BBNS system processes by auto-psi to modify the final emergent, the subject's behavior, so he just happens to be "lucky." Note too that in the PMIR, the auto-psi process need not actually modify the emergent of *conscious experience*: the subject just does the right thing without knowing why, without knowing there is a hidden agenda to the experiment.

I believe the tremendous complexity of the BBNS system and the automatization of much of its action in the course of ordinary socialization offers a partial explanation for why allo-psi about external events usually does not work well in our ordinary state of consensus consciousness. The information processing activity in the BBNS system has become habitual and continuous, and it ties up most or all of the processing capacity of the BBNS system. In terms of possible allo-psi messages being received or allo-psi outputs being initiated (via auto-psi intermediation to the M/L system), this produces a very high "noise" level that makes it unlikely that auto-psi will be able to influence the BBNS system or vice versa. This view is congruent with various experimental data we have that indicate that allo-psi conducive states (such as hypnosis and the states induced by ganzfeld procedures [25]) involve cutting down internal noise levels from irrelevant BBNS system processes. In my extended presentation of my theory—that immediate feedback will help percipients to learn to use psi efficiently [26]—I also stress that learning to discriminate the relevant psi signals from internal BBNS system noise is a major requirement of success.

ALTERED STATES OF CONSCIOUSNESS

In my systems approach to understanding altered states of consciousness [1, 27-32], I defined a *discrete altered state of consciousness* (d-ASC) as a radical pattern change in the functioning of consciousness, a combination both of particular subsystems or aspects of consciousness changing as well as the consequent emergent, system properties of consciousness changing. I was careful not to bring in serious dualistic considerations in these earlier publications in order not to arouse possible prejudices in the largely unprepared psychologist audiences that the theory was primarily intended for. Thus while I defined "awareness" as constituting a kind of activating energy for affecting the operation of subsystems of consciousness, I was careful to legitimatize this usage as primarily a matter of semantic convenience, so it would be consistent with and useful to monistic positions. For the dualistic Psi Mediated Emergent Interactionism position I am now proposing, however, some further distinctions about the nature of altered states of consciousness can be made.

Any *discrete state of consciousness (d-SoC)* consists of a particular pattern of functioning, a system, within both BBNS system and M/L system levels. The d-SoC, the experienced consciousness, is the emergent from the interaction of both of these BBNS and M/L levels of organization. A discrete *altered* state of consciousness, a radical pattern shift compared to some d-SoC we take as our baseline, can be induced by 1) changing the organization of subsystems of the BBNS system alone; 2) changing the organization of subsystems of the M/L system alone; and/or 3) changing the nature of the auto-psi interactions between BBNS and M/L system levels. In terms of observable consequences of this Psi Mediated Emergent Interactionist understanding, some d-ASCs will turn out to be explainable strictly in terms of alterations of BBNS system functioning, but others will not be reducible simply to alterations in BBNS system functioning.

This view that some d-ASC are primarily functions of M/L system changes or auto-psi interaction changes has important implications for parapsychological research as well as more conventional research. We have a scattering of evidence to suggest that various altered states may be conducive to psi functioning. This may be partially due to the fact that well ingrained BBNS system habits (automatisms) that create the noise that interferes with psi functioning in our ordinary state are no longer functioning as strongly in some d-ASCs, due to changes in BBNS system operation. It may also mean that certain d-ASCs have their balance of functioning shifted more toward the M/L system side, for which psi is the direct and natural mode of expression. Thus we might expect some important breakthroughs for enhancing allo-psi by discovering which particular d-ASCs are most favorable in this way.

ORDINARY PSI AND NON-ORDINARY PSI

From the perspective of this Psi Mediated Emergent Interactionist view of consciousness, it becomes clear that psi is frequently used in everyone's life, but is being used, as it were, "internally" and implicitly. We frequently use auto-clairvoyance to read our own BBNS system and auto-PK to affect our BBNS systems. This is ordinary psi, auto-psi. What we observe in parapsychological experiments however, is non-ordinary psi; it is taking a process ordinarily confined "within" a single organism and pushing it outside making it allo-psi.

I have tried to represent the general situation in an amplified model of consciousness in Figure 4. When the M/L system reads the state of its own BBNS system, we term this auto-clairvoyance (auto-CL in the figure); when the M/L system influences BBNS system operation we term it auto-PK. The unusual use of psi outside of the organism results in allo-clairvoyance (allo-CL) to obtain information about the external environment, and allo-PK to affect the external environment. This is a BBNS system to M/L system information flow route, and an M/L system to BBNS system information/energy flow route, respectively.

Communication from one distinct M/L system to another, telepathy, can be subdivided into *receptive telepathy*, picking up information from another M/L system, and *projective telepathy*, sending information to another M/L system, a useful division for maintaining symmetry with the clairvoyance and PK processes. Given our terminological convention, telepathy is inherently a form of allo-psi. Indeed, the fundamental distinction seems to be with psi that deals with M/L system to M/L system interaction, and psi that deals with matter and M/L system interaction.

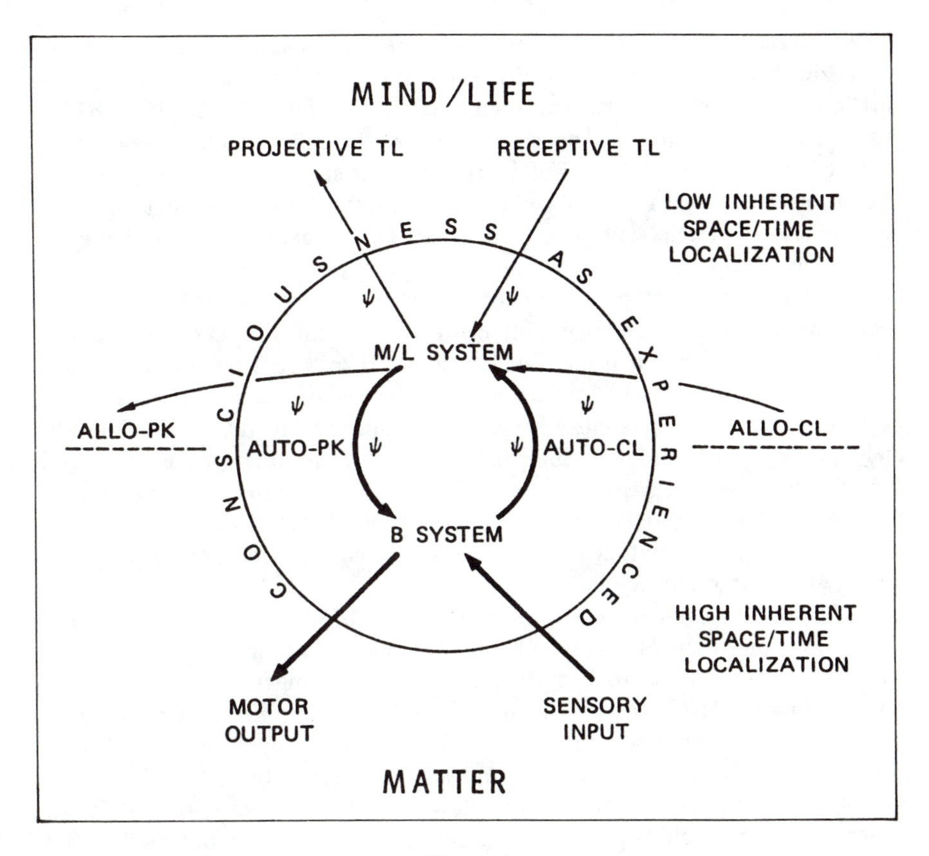

Figure 4.

On the BBNS system side of consciousness, sensory input brings in information about the matter world around us, automatically abstracts this information along consensus consciousness concept and value lines, and creates a continuous simulation of our environment (which we call perceiving the world [22]). Motor output sends, through our various muscles, information and energy back out into that matter world. I have shown the sensory input and motor output arrows, and the auto-CL and auto-PK arrows in heavy lines to represent the most prominent information flow channels ordinarily active in an organism. I have also drawn in "consciousness as experienced" as a circle around these other processes, to remind us that it is an emergent of BBNS system and M/L system auto-psi interaction.

Earlier I listed precognition, prediction of the future when this cannot be done from rational inference, as one of the basic four psi phenomena, but I am inclined not to consider this temporal distinction as to where psi is focused as quite so basic. In Figure 4 I have indicated that the M/L aspect of consciousness has a low inherent degree of localization in space and time (an idea developed further in my discussion of trans-temporal inhibition [33-34]). The BBNS system aspect of consensus consciousness, on the other hand, is very highly localized in space and time. That is, the BBNS system belongs to an order of reality in which you can specify with great confidence that a particular event is happening at a certain time, at a certain location in space and possesses highly specifiable and predictable matter and physical energy properties.

The M/L system, on the other hand, is not so localized in terms of physical space/time measures. While it usually centers around the here and now of BBNS system space and time, it is more widely spread than that. This is why there is a need for the process I have called *trans-temporal inhibition* in efficient ESP, an active inhibition of extrasensorily perceived immediately future and immediately past events in order to sharpen (contrast enhancement, edge detection) the extrasensory perception of the present. The M/L system can volitionally focus at different spatial and temporal locations other than the immediate spatio-temporal present that the BBNS system and its associated sensory and motor apparatus are locked into.

To be more speculative, it may be that the very diffuseness or spatio-temporal nonlocalization of the M/L system is a reason that it is associated with a particular BBNS system. That BBNS system may act as a stabilizing influence on the operation of the M/L system; it focuses and anchors that M/L system to a particular location and moment in space and time for evolutionary reasons. Without this stabilizing focus the M/L system might "lose itself." Indeed, as far as biological survival is concerned, events within the sensory range of the BBNS system are almost always the most important ones for the organism to be concerned with, so the style of M/L system interaction with the BBNS system would evolve toward maximizing the efficiency of the combined BBNS and M/L system/consciousness for biological survival. To the extent to which this becomes habitual and automatized, this would be a reason why allo-psi seems relatively rare; the psi capacity is almost totally used up in auto-psi functioning which is geared to maximizing the functioning of the total organism in its physical environment. Further, allo-psi is only rarely useful for gathering information about the immediate spatio-temporal environment of the BBNS system, as our biological senses are already so effective.

SPECIAL SENSITIVITY OF BBNS SYSTEM TO PSI

The BBNS system, from this Psi Mediated Emergent Interactionism point of view, has two main properties. First are many self-organizing properties, independent of interaction with the M/L system, that are adaptive in dealing with the needs for maintaining homeostasis within the physical organism and dealing effectively with the physical environment. Second, it must have properties that not only make it receptive to M/L system influences via auto-PK, it should be efficiently receptive to these influences in order to maximize survival potential. This means semi-independent associative and decision making properties, "perceptual" properties, with respect to M/L system influences that compensate for inefficiencies and deficiencies in the interaction.

The BBNS system, for example, should automatically fill in a message from the M/L system that is a little incomplete and, in cases of doubt, fill it along lines which are most relevant to biological survival. If an ambiguous pattern seen in some bushes could be a tiger, it is highly adaptive for simulation of the environment to make you perceive it as a tiger and take fast action, rather than ignore it because you aren't *sure* it's a tiger. The receptive function of the BBNS system, then, for auto-PK, is likely to be elaborative as well as efficiently receptive, and, by being elaborative, it can be prone, like any similar communication system, to produce incorrect outputs.

The line of reasoning has two important consequences for parapsychological research. First, the BBNS system must be especially sensitive to auto-PK. Insofar as auto-PK and allo-PK are probably manifestations of the same fundamental process, investigation of what aspects of BBNS functioning make it especially sensitive to PK should be of great value in designing other physical processes which would be sensitive PK detectors. Second, not only does the M/L system need to use an appropriate allo-psi process to gather the relevant information about some distant target other than the percipient's own BBNS system, this information must be then put into, or influence the BBNS system of the percipient by auto-PK effects on BBNS system functioning. This is in order to get relevant information into the emergent consensus consciousness of the percipient, information which he can then express behaviorally so we can observe it. Auto-PK at least needs to affect relevant aspects of the BBNS system so we can observe a behavioral or physiological effect that manifests the psi information, even if it does not reach the percipient's consensus consciousness. But, the BBNS system is constantly producing an adaptive simulation of the percipient's immediate sensory environment (modified by his psychological concerns) in a way largely independent of current BBNS and M/L system interactions, and this constitutes a high noise level that the auto-PK information carrying the allo-psi information must compete with. Further, the elaborative aspects of the BBNS system's receptivity to auto-PK means that there is a strong probability that the psi message will tend to be elaborated/distorted in ways which fit the ongoing, survival-oriented simulation of the immediate physical environment being continuously constructed by the BBNS system. The very "efficiency" and partial independence of the BBNS system, then, automatically makes some distortion of allo-psi messages likely. Given this as a basic characteristic of the BBNS system, practical measures to increase the incidence of psi in parapsychological experiments would need to involve some combination of BBNS system noise reduction (as in, e.g. ganzfeld techniques), discrimination training (as in immediate feedback training), and enhanced discriminability of the allo-psi targets themselves (distinct remote locations, e.g. versus similar playing cards differing only in number).

COMPLEXITY OF PSI TASKS

The BBNS system is obviously an incredibly complex system, so auto-psi interaction with the M/L system must also be of a very complex nature. This leads to an interesting idea: the kinds of allo-ESP and allo-PK tasks we have given percipients and agents in the laboratory have probably been enormously simple (and perhaps trivial) compared to what is routinely done by auto-clairvoyance and auto-PK. In an earlier modeling of PK along conventional lines [15, 35], for example, I argued that influencing a tumbling die by PK is quite complex, requiring continuous clairvoyant feedback about its three dimensional motion and mass-energy parameters and the surface characteristics of the surface it would bounce against, so just the right amount of PK force could be applied in just the right places and directions at just the right moments. This is, indeed, a formidable task from the viewpoint of physical mechanics as we currently conceive it, but from the point of view of an M/L system used to constantly reading and influencing enormous numbers of cells in a dynamically changing brain, the task may well be so trivial as to be hardly capable of attracting much attention! Similarly, the circuits of the electronic random number generators which have been influenced by allo-PK may also be trivially simple compared to the typical operations of auto-clairvoyance and auto-PK.

This leads to a clear prediction, namely, that allo-PK should work more successfully when directed toward super-complex systems, such as brains or huge computers, rather than when directed toward simply physical tasks: it's what the M/L system is used to doing, and habit is hard to break. Further, we probably can't reliably detect differences in PK efficacy for simple tasks that involve, say, influencing one versus ten decision-making elements. They are all ridiculously simple; we need to compare PK on single element random number generators versus generators that employ millions or more of interacting decision-making elements leading to a random output.

A similar line of thinking might be applied to ESP tasks; perhaps ESP is more successful at detecting the overall pattern of complex elements than at picking out single elements.

OUT-OF-THE-BODY EXPERIENCES

Out-of-the-body experiences (OBEs) are especially interesting from a dualistic point of view. While there are both a wide variety of experiences and much looseness in the use of the term OBE, the basic, "classical" experience that we will consider here has two distinguishing elements. First, the experiencer finds himself located at some location other than where he knows his physical body is located. Second, and of crucial importance in definition, the experiencer knows *during* the experience that his consciousness is basically functioning in the patterns he recognizes as his ordinary state. It is quite similar to consensus consciousness. He can call upon most or all of his ordinary cognitive abilities during the OBE, typically recognizing, e.g., the "impossibility" of his ongoing experience according to what he has been taught. As far as he can tell, he is rather "normal" in all mental ways that matter; it's just that he is obviously located somewhere other than where his physical body is.

Although some people manage to retrospectively talk themselves out of accepting the dramatic dualistic implications of their OBE, most people who have an OBE become confirmed dualists on an experiential basis. No matter what "logical" arguments one may make, they *know* that their consciousness is of a different nature than their physical body, because they've experienced them as separated.

As an outsider, listening to someone else's account of his OBE, we can dismiss the implications of his experience and remain convinced monists without much psychological effort. The OBE, as defined so far, can be seen as an interesting hallucination. It is like a dream in that a realistic, but hallucinatory environment is present, but obviously certain other parts of the BBNS system responsible for ordinary consensus consciousness are also activated. Indeed, if the experiencer would only call his experience a "lucid dream," [36] instead of an OBE, stop insisting that his experience was *real* and agree with our view that it was *hallucinatory*, even if it seemed real, he would not bother a confirmed monist. It is easy from a monistic point of view to model brain functioning that would create a lucid dream.

As defined so far, OBEs could easily be included within the domain of ordinary psychology (although they are not), for I haven't put any psi element into the definition. Indeed, it is useful to define them in purely psychological terms just to make them legitimate subjects for investigation by psychologists who might shy away from psi phenomena. But we know that in some OBEs the person accurately describes a distant location that he could not have known about except by psi. The most dramatic laboratory example occurred when a subject I called Miss Z correctly read a five-digit random number on a shelf above her head while experiencing an OBE [37].

Because of the strong psi component of some OBEs, I am inclined from the Psi Mediated Emergent Interactionist position, to take them as being pretty much what they seem to be, a temporary spatial/functional separation of the M/L system from the BBNS system. The separation is not only temporary (otherwise we wouldn't get any report!), it is probably only partial, with the M/L system still interacting with the BBNS system to some extent. Several aspects of OBEs support this partial separation view.

First, in most OBEs the person experiences his consciousness as very like ordinary, yet consensus consciousness arises as an emergent from BBNS and M/L system interaction and mutual patterning. This suggests that a great deal of this interaction is still occurring, and/or that the *force of habit*, the lifetime practice of this patterning, is still fairly active in the M/L system alone.

Second, in cases of prolonged (more than a few minutes apparent duration) OBEs, or cases of people who have had many OBEs, or cases of OBEs associated with severe disruption of physical functioning as near-death cases, consciousness as experienced tends to drift away from its ordinary patterning into various d-ASCs. The OBE starts to become "ineffable," or more of a "mystical experience," even though it retains the basic feeling of separation of BBNS and M/L systems. This is what we would expect for greatly reduced auto-psi interaction between these two systems; both the BBNS system and the M/L system would start drifting toward unique patterns of functioning determined by their own inherent characteristics, now manifesting as they are freed from mutual, interactive patterning of each other. Indeed, it is these kinds of unusual OBEs that may give use valuable insights into what the M/L system in and of itself may be like, unpatterned by the BBNS system.

IMAGERY

Finally let us briefly consider the role of mental imagery from the Psi Mediated Emergent Interactionist perspective.

From an orthodox monistic, materialistic position, all mental imagery is totally reducible to an electrochemical pattern in some part of the BBNS system. Except when communicated or acted upon through normal sensory or motor channels, an image thus has no direct effect on reality. I suspect, however, that imagery (in all modalities) may sometimes have M/L system reality, that an image may exist in "mental space" independently of the BBNS system, and/or that imagery may be an important carrier of auto-clairvoyant and auto-psychokinetic information.

In most psychic development systems found in traditional societies, as well as in many contemporary systems [38], the ability to create, fix, and control mental imagery, especially visual imagery, is strongly emphasized. The shaman undertakes an inner "journey" to "see" his spirit helpers or to "see" distant scenes that are important to know about [39]. The practitioner of the Western magical tradition [40, ch. 11] learns to fashion a vivid image that represents the outcome he desires, fix this image in his mind during a ceremony, and then release it into some kind of psychic realm where the image will then influence processes toward the desired outcome. Some initial empirical research has suggested that imagery may indeed be a more effective way of producing detectible psychokinetic effects, especially if it is a preferred mode of mental functioning for the agent [41-44]. Note that we are discussing statistically significant deviations from chance here in this research, not obvious macro-PK effects visible to the naked eye.

The classical period of ESP research was almost exclusively done with the twenty-five card Zener deck with its five symbols of square, cross, wavy lines, circle, and star. Although originally selected to represent five readily discriminable visual patterns, the fast pace of response involved (typically only a few seconds per trial) and the fact that a percipient might become analytical about the process ("I've already guessed a lot of stars, I'd better guess something else now.") tended to discourage the use of visual imagery as a way of trying to get the target information. While many *statistically* significant outcomes came from this card guessing procedure, the magnitude of the effects is typically low (say 21% success over a long period instead of the 20% expected by chance) and the procedure does not produce reliable ESP results with most percipients.

A number of parapsychologists found theoretical reasons and/or empirical observations suggesting that imagery was a useful mediating vehicle for conveying information obtained by ESP [see, e.g., 45-51]. Reflecting an interest in altered states as facilitators of imagery, one outcome was an extensive series of ganzfeld studies, where percipients in ESP tests spent their time in a uniform visual and auditory ganzfeld. The visual ganzfeld was produced by light illuminating acetate hemispheres (halved ping pong balls!) which were over their eyes, the auditory ganzfeld by white or pink masking noise in earphones they were wearing. The ganzfeld procedure's effects on ESP functioning have been studied at some length, and are generally considered positive [52], even after multitudinous methodological arguments [53].

A second major outcome of the interest in imagery as a mediator for ESP is an interesting experimental procedure that is fairly reliable and successful in the hands of a number of experimenters, namely the *remote viewing* procedure [16, 54-56]. One experimenter (the traveler) consults a random process which determines some physical location (the target site) he should drive to. A second experimenter (the interviewer) remains at the laboratory with a percipient (the viewer). At a time when the traveler will be at the target site the interviewer asks the viewer to close his eyes and describe any imagery he gets that will tell him about the target site the traveler is at. Some of the impressions of the viewer are visual images and are both described and drawn. Other impressions are imagistic but not visual (such as feeling it is cold at the target site), occasionally some are just "knowings" that are not in the form of a sensory image. Irrelevant impressions and images also arise as noise.

Blind judges compare the viewers' descriptions of a series of target against the actual target sites. Many experimenters show the judges can accurately match descriptions against the sites they were intended to describe. Often the visual images make this matching quite easy, as when a marina target is described by the viewer as "I see a lot of little sailboats . . ." My general impression is that psi-mediated images in successful remote viewing studies tend to remain close to what the actual targets look like, while the ganzfeld procedure produces, if anything, too much imagery. The target related images tend to be drowned in the noise of associated imagery and associated images to associated images, etc.

The most interesting theoretical analysis of the role of imagery in mediating ESP is that of White [57]. She found heavy reliance on imagery was characteristic of successful percipients in older research, before the card guessing era. This research is in its infancy, but I suspect that as our knowledge of imagery generally improves, its usefulness as a mediator of auto-psi processes will also improve.

CONCLUSIONS

Dualistic views of consciousness are inherently appealing as they seem to match our personal experience of consciousness being different from matter. The overwhelming success of the physical sciences has lent great prestige to monistic views of consciousness that reduce all mental functioning to material events, so that many people, including scientists who should know better, believe that somehow science has "proven" that all experience can be completely reduced to brain functioning.

Basic parapsychological phenomena, however, are completely incompatible with reducing all mental events to materialistic monism, at least given our current knowledge of the physical world and reasonable extensions of this knowledge. Thus mental events need to be investigated on their own terms, as well as correlated with physical events. I hope the Psi Mediated Emergent Interactionist perspective presented in this paper will stimulate such research.

REFERENCES

1. C. T. Tart, *States of Consciousness*, Psychological Processes Inc., El Cerrito, California, 1983. Originally published Dutton, New York, 1975.
2. J. Miller, *Living Systems*, McGraw-Hill, New York, 1978.
3. F. Capra, *The Tao of Physics*, Shambala, Berkeley, California, 1975.
4. G. Zukav, *The Dancing Wu-Li Masters*, William Morrow, New York: 1979.
5. A. Greeley, *The Sociology of the Paranormal*, Sage Publications, Beverly Hills, California, 1975.
6. B. Wolman, L. Dale, G. Schmeidler and M. Ullman (eds.), *Handbook of Parapsychology*, New York, Van Nostrand Reinhold, 1977.
7. J. Beloff (ed.), *New Directions in Parapsychology*, Scarecrow Press, Metuchen, New Jersey, 1975.
8. I. Grattan-Guiness (ed.), *Psychical Research: A Guide to its History, Principles and Practices*, Aquarian Press, Wellingborough, England, 1983.
9. R. Jahn (ed.), *The Role of Consciousness in the Physical World*, Westview Press, Boulder, Colorado, 1981.
10. S. Krippner (ed.), *Advances in Parapsychological Research, Volume 1, Psychokinesis*, Plenum Press, New York, 1977.

11. S. Krippner (ed.), *Advances in Parapsychological Research, Volume 2, Extrasensory Perception*, Plenum Press, New York, 1978.
12. S. Krippner (ed.), *Advances in Parapsychological Research, Volume 3*, Plenum Press, New York, 1982.
13. E. Mitchell and J. White (eds.), *Psychic Exploration: A Challenge to Science*, Putnams, New York, 1974.
14. G. Schmeidler (ed.), *Parapsychology: Its Relation to Physics, Biology, Psychology, and Psychiatry*, Scarecrow Press, Metuchen, New Jersey, 1976.
15. C. T. Tart, *Psi: Scientific Studies of the Psychic Realm*, Dutton, New York, 1977.
16. C. T. Tart, H. Puthoff, and R. Targ (eds.), *Mind at Large: Institute of Electrical and Electronic Engineers Symposia on the Nature of Extrasensory Perception*, Praeger, New York, 1979.
17. R. White (ed.), *Surveys in Parapsychology: Reviews of the Literature and Updated Bibliographies*, Scarecrow Press, Metuchen, New Jersey, 1976.
18. C. Tart, The Controversy about Psi: Two Psychological Theories, *Journal of Parapsychology, 46*, pp. 313-320, 1983.
19. ———, Acknowledging and Dealing with the Fear of Psi, *Journal of the American Society for Psychical Research, 78*, pp. 133-143, 1984.
20. C. T. Tart and C. M. Labore, Attitudes Toward Strongly Functioning Psi: A Preliminary Survey, *Journal of the American Society for Psychical Research, 80*, pp. 163-173, 1986.
21. C. Tart, Effects of Electrical Shielding on GESP Performance, *Journal of the American Society for Psychical Research, 82*, pp. 129-146, 1988.
22. ———, *Waking Up: Overcoming the Obstacles to Human Potential*, Shambala, Boston, 1986.
23. R. Stanford, An Experimentally Testable Model for Spontaneous Psi Events. I. Extrasensory Events, *Journal of the American Society for Psychical Research, 68*, pp. 34-57, 1974.
24. ———, An Experimentally Testable Model for Spontaneous Psi Events. II. Psychokinetic Events, *Journal of the American Society for Psychical Research, 68*, pp. 321-356, 1974.
25. C. Honorton, Psi and Internal Attention States, in *Handbook of Parapsychology*, B. Wolman, L. Dale, G. Schmeidler and M. Ullman (eds.), New York, Van Nostrand Reinhold, pp. 435-472, 1977.
26. C. T. Tart, Toward Conscious Control of Psi through Immediate Feedback Training: Some Considerations of Internal Processes, *Journal of the American Society for Psychical Research, 71*, pp. 375-408, 1977.
27. P. Lee, R. Ornstein, D. Galin, A. Deikman and C. T. Tart, *Symposium on Consciousness*, Viking, New York, 1975.
28. C. T. Tart, On the Nature of Altered States of Consciousness, with Special Reference to Parapsychological Phenomena, in *Research in Parapsychology 1973*, W. Roll, R. Morris and J. Morris (eds.), Scarecrow Press, Metuchen, New Jersey, pp. 163-218, 1974.
29. ———, The Basic Nature of Altered States of Consciousness: A Systems Approach, *Journal of Transpersonal Psychology, 8*:1, pp. 45-64, 1976.

30. C. T. Tart, Drug-induced states of consciousness, in *Handbook of Parapsychology*, B. Wolman, L. Dale, G. Schmeidler and M. Ullman (eds.), New York, Van Nostrand Reinhold, pp. 500–525, 1977.
31. ————, Putting the Pieces Together: A Conceptual Framework for Understanding Discrete States of Consciousness, in *Alternate States of Consciousness*, N. Zinberg (ed.), Free Press, New York, pp. 158–219, 1977.
32. ————, A Systems Approach to Altered States of Consciousness, in *The Psychobiology of Consciousness*, J. Davidson, R. Davidson and G. Schwartz (eds.), Plenum Press, New York, pp. 243–269, 1980.
33. ————, Improving Real-Time ESP by Suppressing the Future: Trans-Temporal Inhibition, in *Mind at Large: Institute of Electival and Electronic Engineers Symposia on the Nature of Extrasensory Perception*, C. T. Tart, H. Puthoff and R. Targ (eds.), Praeger, New York, pp. 137–174, 1979.
34. ————, Space, Time and Mind, in *Research in Parapsychology 1977*, W. Roll (ed.), Metuchen: New Jersey: Scarecrow Press, pp. 197-250, 1978.
35. ————, Models for Explanation of Extrasensory Perception, *International Journal of Neuropsychiatry, 2*, pp. 488–504, 1966.
36. S. LaBerge, *Lucid Dreaming: The Power of Being Awake and Aware in Your Dreams*, Jeremy Tarcher, Los Angeles, 1985.
37. C. T. Tart, A Psychophysiological Study of Out-of-the-Body Experiences in a Selected Subject, *Journal of the American Society for Psychical Research, 62*, pp. 3–27, 1968.
38. J. Mishlove, *Psi Development Systems*. Jefferson, North Carolina: McFarland & Co., 1983.
39. M. Harner, *The Way of the Shaman*, Harper & Row, New York, 1980.
40. C. T. Tart, *Transpersonal Psychologies*, Psychological Processes Inc., El Cerrito, California, 1983. Originally published Harper & Row, New York, 1975.
41. R. Morris and K. Bailey, A Preliminary Exploration of Some Techniques Reputed to Improve Free Response ESP, in *Research in Parapsychology 1978*, W. Roll (ed.), Scarecrow Press, Metuchen, New Jersey, pp. 63–65, 1978.
42. Steilberg, B., "Conscious Concentration" versus "Visualization" in PK Tests, *Journal of Parapsychology, 39*, pp. 12–20, 1975.
43. W. Braud, G. Smith, K. Andrew, and S. Willis, Psychokinetic Influences on Random Number Generators during Evocation of "Analytic" versus "Nonanalytic" Modes of Information Processing, in *Research in Parapsychology 1975*, J. Morris, W. Roll, and R. Morris (eds.), Metuchen, New Jersey, Scarecrow Press, pp. 85–88, 1976.
44. R. Morris, M. Nanko, and D. Phillips, A Comparison of Two Popularly Advocated Visual Imagery Strategies in a Psychokinesis Task, *Journal of Parapsychology, 46*, pp. 1–16, 1982.
45. R. Anderson and W. Anderson, Veridical and Psychopathic Hallucinations, *Parapsychology Review, 13*:3, pp. 17–23, 1982.
46. L. George, A Survey of Research into the Relationship between Imagery and Psi, *Journal of Parapsychology, 45*, pp. 121–146, 1981.
47. ————, Psi in the Mind's Eye, *Theta, 10*:2, pp. 31–35, 1982.

48. L. George, Enhancement of Psi Functioning through Mental Imagery Training, *Journal of Parapsychology, 46*, pp. 111–126, 1982.
49. C. Honorton, Psi and Mental Imagery: Keeping Score on the Betts Scale, *Journal of American Society for Psychical Research, 69*, pp. 327–332, 1975.
50. C. Honorton, L. Tierney, and D. Torres, The Role of Mental Imagery in Psi-Mediation, *Journal of the American Society for Psychical Research, 68*, pp. 385–394, 1974.
51. R. Schechter, G. Solfvin, and R. McCollum, Psi and Mental Imagery, *Journal of the American Society for Psychical Research, 69*, pp. 321–326, 1975.
52. C. Honorton, Psi and Internal Attention States, in *Handbook of Parapsychology*, B. Wolman, L. Dale, G. Schmeidler, and M. Ullman (eds.), Van Nostrand Reinhold, New York, pp. 435–472, 1977.
53. R. Hyman and C. Honorton, A Joint Communique: The Psi Ganzfeld Controversy, *Journal of Parapsychology, 50*, pp. 351–364, 1986.
54. R. Targ and K. Harary, *The Mind Race: Understanding and Using Psychic Abilities*, Villard Books, New York, 1984.
55. R. Targ and H. Puthoff, *Mind Reach: Scientists Look at Psychic Ability*, Delacorte, New York, 1977.
56. C. Tart, H. Puthoff, and R. Targ (eds), *Mind at Large: Institute of Electrical and Electronic Engineers Symposia on the Nature of Extrasensory Perception*, Praeger, New York, 1979.
57. R. White, A Comparison of Old and New Methods of Response to Targets in EXP Experiments, *Journal of the American Society for Psychical Research, 58*, pp. 21–56, 1964.

PART II

Research into Psychophysiological Correlations: Images, Dreams, and Hallucinations

CHAPTER 3

*Waking Images and Neural Activity**

EDOARDO BISIACH AND ANNA BERTI

INTRODUCTION

In this chapter, the term *mind* refers to the manifold central nervous activities which may, to variable extent, be traduced into overt behavior. (Whether the concept of mind should more properly apply only to a subset of such activities, may for present purposes be disregarded.) Discerning *mental images*, therefore, is held to depend on the criteria by which we are willing to consider an *image* a manifestation of nervous activity, whether inferred from behavior or more directly detected by some technical means.

Rooted in philosophy, psychology, computer science and neurology, the issue of mental images seems nowadays to be one of the most intricate and controversial. Obstacles such as incompetence areas, ideologies and rhetoric peculiar to each of the involved parties, as well as reluctance to interdisciplinary confrontation (prone to degenerate into theoretical chauvinism), may breed equivocation and soliloquy. Yet, there seems to be more and more room for a sound trial-and-error way of proceeding by drawing advantage from mutual interdisciplinary advice and correction.

Leaving aside the allegiances of the metaphysical functionalist, hesitancy *vis-à-vis* neurological theories of mental images may originate from persuasion that such theories pave the blind alley which leads to stale reductionism. What would be lost to sight in a predicament like this is the fact that this alley may, and should always be walked both ways. It is indeed our contention that no real knowledge of the mind of a living organism can ever be attained by ignoring his brain. Thinking in terms of mere software, indeed, would expose us to the danger of imagining mental organs which are very far from those which actually exist in the brain. A long time has elapsed since epidemiologists discarded

*Preparation of this chapter was aided by a CNR grant 85.00830.04.

miasmata in the search for a tangible origin and adequate explanation of infectious diseases in more "material" entities. True, they had to proceed under social pressures which are more tolerant to contemporary theorists of mind. Sooner or later, however, the latter will probably accept that psychology should be constrained by physiology, as much as epidemiology is by microbiology, and that psychological parochialism would lead us astray as plainly as a parallel neurological parochialism, by ignoring functionalist approaches to the mind, would lead us nowhere.

We will first examine some philosophical and psychological quandaries about mental images. Then we will point to some arguments supporting the hypothesis of a functional similarity between perceptual and representational processes and shortly review suggestions for a neural implementation of structures in which confluence of these processes might take place. The next section will focus on clinical observations which might constitute a critical neurological contribution to the understanding of mental images: namely, on observations relative to a syndrome of unilateral representational disorder (*dyschiria*), of which unilateral neglect of space is the most frequent and best-known, although not unique, manifestation. Finally, we will consider the issue of the contribution of each half of the brain to processes related to mental imagery.

PHILOSOPHICAL AND PSYCHOLOGICAL QUANDARIES

Although brain, behavior, mind and phenomenal experience are the facets of what may appear an impossible tetrahedron, unitary knowledge of mental images can only be attained by integrating these four aspects. This statement may seem a very bad start, since it seems to raise the question of the scientific status of phenomenal experience and misgivings about category mistakes. As far as the first is concerned, our premise is only meant to record the fact that, if we are to push our knowledge beyond the surface of mere behavioral regularities, the development of our collective insight is largely influenced by a manifold of individual, presumably very disparate, phenomenal experiences (e.g., by the remarkably different degree to which people claim to experience mental images) and that shared knowledge merges, in turn, with what each of us knows from his own inner perspective—whatever controversy this might raise. As for the danger of category mistakes occasioned by pitfalls resulting from the collision of idioms peculiar to each of the above mentioned perspectives (e.g. from expressions such as "red mental image"), the reader himself will judge at the end of the chapter.

The concept of mental images has been related to two kinds of representation: namely, to a stored, inactive data base and to information in the course of being processed. The second type of representation is often, but not necessarily, taken as conscious. Although some confusion may be engendered by the lack of uniformity in the use of the words "mental image" with reference to these different states and processes, the context in which they appear is usually sufficient to avoid misunderstanding. Most arguments, however, are centered on processes involving the surfacing of a sensory-like representation which the subject refers with a variable degree of phenomenal experience. It is indeed in this context that arguments are apt to degenerate either by viewing mental images as metaphysical entities mysteriously related to the activity of the nervous tissue or, contrariwise, as simulacra forming in the brain and passively offering themselves for perception by the mind's eye. The first of these two aberrations needs not be taken too seriously, except perhaps when in a somewhat concealed form it insinuates the bizarre idea that something (phenomenal experience) may be the cause or the consequence of itself under another description (nervous activity). The second is worth consideration, not because anybody is likely, these days, to be found toying with the *kitsch* "picture-in-the-head" version of mental images, but because this can be taken as a straw-man for too radical attacks which, although intended to counter misconceptions about mental imagery, may also involve the positive potential of this concept.

What is the origin of the myth of (hypostasized) "pictures-in-the-head?" Block denounces a false parallel between our relation to mental images on one side and to external objects on the other [1]. But objects "are things we see," says Bloch, whereas mental images "are things we *have*." (We would prefer to say, for the purposes of this discussion, that "mental images are things we *are*," in order to wipe out any homunculus or germ of infinite regress.) Likewise, Hebb points out that reports of mental images are not descriptions of the mental image itself but of its apparent object [2]. In this sense, imagery reports would be no more introspective than perceptual reports [3]. Hebb adds that since one is aware of the inexistence of the apparent object, "it is natural to think that it must be the image that one perceives and describes."

By this demystification of the "picture-in-the-head" we are apparently given three true parallels instead of a false one. They may be defined as a three-cornered set of relations. One place is occupied by external objects which exist independently of the presence of any particular observer and by whatever outward manifestation the subject of mental images may show of the intensional object of the latter, as well as of his perception of real objects. The second place is held by the subject engaged in mental imagery or perception. The third, by a witness; to wit, by the scientific community. The first of the three legitimate parallels exists between independent objects and those (drawings, descriptions, etc.) originating from the imaginal or perceptual activity of our subject. The second, between the subject's phenomenal experience in the case of imagery or perception respectively. The third, between the information processing activities corresponding to these two kinds of phenomenal experience. Disregarding the case of discursive representation for a while, it should be uncontroversial that "pictorial" representations exist *outside* our subject's head, in the form, e.g., of drawings he might produce either by copying an external object or by depicting the intensional object of his mental image, as well as *inside* (assuming that our subject does experience sensory-like mental images), where "pictorial" is merely defined on a phenomenological level and by no means implies identical characteristics of experiences related to perception on one side and to mental imagery on the other.

Given this system of parallels, we must first discover what perceptual and imaginal information processing have in common. As we shall see, certain results have already been obtained in this direction. However, in order to answer the question of whether this processing might also, in some sense, be said to be pictorial, another parallel has to be considered: that between the properties of copied or depicted objects and the pattern of corresponding brain activities which can be objectively assessed. We must then ascertain, therefore, whether there are mental processes which retain enough of the properties of external objects to qualify as imaginal. This is in part an empirical question and in part a matter of criteria.

We are now in a position to be more precise and from now on to limit the term "*mental* image" to a putative objective pattern of neural activity, in contrast with "*phenomenal* image." The next step is to determine the role played by this imaginal representation in cognitive processes; this implies a subtler and more problematic question, which must nonetheless be considered here since the very applicability of terms such as "mental" and "representation" to the brain activities at issue depends on the answer we give.

Much of the controversy about the pictoriality of mental representations has apparently developed without a clear understanding of premises such as those formulated above or with the deliberate purpose of preventively undermining any imaginal notion of cognitive processes. Before turning to review some empirical evidence and theoretical proposals in favor of an updated pictorialism, we shall consider some aspects of the controversy and some foundational worries.

Following Rey [4, p. 119], we will make a distinction between x-depicting, x-describing and x-denoting as possible mental representations of an object x; the first imaginal, the second and third belonging to a propositional system. We will also assume that any kind of representation can be derived from any other and that both x-depicting and x-describing can be more or less approximative, according to circumstances. That is to say that both depicting and describing may have a variable degree of indeterminacy; the type of indeterminacy, however, is quite different in the two cases. Whereas a propositional representation of a wooden-legged man needs not specify the side of the wooden leg [5, p. 130], in the putative mental image of a wooden-legged man *qua* wooden-legged the side must either be the left or the right, as in a phenomenal image, although these images might be so rudimentary that the color of a man's eyes is left undefined. Conversely, the propositional representation of a "chiliagon" differs sharply from that of a "999-sided polygon," whereas it would be ludicrous to maintain that the two corresponding imaginal representations would differ in any respect; they would be likely to bear a strict resemblance to the image of a circle, the area and location of which (in striking contrast with propositional representations) cannot help but be defined for each example of such representations. The fact that with a great deal of patience one *could* draw a chiliagon (taken by Dennett as demonstrating that picturing does not proceed from mental representations of a pictorial kind [5, p. 131]) is likely to be due to the ability to draw details from wholes which one is not able to subitize in a mental image while being able to construct, more or less directly, an image of single parts, as in the case of imagining a multidigit number. Obviously, we do not mean to suggest that one could at once form the mental image of a 179° 38′ 24″ angle; we only suggest that the computations involved in chiliagon-drawing might involve a lot of imaginal representation.

The infelicitous locutions to which we usually resort to denote non-propositional mental representation do not imply that forming a mental image is anything like depicting an image on canvas. The fact that in imaging a tiger one may not report the phenomenal experience of a definite number of stripes [5, p. 130] or that the image of the handwriting of a known person might be evoked without imagining any particular words [6, p. 181] shows the naivety of such an idea but constitutes no proof against the existence of mental representation of a non-propositional kind; quite the contrary, it might demonstrate the existence of representations whose constraints are such that they may not be able to faithfully render all propositional particulars of an "*n*-striped tiger." The limits set to imagery find a parallel in perceptual activity: we can easily recognize the voice of a familiar person in the adjoining room without recognizing her words. In the transitions among processes occurring in perception, propositional and non-propositional representation, some information is lost and some added. As Dennett remarks [5, p. 130], what we retain after having seen the film version of "*War and Peace*" is something more like the written Tolstoy than the film, which, on the other hand, "cannot possibly be *faithful* to Tolstoy's words, since the 'picture painted' by Tolstoy does not go into the details the film cannot help but go into (such as the color of the eyes of each filmed soldier)." It must, however, be added that whoever has been fortunate enough to read Tolstoy without having previously been exposed to the film will admit that his own imagery evoked by the book was likewise "unfaithful" to Tolstoy. Indeed, any image derived from a propositional representation of *x* cannot but be one of an *x* with surplus content, in the same way in which a model cannot help but have theory-irrelevant properties.

Unsuccessful attempts at dismantling the notion of mental images altogether may resort to arguments aiming to demonstrate how any trace of iconic representation dissolves at the level of more elaborate cognitive processes. Images are thus viewed as raw material which has to be interpreted and which cannot carry any inherent character of truth or falsehood. Wittgenstein's duck-rabbit drawing, his image of a man who might be interpreted as walking uphill or walking backwards downhill, or variants to the same effect are given as examples.

Fodor asserts that an iconic representational system "does not distinguish the thought that John is tall from the thought that John is fat" [7, p. 137]. What is overlooked in arguments of this kind is the synchronic and diachronic context in which a representation is embedded. A mental image, whatever it might turn out to be, cannot be conceived *in vitro*; it is very far from being a fragment of still-life. Its meaning is determined by the complex of its antecedents and concomitants, which might themselves be icons. There seems to be no reason why the analytic aspect of "John is tall" should not be embedded in an image of John which synthesizes an indefinite number of properties of which a corresponding number of separate analyses are possible. Why should the synthesis be less cognitive than the analysis? The two different "thoughts" about John might simply correspond to two different patterns of activation of a system of links which determines the image of John in an associative network. Indeed, the semantics of inner generated mental images could hardly be conceived in isolation from its syntax. Mental images implausibly conceived as snapshots of mental activity might be as meaningless as a single frame cut off from a film, whereas their dynamics, like a silent film, might carry a fully-fledged thought. Thus, even if it were true that "icons are insufficiently abstract to be vehicles of truth" [7, p. 137], it would only be true of fictional mental images.

Criticism of mental images, on the other hand, cannot be developed in absolute terms, but, unless the concept itself of mental representation is called into question, ought to unfold with reference to alternative forms of representation. It is therefore rather surprising that whereas the notion of iconic representation has been the subject of hyperbole aiming to create fetishes which could be comfortably fought against, a parallel caricature of propositional representations as "sentences-in-the-head" is seldom encountered. Yet, in the same way in which imaginal representations may be underrated as precognitive structures, propositional representations might be demoted to patterns of pre-motor speech activity. The term "quasi-pictorial," which acknoweldges the present unavailability of an adamantine construct of mental image, may look ludicrous, whereas the parallel term "quasi-linguistic," referred to propositional representations purported to be the essence of cognition, has no such overtones. The fact that a compromise is drastically imposed in the latter case by the opportuneness of extending the concept of cognition to animals makes no difference.

Hedging idioms on both fronts leads to the absurd consequence of presenting the two antagonistic forms of representation as "non-propositional" and "non-imaginal" respectively. Anyway, non-imaginal, viz. "sentence-analog," representations are usually said or implied to inhabit the sanctum of cognition. The well designed metaphor of computer programs has been devised for this exclusive representational system, which has so far resisted empirical investigation and might be a phoenix, for all we know. It is indeed significant that, whereas we begin to recognize cognitive disorders due to focal brain damage which is likely to interfere with an imaginal system of representation, no comparable evidence has yet been provided, either in man or in animals, of selective disorders due to disruption of a putative propositional code. Even most severe language disorders seem to leave cognitive processes underlying everyday nonverbal behavior relatively unaffected. Frontal lobe disease, on the other hand, is much more likely to interfere with the manipulation of representations rather than with the possibility of forming representations in one or another representational mode.

If we want to tunnel into the innermost recesses of cognition to obtain an idea of the structure of our representational system at those levels, the most reasonable strategy is that of coordinating a program of concurrent actions starting both from the input and output sides of the system. The two basic steps taken from the input side are meant to ascertain, first, whether and to what extent some degree of isomorphism is preserved between patterns of stimulation at the receptor surface and subsequent information-bearing structures and, secondly, whether isomorphic structures, if actually found, should be considered pre-cognitive or, in all aspects, cognitive inasmuch as isomorphic.

The notion of isomorphism which is inherent to the concept of mental image—not its caricature—needs not imply that represented and representing properties are in the same physical dimension. There is nothing more otiose than arguing that the results of the spectral analysis of nervous tissue engaged in representing a red object are different from those obtained by the analysis of the red object itself. This is why the notion of isomorphism has given way to the more adequate notion of *analog*. This conforms to Shepard's second-order isomorphism by which the relationships between properties of the represented object on a physical dimension are mapped by similar relationships among properties of the representing medium on a different physical dimension [8]. For example, two sounds of differing intensity might be represented by differing rates of discharge in the nervous tissue. This non-propositional representational mode might be in a strong sense *nomological* inasmuch as 1) *it obeys the physical laws* and 2) *is thenceforth fully empowered to represent* (see below). It is worth anticipating, however, that in the special case of space representation a first-order isomorphism (realized on the same physical dimension) might be involved between represented and representing properties. It is also worth observing that the relevant contraposition here is not between analog and digital, but between analog and propositional representation. This should clear at least a part of the ambiguity in the notion of analog representation which worries some authors (e.g., [9, p. 118]). It should also be observed that what is of critical importance for the coding of the black and white of an image in terms of zeroes and ones is not the appearance of these representational atoms *per se*, but *the way they are grouped*. If, for example, in representing the contours of a pattern depicted two-dimensionally their grouping were such as to preserve topological properties on a representing n by n matrix (see Figure 9.3 in [10]), they would constitute an analog in which an unessential limitation might be due to the degree of discontinuity imposed by the grain of the grid. If, on the other hand, this grouping were linear (as in the example discussed by Dennet, [11]), much of the pictorial character of the representation would be lost in the resulting vector. As it will later be shown, a linear transformation of this kind does not seem to be performed by the brain, whose visuo-spatial representation seems indeed to be much more pictorial.

We have already mentioned that the most serious attack on imaginal (i.e. analog) representation does not intend to deny the existence of information-bearing structures of this type, but to reduce them to profane physical instantiation of codes which need a separate act of cognitive interpretation in order to be admitted and manipulated as *true* representations in the computational workspace of cognition. Unless only a change in vocabulary is implied, by which the nomological explanations of neurophysiology are rephrased into—not superseded by—computational explanations (which does not seem to be the case), this Pygmalionic act, in the domain of the natural mind, would seem to demand some sort of supernatural agency. This would be required for the same reason for which external (human) mediation is necessary in order to fix (i.e. stipulate) the semantics of uninterpreted symbols in a computing machine, a mediation whereby a leap from the nomological to the non-nomological, that is arbitrarily rule-governed, is truly made. What is at this point to be settled, is whether or not we should credit imaginal representation with *original* semantics, short of which, except for the intervention of some unknown demiurge, our brain would be lost in referenceless symbols. Since a positive answer to this question seems unescapable, unless we are willing to embrace some form of dualism, much of Pylyshyn's [12] arguments against mental images should perhaps be endorsed to the varying degree of flexibility of mental processes rather than related to a sharp dichotomy between cognitive and non-cognitive processes drawn to classify propositional and analog modes of representation. Pylyshyn's strategy is that of (rightly) assuming that analog representations must be subject to nomological constraints, and then stating that suggested instances of analog representations either resist being affected or *penetrated* by cognitive processes (which would constitute the earmark of the non-cognitive functional architecture of the mind) or undergo cognitive penetration (which would shatter their disguise as sterling, nomologically constrained analogs). According to Pylyshyn what suggests the existence of analog representations is an "objective pull," a "tendency to view the cognitive processes in terms of properties of the represented objects—that is in terms of the semantics of the representation—rather than the structure, or syntax, of the representations" [12, p. 229]. By doing so, one "begs the question why processing occurs in this fashion." Putting side by side two assertions of Kosslyn et al. [13], that "images do represent metrical distance" and that "images have spatial extent," he remarks that "this vacillation between *representing* and *having* is no accident [12, p. 233]. Indeed, the attraction of the theory—what appears to give it a principled explanation—is the strong version . . . but the only one that can be defended is the weaker version . . . indistinguishable from the tacit knowledge view I have been advocating," that is that tacit knowledge of how things happen in the world would induce subjects in mental rotation or mental scanning experiments to behave as if relying on an intrinsically analog representation of space. Which of the two versions is true is in part an empirical question towards the solution of which, as we shall later argue, some steps have been made which seem to favor the strong one. In part it depends on the willingness to accept the view that, first, analog representations do indeed represent actual or possible states of affairs in the world with no need of further semantic investiture and, second, that the fact that such analogs may be shown to be to some extent manipulated top-down, far from downgrading their analog properties to an unessential role, might be a clear indication of how such properties are inextricably involved in cognitive processes.

Yielding to this view of mental representation implies abandoning the sharp distinction between code and its interpretation which is inherent in the digital computer metaphor and which might constitute one of its misleading aspects. One may wonder if, at this point, psychology should retire, under pain of being trivialized to folk-psychology in the negative sense. Block has put forth similar worries: "if cognitive science must postulate pictorial representations . . . much of what it hopes to explain will probably be in the domain of a different discipline: neurophysiology" [1]. Consistent with the beliefs we expressed introducing our chapter, we think that this is not and must not be the case, whatever the depth of the analog layer might turn out to be. What seems to be clear is that a brain metaphor should be exploited along with the digital computer metaphor (the appealing construct of "cell assemblies" was suggested by a psychologist, after all) and, perhaps, that we should take the distinction between different levels of aggregation of mental processes not too literally and welcome some amount of interdisciplinary overflow at their borders.

SIMILARITY AND CONFLUENCE OF PERCEPTUAL AND REPRESENTATIONAL PROCESSES

Answering the question about the functional similarity of perceptual and representational processes, as pointed out e.g. by Block [1], provides no solution of the controversy over the pictorialist vs. descriptionist interpretation of mental representations. It is however a preliminary step necessary to find out analogies and disanalogies apt to suggest and constrain suitable imaginal theories.

There is no need to go into the details of the copious literature relative to the correspondence of perceptual and representational processes, for the reader may find them in the valuable survey recently published by Finke [14]. Finke classifies three kinds of theories: structural, functional and interactive. Structural theories maintain that "internal structures or mechanisms used in the generation of mental images are similar to some used in perception." This is a rather conservative claim, inasmuch as it does not posit actual sharing of any specific processing resources. Functional theories try to explain how the formation and transformation of mental images may contribute to inner operations performed on perceptual data, e.g. in the well-known experiments of mental rotation done by Shepard and his associates (e.g. [8]). Interactive theories make the strongest proposal by envisaging common mechanisms for perception and imagery. All theories are evaluated by Finke on the basis of the empirical support they enjoy and of the strength of alternative accounts in terms of experimenter bias, task-induced demand characteristics and subject's tacit knowledge of how things happen in the world. The results of the scrutiny are far from being clear-cut: each type of theory seems to be vulnerable by at least some accounts. Finke's persuasive conclusion is that since "no single alternative can adequately explain the collective evidence for all three types of theories" credit should be given to the claim shared by most imagery researches that "imagery truly does resemble perception in at least some fundamental respects."

The weakest position seems to be that held by theories which posit an actual confluence of perceptual and representational processes on some common mechanisms. Before submitting what we think constitutes harder evidence in support of this claim, we shall briefly mention some proposals relative to neural mechanisms which might subserve both perception and representation.

Since its initial formulation, the concept of cell assembly [15] was meant as the foundation stone of a theory suited to account for representational, as well as perceptual theories in the nervous system. Hebb reiterated this claim, more specifically, in his 1968 and 1980 papers [2, 16]. Although it may be said to be in some respects too vague [17], this theory offers a valuable heuristic scheme for conceiving in neural terms processes which have not yet been encompassed by neurophysiological investigation, or are very unlikely to prove within reach of neurophysiology. It also offers a basis for a general analog conception of cognitive processes.

Konorski [6, pp. 86ff.] has suggested a model, largely influenced by clinical knowledge about different forms of cortical blindness, in which initially naive "gnostic units" fed by cortical sensory areas develop the ability to process sensory information in the context of previous experience and to generate autochthonous mental representations. Konorski's model is endowed with a redundancy mechanism fit to account for important aspects of representational processes such as Ribot's law, by which earlier memories are more robust than those laid down later, and the comparatively low vulnerability of the stock of memories in case of focal brain injury. It is however mute concerning the format of surface mental images and, although inspired by clinical evidence, fails to account for the important phenomena which are the subject of the next section. In some respects it is therefore similar to Pribram's model [18, 19], which also provides for a convergence of perception and representation in the mechanism of a neural hologram granting a good deal of redundancy. Designed to replace Köhler's isomorphic visuo-spatial theory of cortical fields of electrical potentials, however, Pribram's model is explicitly directed against a first-order spatial isomorphism of mental images which, as we shall see, provides the main thrust of our model.

Although not directly concerned with the format of mental images, Mishkin's model [20], relative to the establishment and reactivation of central visual representations and consisting of a circuit involving the monkey's area TE, lymbic and thalamic structures, cannot be ignored by the reader interested in the neural correlates of imagery, who is advised to look at the original paper for what space limits prevent us from expounding here. Likewise, the anatomical argument put forth by Merzenich and Kaas [21] cannot be ignored. Dealing with the manifold of separate topologically organized areas which have been found over the surface of the so-called association cortex, these authors point out that, given their considerable extent, these areas are likely to subserve mental representation as well as perceptual activities. The topological structure of such areas fits in with a notion of spatial isomorphism of mental representations.

A spatial analog is embodied in the topological indexing system of Trehub's neuronal model [22, 23]. Although this model, sufficiently implemented to perform a wide spectrum of the operations implied in visuo-spatial cognition, has been criticized as being inadequate in some respects [17], it constitutes an important step forward after Hebb's theory (into which it might presumably be incorporated) in providing a way of conceiving cognitive processes in terms of neural circuitries. Up to now, it is the neural model which offers the best suggestion relative to a medium for the surfacing of phasic visuo-spatial images in active memory; the spatial analog module ("retinoid") on which such images appear may also help to explain phenomena of hemi-spatial misrepresentation in brain-damaged patients.

DYSCHIRIA: A UNILATERAL REPRESENTATIONAL DISORDER

In 1913, Hermann Zingerle adopted the term *dyschiria* (from Greek *chèir, cheiròs:* 'hand' and, by extension, 'side') to designate a syndrome an early profile of which appeared in sparse clinical writings towards the end of the last century [24]. Its dominant symptom being the singular oblivion of the half of space contralateral to the brain lesion, this syndrome was eventually listed under the prejudicial appelations of *hemi-spatial neglect* or *spatial hemi-inattention*. Indeed, most patients severely affected by this syndrome behave as if one half of space had ceased to exist: perception and exploration of the environment, although apparently normal on one side, may be completely abolished on the other. Such patients may draw one half of a figure, leaving the other half unfinished, or may execute orders involving one half of their body while ignoring those related to the opposite half; they may enter into conversation with a person talking from their affected side, though obstinately addressing their speech to a silent bystander on their normal side; etc. Usually these patients show unilateral anosognosia, that is they fail to recognize sensory or motor disorders affecting the neglected side of their body.

Early explanations of these disorders in terms of defective sensory processing or in terms of defective actuation of programs for the exploration of the environment (either ascribed to a more central attentional disfunction or to a relatively more peripheral pre-motor impairment) had to be abandoned or reconceived to account for the recent findings that neglect phenomena are not confined to perception and action in outer space but extend to the domain of mental representation. Such findings, which lend support to the representational interpretation of dyschiria given by Zingerle, concern mental representation of both short-term and long-term memory contents. An instance of the first kind is the misapprehension of one half of shapes presented in horizontal motion behind a stationary slit [25, 26]. The second eventuality is exemplified by the omission of details belonging to one side during the description from memory of a familiar setting from a given vantage point, such that details neglected in a given perspective may be reported during the description of the opposite one and vice-versa [27, 28], or by disorders of spelling limited to one half of words [29].

The effacement of one half of space from the patient's awareness may be sometimes substituted by misrepresentation of its content. Although this usually surfaces in the form of pathological completion of one half of shapes or words [30-32], it may—as already observed by Zingerle—relate to one side of the body or, less frequently, of the environment. The delusional, and often amazingly bizarre beliefs concerning the misrepresented half of the body in patients who manifest this form of dyschiria are well-known to all clinical neurologists under Gerstmann's term of *somato-paraphrenia* [33]. They may be associated with a variable degree of attention to the affected side, ranging from mild inattention to hyperattention, thus vindicating the more comprehensive name given to the syndrome by Zingerle.

The site of the lesion responsible for the appearance of dyschiria is variable: lesions may encroach the temporo-parieto-occipital junction, the frontal lobe or subcortical structures (see [34] for a review). This suggests that multistage or heterarchical mechanisms are involved in mental representation of space. Of utmost importance, however, is the fact that the lesion may involve a spatially circumscribed brain area and that damage to such an area may cause contralateral losses or aberrations of mental representation which are as spatially circumscribed as are perceptual disorders due to local breakdown of relatively more peripheral sensory apparata. This suggests that *the analog structure which characterizes earlier information-processing stages is preserved in the nervous system up to levels the lesion of which is followed by a similar impairment of sensory-driven and of autochthonous representation*.

As we have argued elsewhere [35], the first-order spatial isomorphism between outer and mental space, inferred from clinical findings, is cognitively irrelevant *per se* since it is only a consequence of the convenient way in which the spatial arrangement of complex nervous circuits has evolved. It is cognitively relevant, however, inasmuch as it reveals the analog structure of processes involved in spatial cognition which otherwise might have gone unnoticed. In fact, whereas an analog space representation does not necessarily imply a first-order isomorphism, the reverse is not true. The spatial characteristics of representational lacunae are such that they could not be accounted for by any selective disorder of a propositional system (i.e., by whatever kind of dysphasic disorder). Clinical findings thus invite the conclusion that the medium for space representation is likely to be implemented in the nervous tissue roughly in the form of the two-dimensional array posited by Kosslyn and his associates (see [36] for a general review), which implies that representations forming in this medium do have imaginal properties.

Before arguing for the cognitive capacity of the spatial analog inferred from the behavioral disorders which characterize dyschiria, it is necessary to shield our inferences against possible counterarguments in terms of task-induced demand characteristics, subjects' tacit knowledge and experimenter's bias. To this end it must first be observed that any spuriousness due to the subject's beliefs, expectations or compliance can be easily ruled out in the experiments aimed at demonstrating unilateral neglect in a merely representational domain. As already indicated elsewhere [37] (see also [38, p. 70]) the obtained results, indeed, cannot be viewed as simulating the behavioral consequences of elementary sensory-motor disorders which, if present, are as a rule underestimated, if not utterly denied, by the patients themselves. As for the experimenter's bias, which could very easily fake experiments such as those requiring description of remembered views, it seems to be dismissed by the unexpected finding that unilateral representational neglect was not apparent in the records of the patients who gave descriptions including foreign items [28]. Such an outcome might be due to the fact that, because of the concomitance of spatial confusion revealed by intrusion of foreign items, left and right details of the view were mixed up in the patients' representation. Finally, it is impossible to see how any of these contaminating factors could explain unilateral anosognosia or the misbeliefs of somato-paraphrenia. (See [39] for an argument against the "psycho-dynamic" interpretation of unilateral anosognosia).

A formal model of a spatial analog involved *in perception as well as in mental representation* and accounting for both the negative and the positive aspects of dyschiria (that is for hemi-neglect and for delusional phenomena confined to the affected side of space) has been presented elsewhere [35, 40]. We will not expound it again, limiting ourselves to a recapitulation of our earlier arguments concerning the status of the suggested analog in the domain of cognitive activities.

As we have already observed, even if disposed towards cautious acceptance of evidence in favor of some kind of mental images, sceptically inclined people are left the further move of demurring at such images in so far as it is unclear whether they are cognitively more significant than, say, the pattern projected onto the retina by a distal object. Finding that mental representations with spatial properties are nomologically constrained by the analog medium provided by the nervous tissue in the same way as sensory-driven representations are, far from constituting a reason for considering images (nomologically constrained mental representations) fully-fledged cognitive structures, might suggest the existence of a print-out stage in which more "abstract" representations are laid-down in the stupid medium which is made available to them.

Against such a view, we have argued [35, 38-40] that clinical findings related to cortical blindness accompanied by anosognosia and to various aspects of dyschiria show that analog structures, such as those we have been discussing so far, are crucially involved in the microgenesis of perceptual awareness and constitute the building blocks of a distributed control mechanism which finds no replica in a superordinate, unitized cognitive module.

Knowledge of the mechanisms responsible for conscious monitoring of the flow of information coming from sense organs and interfacing the nervous system with its environment began to develop nearly one hundred years ago; Anton's paper on anosognosia related to cortical deafness and cortical blindness constitutes its cornerstone [41]. In that paper Anton showed that awareness of blindness may be retained, even when the defect is due to destruction of cerebral cortex, unless some brain structures near to the visual areas are also compromised. In the latter case, the subject is no longer aware of his sensory loss and may report delusional visual experiences. In sharp contrast with this severe disorder, other cognitive activity may appear unchanged. This was the first intimation of a highest-level *modality-specific* processing stage which might constitute the basic component of a modular, distributed consciousness. Although Anton himself mentioned instances of unawareness of motor disorders affecting one half of the body, Zingerle's paper made the second critical step by implying an analog structure of the putative module, that is by showing that unawareness and misrepresentation may disguise one half of the environment while leaving the other half apparently incontaminate. The unyielding imperviousness of these disorders to the pool of unimpaired cognitive resources demonstrates that no effective general purpose control unit is superimposed onto the modules from the disfunction of which they originate. Cognitive control over sensory experience and mental representation seems therefore to be mainly a distributed function inherent in the modules at issue, which would thus constitute much more than a menial infrastructure.

DISTINCTIVE HEMISPHERIC CONTRIBUTION TO IMAGINAL PROCESSES

In the foregoing section, in order to defend the notion of mental image, we have argued for the existence of surface mental representation occurring in modality-specific analog components of the nervous system. No mention has been made of the mechanisms by which information coming either from without or from within the system is processed and transferred to the inferred analog, nor of the processes such information may undergo once loaded into an analog. Although these issues exceed the scope of our chapter, they are of primary relevance to problems concerning possible differences between the roles played by the left and by the right hemisphere in mental imagery.

The question of whether each hemisphere is equally equipped to host mental images is a most variegated one and ought to be considered with a clear understanding of its separate aspects and, possibly, within the frame of an explicit theory of the dynamics of mental imagery. This has seldom been done, as is apparent from the reviews by Ley [42, 43], and Ehrlichman and Barrett [44]. Thus, it is no surprise that these authors disagree in their conclusions on an hemispheric specialization for mental imagery.

Indeed, much of the alleged superior competence of the right hemisphere in imaginal processes is inferred from performance of tasks—mainly visuospatial tasks—in which the role of visual images is far from being clear. In this section we will not examine this aspect of the issue, and will also disregard the rather inconclusive evidence afforded by indicators such as EEG, galvanic skin responses, ocular deviations, etc., which is reported in the above mentioned reviews.

Very little can be drawn about hemispheric asymmetries in imaginal processes from Penfield's otherwise very remarkable studies with electrical brain stimulation [45]. With all due reservations relative to inferring any such asymmetries from cases in which long-standing epileptogenic lesions may have caused extensive readjustment of the cerebral architecture, the single relevant datum offered by these studies is the fact that, although electrical stimulation of the temporal cortex was apt to elicit complex sensory-like experiences in the same proportion in left and right hemispheres, the spread of the responsive area was found to be larger in the right temporal lobe. Thus, Penfield's data cannot be taken as either supporting or disconfirming the hypothesis of a right-hemisphere specific mediation of imaginal processes. The single conclusion they license is that some activities preluding the appearance of mental images can be carried out by *each* hemisphere.

Indubitable evidence of hemispheric asymmetry is, by contrast, constituted by the fact that, nearly in the same way in which dysplasia ensues from left-hemisphere lesions, dyschiria ensues from lesions of the right hemisphere. This shows that the analog medium in which, according to our interpretation, sensory-driven and autochthonous mental representations are displayed while surfacing in active memory is unevenly distributed in the brain. Whereas the right hemisphere is equipped with an analog of the whole egocentric space, the left, in normal conditions, contributes an effective analog relative only to the right side of space [35]. This analog, however, may not only support perceptual activity related to the right hemi-space, but also imaginal activity such as the right hemi-spatial hallucinations observed in left hemi-neglect patients by Silberpfennig [46] and by Mesulam [47]. Since, as a rule, all phenomena which constitute dyschiria appear after acute or subacute right hemisphere damage and disappear over time, even in case of lasting, extensive damage, it may be conjectured that under these circumstances the left-hemisphere analog acquires the ability to represent the whole egocentric space. This conjecture would be undermined by clear evidence of reappearance of the same pathological phenomena after a second lesion of the right hemisphere; this would indeed suggest that compensation for the earlier disorder was due to reduplication of functions by different structures of the right hemisphere. That at least in some instances the left hemisphere might take on the job of representing both halves of egocentric space is, however, documented by the possible absence of left hemi-neglect after right hemispherectomy [48].

Intricate obstacles for the issue of the comparative involvement of the left and right hemisphere in imaginal representation are set by sparse records concerning patients who started complaining of loss of visual imagery following focal brain damage. It is hard, if not impossible, to form an opinion based on the available literature, since all cases appear, *a posteriori*, more or less insufficiently investigated and reported. A sound move to begin with may be that of renouncing any attempt at making some sense out of clinical records of loss of dreaming activity, since this has been found after damage of either hemisphere, and even after damage (pre-frontal leucotomy) not involving post-Rolandic brain structures [49]. Against the thesis of a right-hemisphere "mediation" of imaginal processes [43], however, is Greenwood, Wilson and Gazzaniga's [50] unequivocal finding that their patient JH, with complete telencephalic commissurotomy, awakened from REM sleep, verbally reported dreams with fully-fledged visual content.

On the contrary, cases in which loss of visual imagery is either explicitly referred or inferred from the patient's behavior–in isolation or associated with disorders of visual perception of agnosic character–deserve consideration. In a paper which has the unprecedented merit of addressing the issue within the frame of an explicit imagery model, Farah concludes that posterior areas of the left hemisphere are "critical for the image generation process" [51]. We cannot fully share these conclusions for a number of reasons.

First, whereas it is true that loss of visual imagery (either subjectively experienced by the patient himself or inferred from his inability to describe his visual images or to make drawings from memory) seems to be more often associated with lesions apparently confined to the left than with lesions apparently confined to the right hemisphere, subjectively experienced loss of visual imagery does not necessarily imply that such images cannot be generated. In spite of his denial of any sort of phenomenological correlate, our patient MG [52] was perfectly able to carry into active memory a map of his immediate surroundings to appropriately guide any kind of behavior. He could do that anytime, provided he abstained from deliberately programming the course of his actions; on one occasion, for example, we observed that in stepping back over the threshold of the testing room while keeping his eyes fixed on those of the experimenter he had made a half-turn towards the right direction he was to take, unaided by any visual cue. The association with other troubles which may be explained on the basis of a selective visuo-verbal disconnection made us suggest the same explanation for MG's imaginal disorder; this interpretation might apply to other patients with similar defects, including patients who, although not complaining of loss of subjectivity experienced visual images, are not able to describe their content.

Second, a parallel interpretation might be advanced for the inability to make drawings from memory, which Farah offers as evidence of an image generation defect. Other forms of apraxia, indeed, have been interpreted as due to intrahemispheric disconnection [53].

Third, although it is possible that disorders in image generation are sometimes due to the same disfunction which results in some forms of visual agnosia, Farah's empirical distinction between published cases of loss of mental imagery without and with visual agnosia and her corresponding theoretical distinction between disorders of image generation and of long-term visual memory, respectively, are too sharp. Our case MG, for example, could give a precise description of his wife's aspect and could recognize her promptly, though denied being able to form any visual image of her after the onset of his illness. Admittedly, he showed symptoms which are usually interpreted as "associative visual agnosia:" he proved unable, for instance, to identify at once the Royal palace in his town, but was able to suggest a correct identification on the basis of its architectural features. However, the relationships between "associative visual agnosia" and language disorders are still an unsettled question [54-58] and the agnosic features of our case, once again, may hint at a borderline pathology rather than a disorder of image generation or of the long-term visual store.

Fourth, the results of a subsequent investigation of two split-brain patients by Kosslyn, Holtzman, Farah and Gazzaniga [59], suggest that both hemispheres are able to generate visual images. A superiority of the left hemisphere, according to this study, seems to be only related to the structuring of precise spatial relations among parts of the image (a conclusion which is in apparent contrast with the right hemisphere superiority in assembling visually presented fragmented patterns in a meaningful percept [60, 61]).

Thus, it appears that the issue of the specific contribution of each half of the brain to the sequence of processes involved in generating and manipulating mental images is far from being settled. The above mentioned studies by Farah and by Kosslyn et al., however, are the first indication of a shift in approaching the problem which is very likely to provide decisive data in the near future.

SUMMARY AND CONCLUSIONS

The concept of mental image has been defended in this chapter from the stand point of clinical neurology. What survives of this concept is perhaps too removed from the qualities of external objects and from the appearances of phenomenal images to warrant the name 'image' any longer. This is a trifle, however. What we have been trying to argue is that patterns of neural activity which deserve the name of image inasmuch as they instantiate an analog model of outside reality, far from being the slave carriers of a message, embody cognitive activity. That is, they embody neurodynamic structures in which awareness is likely to originate and which are likely to participate in the composite of control functions inherent in cognitive activity. To the extent that mental images, thus conceived, are *processes* occurring in the brain, one may wonder what contribution is made to such processes by each hemisphere. As we have shown, apart from the asymmetry revealed by hemi-spatial neglect and related disorders, little is known. Refraining from forcing conclusions on the grounds of the equivocal data so far available, we have indicated the first steps undertaken along what seems to be a promising line of inquiry.

REFERENCES

1. N. Block, Mental Pictures and Cognitive Science, *The Philosophical Review, 92*:4, pp. 499–541, 1983.
2. D. O. Hebb, Concerning Imagery, *Psychological Review, 75*:6, pp. 466–472, 1968.
3. D. F. Marks, Mental Imagery and Consciousness: A Theoretical Review, in *Imagery. Current Theory, Research, and Application*, A. A. Sheikh (ed.), Wiley, New York, pp. 96–130, 1983.
4. G. Rey, Introduction: What Are Mental Images? in *Readings in Philosophy of Psychology*, N. Block (ed.), Harvard University Press, Cambridge, Massachusetts, pp. 117–127, 1981.
5. D. C. Dennett, The Nature of Images and the Introspective Trap, (1969), reprinted in *Readings in Philosophy of Psychology*, N. Block (ed.). Harvard University Press, Cambridge, Massachusetts, pp. 128–134, 1981.

6. J. Konorski, *Integrative Activity of the Brain*, The University of Chicago Press, Chicago, 1967.
7. J. A. Fodor, Imagistic Representation, (1975), reprinted in *Readings in Philosophy of Psychology*, N. Block (ed.), Harvard University Press, Cambridge, Massachusetts, pp. 135-149, 1981.
8. R. N. Shepard, Form, Formation and Transformation of Internal Representations, in *Information Processing and Cognition: The Loyola Symposium*, R. L. Solso (ed.), Lawrence Erlbaum Associates, Hillsdale, New Jersey, pp. 87-122, 1975.
9. R. Schwartz, Imagery–There's More to It than Meets the Eye, in *Imagery*, N. Block (ed.), The MIT Press, Cambridge, Massachusetts, pp. 109-130, 1981.
10. S. E. Palmer, Fundamental Aspects of Cognitive Representation, in *Cognition and Categorization*, E. Rosch and B. B. Lloyd (eds.), Lawrence Erlbaum Associates, Hillsdale, New Jersey, pp. 259-303, 1978.
11. D. C. Dennett, How to Study Human Consciousness or Nothing Comes to Mind, *Synthese, 53*, pp. 159-180, 1982.
12. Z. W. Pylyshyn, *Computation and Cognition*, The MIT Press, Cambridge, Massachusetts, 1984.
13. S. M. Kosslyn, S. Pinker, G. Smith, and S. P. Schwartz, On the Demystification of Mental Imagery, *Behavioral and Brain Sciences, 2*:4, pp. 535-548, 1979.
14. R. A. Finke, Theories Relating Mental Imagery to Perception, *Psychological Bulletin, 98*:2, 236-259, 1985.
15. D. O. Hebb, *Organization of Behavior*, Wiley, New York, 1949.
16. ————, The Structure of Thought, in *The Nature of Thought*, P. W. Jusczyk and R. M. Klein (eds.), Lawrence Erlbaum Associates, Hillsdale, New Jersey, pp. 19-35, 1980.
17. S. Pinker and S. M. Kosslyn, Theories of Mental Imagery, in *Imagery. Current Theory, Research, and Application*, A. A. Sheikh (ed.), Wiley, New York, pp. 43-71, 1983.
18. K. H. Pribram, *Languages of the Brain*, Prentice-Hall, Inc., Englewood Cliffs, New Jersey, 1971.
19. K. H. Pribram, M. Nuwer, and R. Baron, The Holographic Hypothesis of Memory Structure in Brain Function and Perception, in *Contemporary Developments in Mathematical Psychology*, R. C. Atkinson, D. H. Krantz, R. C. Luce, and P. Suppes (eds.), Freeman, San Francisco, pp. 416-457, 1974.
20. M. Mishkin, A Memory System in the Monkey, *Philosophical Transactions of the Royal Society*, London, *B 298*, 85-95, 1982.
21. M. M. Merzenich and J. H. Kaas, Principles of Organization of Sensory-Perceptual Systems in Mammals, *Progress in Psychobiology and Physiological Psychology, 9*:1, pp. 1-41, 1980.
22. A. Trehub, Neuronal Models for Cognitive Processes: Networks for Learning, Perception and Imagination, *J. Theoretical Biology, 65*:1, 141-169, 1977.
23. A. Trehub, A Confusion Matrix for Hand-Printed Alphabetic Characters: Testing a Neuronal Model, Paper presented at the *Eighth Symposium and Quantitative Analysis of Behavior at Harvard*, 1985.

24. H. Zingerle, Ueber Stoerungen der Wahrnehmung des eigenen Koerpers bei organischen Gehirnerkrankungen, *Monatschrift für Psychiatrie und Neurologie, 34*: 1, pp. 13-36, 1913.
25. E. Bisiach, C. Luzzatti, and D. Perani, Unilateral Neglect, Representational Schema and Consciousness, *Brain, 102*:3, pp. 609-618, 1979.
26. J. A. Ogden, Contralesional Neglect of Constructed Visual Images in Right and Left Brain-Damaged Patients, *Neuropsychologia, 23*:2, pp. 273-277, 1985.
27. E. Bisiach and C. Luzzatti, Unilateral Neglect of Representational Space, *Cortex, 14*:1, pp. 129-133, 1978.
28. E. Bisiach, E. Capitani, C. Luzzatti, and D. Perani, Brain and Conscious Representation of Outside Reality, *Neuropsychologia, 19*:4, pp. 543-551, 1981.
29. D. M. Baxter and E. K. Warrington, Neglect Dysgraphia, *J. Neurology, Neurosurgery and Psychiatry, 46*:12, pp. 1073-1097, 1983.
30. E. K. Warrington, The Completion of Visual Forms across Hemianopic Field Defects, *J. Neurology, Neurosurgery and Psychiatry, 25*:3, pp. 208-217, 1962.
31. M. Kinsbourne and E. K. Warrington, A Variety of Reading Disability Associated with Right Hemisphere Lesions, *J. Neurology, Neurosurgery and Psychiatry, 25*:4, pp. 339-344, 1962.
32. E. K. Warrington, The Effect of Stimulus Configuration on the Incidence of the Completion Phenomenon, *British J. Psychology, 56*:4, pp. 447-454, 1965.
33. J. Gerstmann, Problem of Imperception of Disease and of Impaired Body Territories with Organic Lesions. Relation to Body Scheme and Its Disorders, *Archives of Neurology and Psychiatry, 48*:4, pp. 890-913, 1942.
34. G. Vallar and D. Perani, The Anatomy of Spatial Neglect in Humans, in *Neurophysiological and Neuropsychological Aspects of Spatial Neglect*, M. Jeannerod (ed.), North Holland, Amsterdam, 1987.
35. E. Bisiach and A. Berti, Dyschiria. An Attempt at Its Systemic Explanation, in *Neurophysiological and Neuropsychological Aspects of Spatial Neglect*, M. Jeannerod (ed.), North Holland, Amsterdam, 1987.
36. S. M. Kosslyn, *Image and Mind*, Harvard University Press, Cambridge, Massachusetts, 1980.
37. E. Bisiach, A. Berti, and G. Vallar, Analogical and Logical Disorders Underlying Unilateral Neglect of Space, in *Attention and Performance XI*, M. I. Posner and O. S. M. Marin (eds.), Lawrence Erlbaum Associates, Hillsdale, New Jersey, pp. 239-249, 1985.
38. S. M. Kosslyn, *Ghosts in the Mind's Machine*, Norton and Co., New York, 1983.
39. E. Bisiach, G. Vallar, D. Perani, C. Papagno, and A. Berti, Unawareness of plegia and Anosognosia for Hemianopia, *Neuropsychologia, 24*:4, pp. 471-482, 1986.
40. E. Bisiach, S. Meregalli, and A. Berti, Mechanisms of Production-Control and Belief-Fixation in Human Visuospatial Processing. Clinical Evidence from Hemispatial Neglect, Paper presented at the *Eighth Symposium on Quantitative Analysis of Behavior, at Harvard*, 1985.

41. G. Anton, Ueber die Selbstwahrnehmung der Herderkrankungen des Gehirns durch den Kranken bei Rindenblindheit und Rindentaubheit, *Archiv f. Psychiatrie und Nervenkrankheiten, 32*:1, 86–127.
42. R. G. Ley, Cerebral Asymmetries, Emotional Experience, and Imagery: Implications for Psychotherapy, in *The Potential of Fantasy and Imagination*, A. A. Sheikh and J. T. Shaffer (eds.), Brandon House, Inc., New York, pp. 41–65, 1979.
43. R. G. Ley, Cerebral Laterality and Imagery, in *Imagery, Current Theory, Research, and Application*, A. A. Sheikh (ed.), Wiley, New York, pp. 252–287, 1983.
44. H. Ehrlichman and J. Barrett, Right Hemisphere Specialization for Mental Imagery: A Review of the Evidence, *Brain and Cognition, 2*:1, pp. 55–76, 1983.
45. W. Penfield and P. Perot, The Brain's Record of Auditory and Visual Experience, *Brain, 86*:4, pp. 595–696, 1963.
46. J. Silberpfennig, Contributions to the Problem of Eye Movements, *Confinia Neurologica, 4*:1–2, pp. 1–13, 1941.
47. M.-M. Mesulam, A Cortical Network for Directed Attention and Unilateral Neglect, *Annals of Neurology, 10*:4, pp. 309–325, 1981.
48. A. Smith, Nondominant Hemispherectomy, *Neurology, 19*:5, pp. 442–445, 1969.
49. M. E. Humphrey and O. L. Zangwill, Cessation of Dreaming after Brain Injury, *J. Neurology, Neurosurgery and Psychiatry, 14*:4, pp. 322–325, 1951.
50. P. Greenwood, D. H. Wilson, and M. S. Gazzaniga, Dream Report Following Commissurotomy, *Cortex, 13*:3, pp. 311–316, 1977.
51. M. J. Farah, The Neurological Basis of Mental Imagery: A Componential Analysis, *Cognition, 18*:1–3, pp. 245–272, 1984.
52. A. Basso, E. Bisiach, E. Capitani, and C. Luzzatti, Loss of Mental Imagery: A Case Study, *Neuropsychologia, 18*:4–5, pp. 435–442, 1980.
53. N. Geschwind, Disconnexion Syndromes in Animals and Man, *Brain, 88*:2–3, pp. 237–294 and 585–644, 1965.
54. E. Bisiach, Perceptual Factors in the Pathogenesis of Anomia, *Cortex, 2*:1, pp. 90–95, 1966.
55. A. L. Benton and K. C. Smith, Stimulus Characteristics and Object Naming in Aphasic Patients, *J. Communication Disorders, 5*:1, pp. 19–24, 1972.
56. H. Goodglass, Disorders of Naming Following Brain Injury, *American Scientist, 68*:6, pp. 647–655, 1980.
57. F. Lhermitte and M. F. Beauvois, A Visual-Speech Disconnexion Syndrome, Report of a Case with Optic Aphasia, Agnosic Alexia, and Colour Agnosia, *Brain, 96*:4, pp. 695–714, 1973.
58. R. M. Bauer and A. B. Rubens, Agnosia, in *Clinical Neuropsychology*, K. M. Heilman and E. Valenstein (eds.), Oxford Press, New York, pp. 187–242, 1985.
59. S. M. Kosslyn, J. D. Holtzman, M. J. Farah, and M. S. Gazzaniga, A Computational Analysis of Mental Image Generation: Evidence from Functional Dissociations in Split-Brain Patients, *J. Experimental Psychology: General, 114*:3, pp. 311–341, 1985.

60. E. De Renzi and H. Spinnler, Visual Recognition in Patients with Unilateral Cerebral Disease, *J. Nervous and Mental Diseases, 142*:6, pp. 515–535, 1966.
61. E. K. Warrington and M. James, Disorders of Visual Perception in Patients with Localised Cerebral Lesions, *Neuropsychologia, 5*:3, pp. 252–266, 1967.
*62. M. Denis, J. Engelkamp, and J. T. E. Richardson (eds.), *Cognitive and Neuropsychological Approaches to Imagery*, Martinus Nijhoff Publishers, Dordrecht, 1988.
*63. G. Goldenberg, The Ability of Patients with Brain Damage to Generate Mental Visual Images, *Brain, 112*, pp. 305–325, 1989.

*These works were published too recently to be included in the text of this chapter, but are called to the attention of interested readers.

CHAPTER 4
Creative Imagination and Neural Activity

COLIN MARTINDALE

INTRODUCTION

A creative idea is one that is both original and appropriate for the situation in which it occurs. It would seem that creative productions always consist of novel combinations of preexisting mental elements. As Poincaré noted, "To create consists of making new combinations of associative elements which are useful" [1]. Creative ideas, he further remarked, "reveal to us unsuspected kinships between other facts well known but wrongly believed to be strangers to one another."

To create, then, involves the realization of an analogy between previously unassociated mental elements. There is every reason to believe that, in all fields of endeavor, mental imagery plays a key role in this process [2, 3]. Ghiselin collected a number of self-reports by eminently creative people that are supportive of this view [4]. The importance of mental imagery is clear enough in the arts. For example, composition was quite easy for Mozart, since he essentially just copied down the melodies he "heard" in his mind. Though composition has not been so easy for others, a process analogous to this seems to have occurred with all great composers. Something similar occurs in the creation of literature. A large number of great authors have said that they created by copying down auditory mental images or by describing visual mental images. Blake's comment is not especially unusual: "I have written this poem from immediate dictation, 12 or sometimes 20 or 30 lines at a time without premeditation, and even against my will" [5]. Though scientists deal with abstract concepts, their creative ideas very often arise as concrete mental images. Examples would be Kekule's discovery of the benzene ring by dreaming about a snake biting its own tail [4] or the discovery of the structure of DNA [6].

THE CREATIVE PROCESS

It is conventional to divide the creative process into several stages originally suggested by Helmholtz [7] and Wallas [8]. The four successive stages are preparation, incubation, illumination or inspiration, and verification or elaboration. Preparation involves thinking about or learning the mental elements presumed to be relevant to the problem at hand. Helmholtz remarked that a solution was often not found at this time. His own practice was to set the problem aside. This is the period of incubation. After some time, the solution simply occurred to him. This is the stage of illumination or inspiration. Creative inspiration is almost universally held to be an effortless and automatic process [4]. Ghiselin concluded that "production by a process of purely conscious calculation seems never to occur" [4]. Finally, during the stage of elaboration, the idea is subjected to logical scrutiny and put into its final form.

THEORIES OF CREATIVITY

Primary Process Cognition

Kris proposed that creative individuals are better able to alternate between primary process and secondary process modes of thought than are uncreative people [9]. The primary process-secondary process continuum is hypothetically the main axis along which cognition varies [10]. Primary process thought is found in normal states such as dreaming and reverie as well as in abnormal states such as psychosis and hypnosis. It is autistic, free-associative, analogical, and characterized by concrete images as opposed to abstract concepts. Secondary process cognition is the abstract, logical, reality-oriented thought of everyday waking consciousness. According to Kris, creative inspiration constitutes a "regression" to a primary process state of consciousness. Since primary process cognition is associative, it facilitates the discovery of new combinations of mental elements. On the other hand, creative elaboration constitutes a return to a secondary process state. Since uncreative people are more or less "stuck" at one point on the primary process-secondary process continuum, they are unable to come up with creative ideas. Kris' hypothesis is similar to Schopenhauer's formulation that "A great poet . . . is a man who, in his waking state, is able to do what the rest of us do in our dreams" [11].

A good deal of evidence is supportive of Kris' theory that creative people have easier access to primary process modes of thought. They report more fantasy activity [12], remember their nighttime dreams better [13], and are more easily hypnotized than uncreative people [14]. Wild showed directly that they are better able to shift between use of primary process and secondary process cognition [15]. Schizophrenia–a primary process state according to psychoanalytic theory–and creativity are related in a number of ways. Since highly creative individuals are over-represented among the relatives of schizophrenics [16-18], there is evidently some type of direct genetic link [19]. Creative people obtain quite high scores on tests of psychoticism [20-22]. Furthermore, schizophrenics and normal highly creative subjects do not differ in the extreme unusualness of their performance on object-sorting tasks [23].

Defocused Attention

Mendelsohn has proposed that individual differences in focus of attention are the cause of differences in creativity [24]: "The greater the attentional capacity, the more likely the combinatorial leap which is generally described as the hallmark of creativity." In order to become aware of a creative idea, one must obviously have the elements to be combined in the focus of attention at the same time. If one can attend to only two things at the same time, only one possible analogy can be discovered at that time. If one could attend to four things at once, six possible analogies could be discovered, etc. There is in fact a good deal of evidence that uncreative individuals do seem to have more narrowly focused attention than do creative ones [23, 25-26].

Associative Hierarchies

Mental elements are associated with one another to varying degrees. For example, on a word association task, if the stimulus word is TABLE, the most likely response is CHAIR. FOOD is a somewhat less probable response, but VICTORY is much less probable. Since people are fairly consistent in the probabilities of the responses they make to any given stimulus, we may plot an associative hierarchy (see Figure 1) for the stimulus. People differ in the steepness of their associative hierarchies. A person with steep hierarchies has just a few responses to make to a stimulus. Hypothetically, the mental representation of the stimulus is strongly bonded to just a few other mental representations. On the other hand, a person with a flat associative hierarchy has more associations to the stimulus. Note that, in this case, the close associates are less strongly connected to the stimulus and the remote associates are more strongly connected to the stimulus than is the case for the person with steep associative hierarchies. Mednick proposed that creative individuals have relatively flat associative hierarchies, whereas uncreative individuals have relatively steep associative hierarchies [27]. This, he argues, accounts for ability of the creative person to make the remote associations that are the basis of creative ideas.

In order to test his theory, Mednick devised the Remote Associates Test. On this test, a subject is confronted with thirty sets of three words and, in each case, must respond with a fourth word that is associated with the other three. The fourth word is one that is associatively rather than logically related to the three stimulus words. Highly creative subjects obtain significantly higher scores than do less creative people on this test. According to Mednick's theory, the relative ordering of elements on associative hierarchies is the same for creative and uncreative people. What differs is the relative strength of the responses. Research with continuous word association supports this contention [27]. At first, creative and uncreative people give similar responses in a similar order. However, creative people continue to respond at a fairly steady rate, whereas uncreative people run out of responses.

A Cognitive Integration

In reality, Kris', Mednick's, and Mendelsohn's theories are more or less identical theories expressed in very different vocabularies. Defocused attention is a property of primary process cognition [28]. Defocused attention and flat associative hierarchies are cognitive and behavioristic ways of describing exactly the same phenomenon [26, 28]. The three theories can be restated in terms of modern cognitive science.

The current consensus is that mind may be represented as a vast set of nodes and relationships among these nodes. The nodes may be activated to varying degrees. The relationships may be either excitatory or inhibitory. An activated node influences the activation of nodes with which it is connected via spreading activation or inhibition. It would seem reasonable to identify nodes with neurons or groups of neurons in the neocortex and relationships with the axonal and dendritic connections amongst these neurons. The nodes may be seen as being partitioned into various "analyzers" [28]. For example, there are separate analyzers for perception of printed words, faces, spoken words, and so on. The nodes in these analyzers are activated by the presence of the relevant stimulus. Nodes in all of the analyzers also hypothetically receive non-specific input from the reticular activating system [28]. Semantic memory hypothetically contains nodes that code concepts and relationships among these nodes. The relationships code attributes of concepts and also connect related concepts to nodes coding superordinate categories.

Consciousness corresponds to the set of nodes that is currently activated. It is usually divided into attention (the one or two most activated nodes) and short-term memory or the fringe of awareness (the remaining less-activated nodes). In Figure 1, an example of differential activation of nodes in semantic memory is shown. The correspondence with steep and flat associative hierarchies is also shown.

We have argued that creative inspiration consists of noticing an analogy between at least two things. Another way of putting this is that it consists of discovering that they share a common superordinate category. The more nodes and relationships that are activated at a given time, the greater the likelihood of this is [28, 29]. Of course, this is merely a cognitive restatement of the theories described above.

The cognitive restatement does shed some light on the preparation-incubation-inspiration sequence. During preparation, attention is probably too focused. One attends to ideas presumed to be relevant to the problem at hand. The

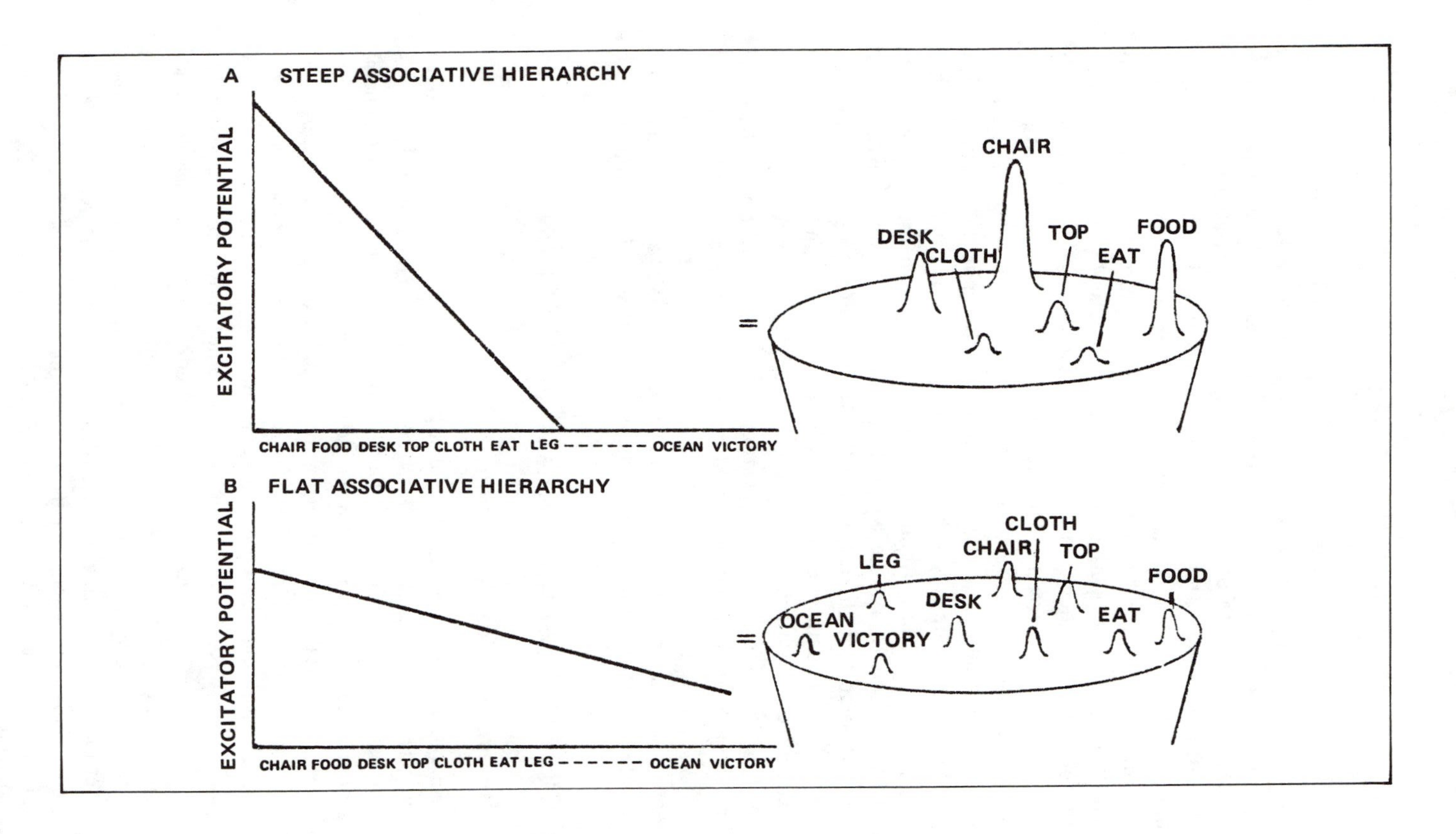

Figure 1. Examples of steep (A) and flat (B) associative hierarchies and correpsonding patterns of activation in semantic memory. The hierarchy of possible responses to the stimulus word, TABLE, is shown. (From 28)

difficulty is that the solution lies in ideas thought to be irrelevant. During incubation, the nodes coding the problem remain partially activated on the fringe of awareness. As the creator goes about his business, huge numbers of other nodes are activated. If one of these nodes happens to be related to the nodes coding the problem, the latter will become activated and leap into attention. This constitutes inspiration, the discovery of the creative analogy. Note that this would not have occurred if the nodes coding the problem were not already partially activated, since the path connecting the two sets of nodes is presumably long and circuitous. Furthermore, the more nodes that can be simultaneously activated (the more creative the person), the more likely it is that inspiration will occur since more paths among nodes can be simultaneously activated.

In order to be creative, as many nodes as possible must be simultaneously activated. How can this be accomplished? The best way it can be accomplished is by being in a state of low overall cortical arousal. In such a state, more nodes will be activated and to a more equal degree than in a state of high arousal [28]. It would seem that the reason for this is that non-specific input from the reticular activating system affects activation of nodes in a multiplicative rather than an addictive fashion: All nodes receive the same amount of non-specific input, but this input increases the activation of the most activated nodes much more than the activation of less activated nodes. There is also reliable evidence that primary process thought, defocused attention, and flat associative hierarchies are associated with states of low cortical activation [see 28 for reviews]. It must be the case, then, that creativity is related to level of cortical activation.

CREATIVITY AND CORTICAL ACTIVATION

Induced Cortical Activation

Though he did not say it explicitly, Hull was probably the first to imply that there is a relationship between creativity and arousal [30]. His "Behavioral Law" is that increases in Drive (what we would today call general level of arousal) make the dominant response to a stimulus even more dominant: i.e., increases in arousal make behavior more stereotypical and decreases in arousal make behavior more variable. Of course, Hull himself produced experimental evidence for this law with studies of lower animals. Osgood [31] and Meisels [32] showed that written language becomes more stereotyped under conditions of increased arousals. A number of studies of word-association tasks [33-37] and creativity tests [38-40] have demonstrated that stress reliably produces decreases in originality. Brainstorming techniques were originally proposed as methods of facilitating creative ideas. In fact, they decrease creativity [e.g., 41, 42]. This makes sense in light of Zajonc's hypothesis that the mere presence of others increases arousal [43]. Finally, intense white noise—which increases cortical arousal—has been shown to produce decrements on tests of creativity [44]. It would seem safe to conclude that induced increases in arousal cause decreases in creativity, originality, and variability of behavior.

Resting Level of Arousal

The simplest explanation of the hypothesized relationship between creativity and low arousal would be that creative people are in a continual state of low arousal. Given the arguments outlined above, it is somewhat surprising that there is a good bit of evidence suggesting that highly creative people in fact exhibit *higher* levels of basal or resting-level arousal than do less creative people. Subjects who are more original in their word associations [e.g., 45, 46] or on paper-and-pencil tests of creativity [47, 48] score higher on tests of anxiety than their low-scoring counterparts. Martindale found positive correlations between basal skin conductance and two tests of creativity [48]. Florek found that creative painters have a very fast basal heart rate, but there was not a control group per se included in the study [49]. On the other hand, Cropley, Cassell, and Maslany [50] and Kennett and Cropley [51] report that creative subjects have low levels of serum uric acid. This implies low basal arousal. However, serum uric acid is correlated with physical activity, and there is evidence that creative people are less physically active than uncreative people [52, 53]. Of course, this evidence of inactivity could, itself, be interpreted as a behavioral sign of low arousal.

Wyspiansky, Barry, and Dayhaw found that highly creative subjects have lower basal EEG alpha-wave amplitude (an inverse measure of cortical activation) than do less creative subjects [54]. My colleagues and I have conducted a series of seven studies concerning creativity and EEG measures [55-58]. In only two of these studies were significant differences between high- and low-creative subjects on basal EEG measures of cortical arousal detected. However, in almost all of the studies, more creative people tended to exhibit slightly higher basal levels of cortical arousal. It is probably the case that creativity is associated with a high resting level of arousal, but the relationship is rather slight. It would seem that we must look elsewhere to find any strong linkage between creativity and neural activity.

Creative Cognition and Cortical Arousal

If creativity is not strongly related to one's general level of cortical arousal, then perhaps it is related to arousal whilst one is engaged in the act of creation. This does, in fact, seem to be the case. Martindale and Hines [56] measured amount of alpha-wave activity—an inverse measure of cortical arousal—while subjects took the Alternate Uses Test (a fairly pure measure of creativity), the Remote Association Test (an index of both creativity and intelligence), and the IPAT (a pure measure of intelligence). Their results are shown in Figure 2. As may be seen in the figure, the highly creative subjects showed differential

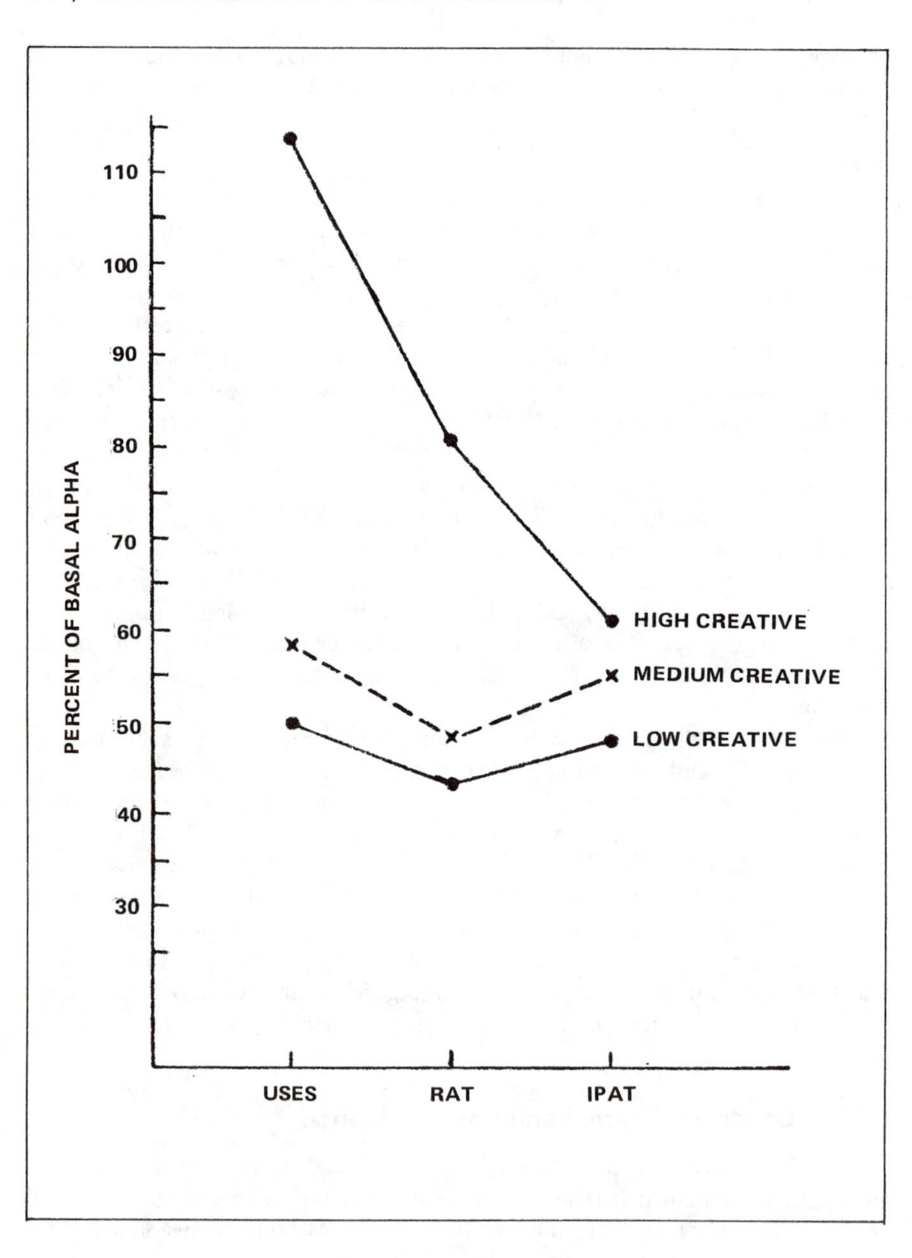

Figure 2. Percentage of basal alpha exhibited by high, medium, and low creative subjects during creative and intellectual performance. (From 48)

amounts of cortical activation across the three tasks whereas the medium- and low-creative subjects did not. The pattern is the one we would expect if creative activity requires the defocused attention produced by low levels of cortical activation. Virtually any task involving mental effort produces an increase in cortical activation. Thus, it is noteworthy that the highly creative group was actually less aroused while taking the Alternate Uses Test than during baseline recording.

These findings lead to the hypothesis that, when asked to be original, as they are on the Alternate Uses Test, creative people exhibit defocused attention accompanied by low levels of cortical activation. On the other hand, uncreative people focus their attention too much, and this prevents them from thinking of original ideas. These differences should be most apparent during the inspirational phase of the creative process, since this is the stage where defocused attention is useful. Elaboration requires focused attention. Thus, there should be no differences in arousal during this stage. Martindale and Hasenfus tested this hypothesis [57]. EEG activity was measured while people thought about a story they would write (the analogue of the inspirational phase) and while they wrote the story (the analogue of the elaboration phase). All of the subjects were asked to be as creative as possible in making up their stories. As predicted, highly creative people exhibited lower levels of cortical activation during the inspirational phase than did less creative people, and no differences in activation were present during the elaboration phase. In a second study, half of the subjects were urged to be as creative as possible, whereas nothing was mentioned about creativity or originality to the other half of the subjects. Creative subjects showed lower levels of cortical activation during the analogue of the inspirational stage *if* they were told to be creative. However, no differences were found when subjects were not asked to be creative.

These studies lead to the conclusion that creative and uncreative people differ in cortical activation only under quite specific circumstances: during the inspirational phase of the creative process. Furthermore, this difference is found only when people are trying to be creative. Thus, when creative people were asked to make up a story but the importance of making it creative was not mentioned, they did not differ from uncreative people in their pattern of cortical activation.

Self-Control of Cortical Arousal

How can we explain the above results? One possible explanation would be that creative people are more capable of controlling their own level of arousal. When asked to be creative, they use this ability to induce the low level of arousal that is necessary for creative inspiration. Kamiya was the first to show that people can in fact control their level of cortical arousal [59]. In his biofeedback paradigm, subjects are asked to keep a light (or tone) on or off. The light is controlled by the person's own brain waves. For example, the only way to turn the light on may be to produce alpha waves. Kamiya showed that subjects can keep the light on or off at above-chance levels and that they get better with practice.

If creative people are adept at self-control of cortical arousal, they should perform well on biofeedback tasks. Two experiments [55, 56] designed to test this hypothesis yielded consistent results: Creative people are not, in fact, very good at biofeedback tasks. Initially, their performance is better than that of less creative people. However, this advantage is lost after only several minutes. After that, uncreative people become better and better at controlling the amount of alpha that they produce. On the other hand, performance of highly creative people actually deteriorates. Specifically, amount of alpha drifts upwards across trials regardless of whether they are trying to produce alpha waves or to suppress them.

Creativity, Disinhibition, and Reactivity

The poor performance of creative people on biofeedback tasks should not really be surprising. When creative subjects are asked to describe themselves, they use words that stress disinhibition and lack of control [60]. Self-reports by highly creative individuals almost all stress the effortlessness of creative inspiration [4]. Creativity seems not to be based upon self-control or will power. Precisely the opposite appears to be the case.

Creative people have used a variety of often bizarre methods which they believed helped them to be more creative. These methods do not include self-control; rather, they tend to involve an automatic reaction to some stimulus [28]. For example, a number of creators have used drugs and alcohol in the (probably false) belief that they facilitate creativity. Clearly, no self-control is involved in this case, since such substances quite automatically induce changes in cortical arousal. Other methods that would seem to be nothing more than odd eccentricities in fact produce physiological effects. To take perhaps the most extreme example, the German poet Schiller's practice of writing whilst his feet were plunged in ice water was in fact an efficient method of increasing blood flow to his brain [61]. Perhaps the most common method used by creators is withdrawal so extreme that it amounts to sensory deprivation, a condition that lowers cortical arousal [62]. The image of the withdrawn artist is ubiquitous: Vigny advocating withdrawal into a "tower of ivory," Hölderlin imprisoned in his tower at Tügingen, Proust isolating himself in his cork-lined room.

Creativity, Oversensitivity, and Habituation

Why do creators withdraw in the first place? Generally, it is not because they know that such a procedure may facilitate creativity. Rather, it is because of oversensitivity. Proust's withdrawal was forced upon him because normal levels of light and noise were painfully intense for him. Creative people quite often say that they are sensitive or oversensitive. While such claims are often dismissed as mere posing, it would seem that such people are reporting accurate self-assessments.

There is a good bit of evidence that creative people are in fact physiologically over-reactive. Martindale and Armstrong found more alpha blocking in response to onset of a tone in highly creative subjects than in less creative ones [55]. Martindale delivered a series of electric shocks to subjects [48]. The more creative a person was, the more intense he rated any given shock. Martindale also found a correlation between creativity and augmentation on a kinaesthetic aftereffect task [48]. Augmentation on this task is conventionally interpreted as meaning that the individual "amplifies" the intensity of stimuli. Rosen, Moore, and Martindale measured skin potential responses to a series of moderately intense tones [63]. (Skin potential is believed to covary directly with cortical activation.) Two findings were of interest. More creative subjects showed much larger skin potential response to the tones than did less creative people. Furthermore, they took two times longer to habituate to the tones than did uncreative subjects.

Creativity and Need for Novelty and Stimulation

Creative people show a trait that seems to be at odds with their oversensitivity and slow rate of habituation: They love novelty, which is known to *increase* cortical arousal [64]. The French poet, Charles Baudelaire expressed the attitude of many creative people when he remarked that "the beautiful is always bizarre." Going along with this preference is an active dislike for things that are not novel. As the English writer George Moore put it [65], "the commonplace, the natural, is constitutionally abhorrent." Koestler [66] notes that scientific geniuses tend to have "on the one hand skepticism, often carried to the point of iconoclasm, in their attitude toward traditional ideas and dogmas" as contrasted with "an open-mindedness that verges on naive credulity towards new concepts." There is experimental evidence that creativity is correlated with preference for novelty [67] as well as with need for stimulation in general [2].

Theoretical Integration

How can creative people crave stimulation if they are oversensitive? Martindale has suggested the following explanation [28]. It is generally the case that the more intense a stimulus, the more cortical activation it produces. Up to some level of intensity, the curve relating cortical activation to stimulus intensity is much steeper for creative than for uncreative people. Thus, conventional ideas or moderately loud noises or bright lights produce "too much" arousal and consequent displeasure in the creative person. The same stimuli induce only moderate arousal and, hence, pleasure in the uncreative person. (There is evidence that moderate increases in arousal induce pleasure, whereas large increases in arousal produce displeasure [64].) At some level of intensity, there is a "paradoxical" dip in the curve relating stimulus intensity to cortical arousal in creative people. Such a paradoxical relaxation response to stimulation has often been observed [see 68], but, to my knowledge, there have been no studies of its relationship with creativity. On the other hand, there is no such dip in the curve for uncreative people. For them, the relationship between stimulus intensity and cortical activation is monotonic. This dip in the curve for creative individuals would correspond to novel ideas and the sort of stimulation that creative people seek. Because such stimuli induce only moderate arousal responses, creative people find them pleasurable. On the other hand, these stimuli induce too much arousal in uncreative people, and this causes them to dislike the stimuli. Recall that telling creative people to be creative induces a decline in cortical arousal. Such a demand may have sufficient impact value to produce the paradoxical decline in arousal. One potentially fatal problem with this explanation concerning the shape of the curves relating stimulus intensity and cortical arousal in more and less creative people is that it is testable. However, to my knowledge, no research has been conducted on the topic.

CREATIVITY AND HEMISPHERIC ASYMMETRY

Theoretical Rationale

There are reasons to believe that creativity should also be related to differential activation of the right and left hemispheres of the brain as well as to general level of cortical arousal. Galin [69] and Hoppe [70] have aruged that the right hemisphere operates in a primary process manner, whereas the left hemisphere operates in a secondary process fashion. Their arguments are based upon findings that verbal, sequential, and analytical processes tend to be carried out in the left hemisphere, whereas global, parallel, and holistic processes are carried out in the right hemisphere. If this is the case, then we can neurologize Kris' theory of creativity: Since creative people have more access to primary process cognition, they should show more right hemisphere—as compared with left hemisphere—activation than less creative people, at least during periods of creative activity.

A number of theorists have proposed similar hypotheses [71-75]. Others, however, have proposed that hemispheric balance may be crucial for creativity [76-78]. The difference in opinion may be a mere semantic one. In a resting state, the left hemisphere is generally more activated than the right. A task that induces right hemisphere activation and left hemisphere deactivation may in absolute terms produce balance—i.e., both hemispheres are equally activated. However, taken in reference to baseline levels, the task would be interpreted as having activated the right hemisphere more than the left.

There are other reasons for suspecting that the right hemisphere should be connected with creativity. A good deal of evidence shows that most brain centers involved in the perception and production of music are located in the right-hemisphere [see 28 for a review]. Similarly, a number of centers necessary for creation of visual art are segregated in the right hemisphere. We argued above that mental imagery is probably involved in creativity of any type. There is evidence that the right hemisphere is more involved in the production of mental images than is the left [79, 80]. Based on research on split-brain patients [e.g., 81], it would seem that the right hemisphere possesses a rather comprehensive lexicon but that it is chaotically arranged. That is, it understands words but not how they go together in a grammatical or propositional manner. Access to scuh an "alternative" lexicon could certainly be of use to a poet.

Penfield and Roberts performed experiments in which exposed cortex was mildly stimulated [82]. When certain areas of the right temporal cortex were stimulated, their patients reported extremely vivid auditory and visual images. Recall that large numbers of literary creators have argued that their work was essentially "dictated." Jaynes has argued that such quasi-hallucinatory experience is a product of intense right hemisphere activity [83].

Induced Right-Hemisphere Activation

There is some evidence that procedures known to increase right-hemisphere activation can facilitate creativity. At least in highly hypnotizable subjects, hypnosis increases right-hemisphere activation. Gur and Raynor found that such subjects performed better on tests of creativity when hypnotized than when not hypnotized [84]. Marijuana also increases right hemisphere activation. At least in low doses, it facilitates performance in tests of creativity; however, higher doses produce decrements in performance [85]. Music also has been shown to facilitate performance on creativity tests [86].

A word displayed in the left visual field is processed first by the right hemisphere, whereas a word displayed in the right visual field is processed first by the left hemisphere. Words presented in the left visual field elicit more unusual word associations than do words presented in the right visual field [87]. Right-hemisphere activation is accompanied by leftward eye movements, while left-hemisphere activation is accompanied by rightward eye movements. Subjects perform slightly better on creativity tests if they are forced by specially constructed goggles to look leftwards as opposed to rightwards while taking the tests [88].

Individual Differences on Noncreative Tasks

Several studies have found positive correlations between creativity and a tendency to make leftward eye movements (indicative of right hemisphere activation) when answering questions [89, 90]. Katz compared the performance of more and less creative architects, scientists, and mathematicians on paper-and-pencil tests hypothetically tapping right and left hemisphere dominance [91]. More creative architects tended to be left dominant and more creative mathematicians and scientists tended to be right dominant. Katz interpreted his findings as implying that more creative individuals have sufficient capabilities in the hemisphere needed for their profession (right hemisphere for architects and left hemisphere for scientists and mathematicians) and that their creativity arises from their extra abilities in the contralateral hemisphere.

Katz and Uemura carried out a series of studies examining the performance of more and less creative subjects on dichotic listening and split-visual-field tachistoscopic tasks [90, 92]. In a dichotic listening task, a stimulus is presented to either the right or left ear. Stimuli presented to the right ear are first processed by the left hemisphere and vice versa. With such tasks there is generally a left-hemisphere advantage for verbal material and a right-hemisphere advantage for recognition of musical melodies. In a split-visual-field tachistoscopic task, a stimulus is briefly presented in either the right or the left visual field. As indicated above, stimuli presented in the left visual field are processed first by the right-hemisphere and vice versa. The general finding is one of a left-hemisphere advantage for linguistic stimuli and a right hemisphere advantage for complex spatial stimuli (see [28] for reviews).

In both studies, creativity was positively correlated with a left-hemisphere advantage for verbal stimuli when presented either verbally or auditorially [90, 92]. That is, the more creative a person was, the better he or she did when the stimuli were processed by the left hemisphere. Uemura found a negative correlation between creativity and right-hemisphere advantage on a split-visual-field spatial task [92]. Katz found that more creative people did not show the usual right-hemisphere advantage on a dichotic listening melody-recognition task. It would seem that on all of the tasks more creative subjects used the left hemisphere more than would be expected on the basis of previous findings with the general population. This does not, of course, conform with our hypothesis. However, none of Katz' or Uemura's tasks involved creative performance. As was the case with general arousal, it may be that the predicted differences tend to be found only during creative activity.

Hemispheric Asymmetry during Creative Activity

Martindale et al. reported on three experiments concerning the relationship between creativity and hemispheric asymmetry as measured by EEG activity [58]. In none of the experiments were their significant differences in resting or basal asymmetry between more and less creative subjects. In two of the experiments, creativity was assessed with paper-and-pencil tests. In these experiments, the creative tasks was to either write down or speak aloud a fantasy story. Hemispheric activity during creative activity showed the same pattern in both experiments: Highly creative subjects exhibited more right- than left-hemisphere activation; those of medium creativity showed strong asymmetry in the opposite direction; and very uncreative subjects showed about equal activation in both hemispheres.

In the third experiment, student artists were compared with artistically naive subjects. EEG was recorded while subjects made a drawing of a cow's vertebra and while they read an article on economics in *Time* magazine. As expected, the student artists showed much greater right-hemisphere than left-hemisphere activity during the drawing task than did the control group. The reading task was included in order to measure asymmetry during a noncreative task. On this task, the artists also showed more asymmetry than did the control group but in the opposite direction from that found during the drawing task. Left-hemisphere activation was greater than right-hemisphere activation, and this was more the case for the artists than for the non-artists. Thus, it would seem that creative people rely more on the right hemisphere than on the left not in general but only during the creative process.

SUMMARY

We have seen that the creative act involves the discovery of an analogy between two or more ideas or images previously thought to be unrelated. This discovery does not arise from logical reasoning but, rather, emerges as a sudden insight. All of the theories of creativity reviewed say essentially the same thing—that creative inspiration occurs in a mental state where attention is defocused, thought is associative, and a large number of mental representations are simultaneously activated. Such a state can arise in two ways: low levels of cortical activation and comparatively more right- than left-hemisphere activation. Creative people do exhibit both of these traits not in general but only while engaged in creative activity.

REFERENCES

1. H. Poincaré, *The Foundations of Science*, Science Press, Lancaster, Pennsylvania, 1913.
2. F. Farley, Psychobiology and Cognition: An Individual Differences Model, in *The Biological Bases of Personality and Behavior*, Vol. 1, J. Strelau, F. Farley, and A. Gale (eds.), Hemisphere, Washington, D.C., 1985.
3. A. Rothenberg, *The Emerging Goddess: The Creative Process in Art, Science, and Other Fields*, University of Chicago Press, Chicago, 1979.
4. B. Ghiselin (ed.), *The Creative Process*, University of California Press, Berkeley, 1952.
5. W. Blake, Letter to Thomas Butts, in *The Letters of William Blake*, A. G. B. Russell (ed.), Methuen, London, 1906. (Originally written, 1803).
6. J. Watson, *The Double Helix: A Personal Account of the Discovery of the Structure of DNA*, Antheneum, New York, 1968.

7. H. von Helmholtz, *Vorträge und Reden*, Friedrich Vieweg und Sohn, Brunswick, Germany, 1896.
8. G. Wallas, *The Art of Thought*, Harcourt, Brace & World, New York, 1926.
9. E. Kris, *Psychoanalytic Explorations in Art*, International Universities Press, New York, 1952.
10. E. Fromm, Primary and Secondary Process in Waking and in Altered States of Consciousness, *Journal of Altered States of Consciousness, 4*, pp. 115–128, 1978.
11. J.-P. Weber, *The Psychology of Art*, Delacorte, New York, 1969.
12. J. L. Singer and V. G. McCraven, Some Characteristics of Adult Daydreaming, *Journal of Psychology, 51*, pp. 151–164, 1961.
13. L. Hudson, *Human Beings: The Psychology of Human Experience*, Anchor, New York, 1975.
14. P. Bowers, Hypnosis and Creativity: The Search for the Missing Link, *Journal of Abnormal Psychology, 88*, pp. 564–572, 1979.
15. C. Wild, Creativity and Adaptive Regression, *Journal of Personality and Social Psychology, 2*, pp. 161–169, 1965.
16. L. L. Heston, Psychiatric Disorders in Foster Home Reared Children of Schizophrenic Mothers, *British Journal of Psychiatry, 112*, pp. 819–825, 1966.
17. J. L. Karlsson, Genealogical Studies of Schizophrenia, in *The Transmission of Schizophrenia*, D. Rosenthal and S. S. Kety (eds.), Pergamon Press, Oxford, 1968.
18. T. F. McNeil, Prebirth and Postbirth Influence on the Relationship between Creative Ability and Recorded Mental Illness, *Journal of Personality, 39*, pp. 391–406, 1971.
19. I. F. Jarvik and S. B. Chadwick, Schizophrenia and Survival, in *Psychopathology*, M. Hammer, K. Salzinger, and S. Sutton (eds.), Wiley, New York, 1973.
20. F. Barron, *The Creative Person and the Creative Process*, Holt, New York, 1969.
21. H. J. Eysenck, The Roots of Creativity: Cognitive Ability or Personality Trait?, *Roeper Review, 5*:4, pp. 10–12, 1983.
22. E. Woody and G. Claridge, Psychoticism and Thinking, *British Journal of Social and Clinical Psychology, 16*, pp. 241–248, 1977.
23. M. Dykes and A. McGhie, A. Comparative Study of Attentional Strategies in Schizophrenics and Highly Creative Normal Subjects, *British Journal of Psychiatry, 128*, pp. 50–56, 1976.
24. G. A. Mendelsohn, Associative and Attentional Processes in Creative Performance, *Journal of Personality, 44*, pp. 341–369, 1976.
25. K. Dewing and G. Battye, Attention Deployment and Nonverbal Fluency, *Journal of Personality and Social Psychology, 17*, pp. 214–218, 1971.
26. G. A. Mendelsohn and B. B. Griswold, Assessed Creative Potential, Vocabulary Level, and Sex as Predictors of the Use of Incidental Cues in Verbal Problem-Solving, *Journal of Personality and Social Psychology, 4*, pp. 423–431, 1966.
27. S. A. Mednick, The Associative Basis of the Creative Process, *Psychological Review, 69*, pp. 220–232, 1962.

28. C. Martindale, *Cognition and Consciousness*, Homewood, Illinois, Dorsey, 1981.
29. C. S. Findlay and C. J. Lumsden, The Creative Mind: Toward an Evolutionary Theory of Discovery and Innovation, *Journal of Social and Biological Structures, 11*, pp. 3-55, 1988.
30. C. L. Hull, *Principles of Behavior*, Appleton-Century-Crofts, New York, 1943.
31. C. E. Osgood, Some Effects of Motivation on Style on Encoding, in *Style in Language*, T. A. Sebeok (ed.), M.I.T. Press, Cambridge, 1960.
32. M. Meisels, Test Anxiety, Stress, and Verbal Behavior, *Journal of Consulting Psychology, 31*, pp. 577-582, 1967.
33. I. Sarason, Relationships of Measures of Anxiety and Experimental Instructions to Word Association Test Performance, *Journal of Abnormal and Social Psychology, 59*, pp. 37-42, 1959.
34. I. Sarason, A Note on Anxiety, Instructions and Word Association Performance, *Journal of Abnormal and Social Psychology, 62*, pp. 153-154, 1961.
35. J. J. Jenkins, Commonality of Association as an Indicator of More General Patterns of Verbal Behavior, in *Style in Language*, T. A. Sebeok (ed.), M.I.T. Press, Cambridge, 1960.
36. D. L. Horton, D. Marlowe, and D. Crowne, The Effect of Instructional Set and Need for Social Approval on Commonality of Word Association Responses, *Journal of Abnormal and Social Psychology, 66*, pp. 67-72, 1963.
37. S. Coren and M. Schulman, Effects of an External Stress on Commonality of Verbal Associates, *Psychological Reports, 28*, pp. 328-330, 1971.
38. R. A. Dentler and B. Mackler, Originality: Some Social and Personal Determinants, *Behavioral Science, 9*, pp. 1-7, 1964.
39. D. Hedley, Experimental Relationships between Creativity and Anxiety, *Dissertation Abstracts, 26*, pp. 2586-2587, 1965.
40. H. D. Krop, C. E. Alegre, and C. D. Williams, Effects of Induced Stress on Convergent and Divergent Thinking, *Psychological Reports, 24*, pp. 895-898, 1969.
41. D. W. Taylor, P. C. Berry, and C. H. Block, Does Group Participation When Using Brainstorming Facilitate or Inhibit Creative Thinking?, *Administrative Science Quarterly, 3*, pp. 23-47, 1958.
42. H. C. Lindgren and F. Lindgren, Brainstorming and Orneriness as Facilitators of Creativity, *Psychological Reports, 16*, pp. 577-583, 1965.
43. R. Zajonc, Social Facilitation, *Science, 149*, pp. 269-274, 1965.
44. C. Martindale and J. Greenough, The Differential Effects of Increased Arousal on Creative and Intellectual Performance, *Journal of Genetic Psychology, 123*, pp. 329-335, 1973.
45. E. Trapp and D. Kausler, Relationship between MAS Scores and Association Values of Nonsense Syllables, *Journal of Experimental Psychology, 59*, pp. 233-238, 1960.
46. J. Worrell and L. Worrell, Personality Conflict, Originality of Response and Recall, *Journal of Consulting Psychology, 29*, pp. 55-62, 1965.
47. S. R. Maddi and S. Andrews, The Need for Variety in Fantasy and Self Description, *Journal of Personality, 34*, pp. 610-625, 1966.

48. C. Martindale, Creativity, Consciousness, and Cortical Arousal, *Journal of Altered States of Consciousness, 3*, pp. 69–87, 1977.
49. H. Florek, Heart Rate During Creative Ability, *Studia Psychologia, 15*, pp. 158–161, 1973.
50. A. J. Cropley, W. A. Cassell, and G. W. Maslany, A Biochemical Correlate of Divergent Thinking, *Canadian Journal of Behavioral Science, 2*, pp. 174–180, 1970.
51. K. F. Kennett and A. J. Cropley, Serum Uric Acid: A Biochemical Correlate of Divergent Thinking, Paper presented at the Annual Conference of the British Psychological Society, London, 1973.
52. S. R. Maddi, Motivational Aspects of Creativity, *Journal of Personality, 33*, pp. 330–347, 1965.
53. J. Singer and R. Schonbar, Correlates of Daydreaming: A Dimension of Self-Awareness, *Journal of Consulting Psychology, 25*, p. 166, 1961.
54. J. O. Wyspianski, W. F. Barry, and L. T. Dayhaw, Brain Wave Amplitude and Creative Thinking, *Revue de l'Université d'Ottawa*, pp. 269–276, 1963.
55. C. Martindale and J. Armstrong, The Relationship of Creativity to Cortical Activation and its Operant Control, *Journal of Genetic Psychology, 124*, pp. 311–320, 1974.
56. C. Martindale and D. Hines, Creativity and Cortical Activation During Creative, Intellectual, and EEG Feedback Tasks, *Biological Psychology, 3*, pp. 71–80, 1975.
57. C. Martindale and N. Hasenfus, EEG Differences as a Function of Creativity, Stage of the Creative Process, and Effort to be Original, *Biological Psychology, 6*, pp. 157–167, 1978.
58. C. Martindale, D. Hines, L. Mitchell, and E. Covello, EEG Alpha Asymmetry and Creativity, *Personality and Individual Differences, 5*, pp. 77–86, 1984.
59. J. Kamiya, Operant Control of EEG Alpha Rhythm and Some of Its Reported Effects on Consciousness, in *Altered States of Consciousness*, C. Tart (ed.), Wiley, New York, 1969.
60. C. Martindale, Feminity, Alienation, and Arousal in the Creative Personality, *Psychology, 9*, pp. 3–15, 1972.
61. T. Ribot, *Essay on the Creative Imagination*, Kegan Paul, London, 1906.
62. D. P. Schultz, *Sensory Restriction: Effects on Behavior*, Academic Press, New York, 1965.
63. K. Rosen, K. Moore, and C. Martindale, Creativity and Rate of Habituation, Paper presented at Eighth International Colloquium on Empirical Aesthetics, Cardiff, U.K., 1983.
64. D. E. Berlyne, *Aesthetics and Psychobiology*, Appleton-Century-Crofts, New York, 1971.
65. G. Moore, *Confessions of a Young Man*, Capricorn, New York, 1959. (Originally published, 1886).
66. A. Koestler, *The Act of Creation*, Macmillan, New York, 1964.
67. J. P. Houston and S. A. Mednick, Creativity and the Need for Novelty, *Journal of Abnormal and Social Psychology, 66*, pp. 137–141, 1963.
68. L. K. Morrell, Some Characteristics of Stimulus-Provoked Alpha Activity, *Electroencephalography and Clinical Neurophysiology, 21*, pp. 552–561, 1966.

69. D. Galin, Implications for Psychiatry of Left and Right Cerebral Specializations: A Neurophysiological Context for Unconscious Processes, *Archives of General Psychiatry, 31*, pp. 572-583, 1974.
70. K. Hoppe, Split Brains and Psychoanalysis, *Psychoanalytic Quarterly, 46*, pp. 220-224, 1977.
71. J. E. Bogen, The Other Side of the Brain: An Appositional Mind, in *The Nature of Human Consciousness*, R. E. Ornstein (ed.), Freeman, San Francisco, 1973.
72. S. Garrett, Putting Our Whole Brain to Use: A Fresh Look at the Creative Process, *Journal of Creative Behavior, 10*, pp. 239-249, 1976.
73. J. C. Gowan, The Production of Creativity through Right Hemisphere Imagery, *Journal of Creative Behavior, 13*, pp. 39-51, 1979.
74. R. Ornstein, *The Psychology of Consciousness*, Freeman, San Francisco, 1972.
75. S. A. West, Creativity, Altered States of Consciousness and Artificial Intelligence, *Journal of Altered States of Consciousness, 2*, pp. 219-230, 1975.
76. S. J. Parnes, CPSI: The General System, *Journal of Creative Behavior, 11*, pp. 1-6, 1977.
77. R. S. McCallum and S. M. Glynn, Hemispheric Specialization and Creative Behavior, *Journal of Creative Behavior, 13*, pp. 263-273, 1979.
78. A. W. Britain, Creativity and Hemisphere Functioning: A Second Look at Katz's Data, *Empirical Studies of the Arts, 3*, pp. 105-107, 1985.
79. K. J. Robbins and D. W. McAdam, Interhemispheric Alpha Asymmetry and Imagery Mode, *Brain and Language, 1*, pp. 189-193, 1974.
80. J. G. Seamon and M. S. Gazzaniga, Coding Strategies and Cerebral Laterality Effects, *Cognitive Psychology, 5*, pp. 249-256, 1973.
81. M. S. Gazzaniga and S. A. Hillyard, Language and Speech Capacity of the Right-Hemisphere, *Neuropsychologia, 9*, pp. 273-280, 1971.
82. W. Penfield and L. Roberts, *Speech and Brain Mechanisms*, Princeton University Press, Princeton, New Jersey, 1958.
83. J. Jaynes, *The Origin of Consciousness in the Breakdown of the Bicameral Mind*, Houghton Mifflin, New York, 1976.
84. R. C. Gur and J. Rayner, Enhancement of Creativity via Free-Imagery and Hypnosis, *American Journal of Clinical Hypnosis, 18*, pp. 237-249, 1976.
85. T. Weckowicz, O. Fedora, J. Mason, D. Radstaak, K. Bay, and K. Yonge, Effect of Marijuana on Divergent and Convergent Production Cognitive Tests, *Journal of Abnormal Psychology, 84*, pp. 386-398, 1975.
86. B. Kaltsounis, Effect of Sound on Creative Performance, *Psychological Reports, 34*, pp. 653-654, 1972.
87. S. Dimond and J. G. Beaumont, Experimental Studies of the Hemisphere Function in the Human Brain, in *Hemisphere Function in the Human Brain*, S. Dimond and J. G. Beaumont (eds.), Halsted Press, New York, 1974.
88. D. Hines and C. Martindale, Induced Lateral Eye Movements and Creative and Intellectual Performance, *Perceptual and Motor Skills, 39*, pp. 153-154, 1974.
89. S. Harnad, Creativity, Lateral Saccades and the Nondominant Hemisphere, *Perceptual and Motor Skills, 34*, pp. 653-654, 1972.

90. A. N. Katz, Creativity and Individual Differences in Asymmetrical Cerebral Hemispheric Functioning, *Empirical Studies of the Arts, 1*, pp. 3–16, 1983.
91. A. N. Katz, The Relationship between Creativity and Cerebral Hemisphericity for Creative Architects, Scientists, and Mathematicians, *Empirical Studies of the Arts, 4*, pp. 97–108, 1986.
92. A. K. Uemura, *Individual Differences in Hemispheric Lateralization*, Unpublished Ph.D. Dissertation, University of Maine, Orono, Maine, 1980.

CHAPTER 5

Brain States of Visual Imagery and Dream Generation

DIETRICH LEHMANN AND MARTHA KOUKKOU

VISUAL IMAGERY AND DREAM GENERATION

Visual Imagery as a Basic Brain Function

Dreaming is the paradigmatic experience of vivid imagery for the healthy adult, and imagery during dreaming is by far most frequent in the visual mode [1]. This chapter explores the role of visual imagery in brain functioning, in particular in its relation to psychophysiological mechanisms of dream generation. Dreaming might be viewed as an extreme case of normal brain functioning in that dream images are totally dissociated from external visual reality, and in that the dreamer typically is not aware that he is dreaming.

On closer scrutiny there appears to be a continuum of visual imagery in normal people, a continuum which ranges from dream imagery without reference to external reality, to wakeful perceptual misinterpretations of incompletely available external images (erroneous percepts such as taking a road sign for a waiting person in a foggy evening), to imagery which is an integral component of wakeful, adequate, visual perception of external reality. One might well consider regular visual perception to be a case of imagery because even the common perception of external visual scenes works with brain mechanisms which use incomplete visual information to produce percepts of complete objects. A visual scene consisting of one or more parts of "figures" implies that many crucial parts or features of the perceived figures are so-called "hidden contours" or occluded figure portions whose direct viewing is visually blocked by other parts of the scene. Obviously, the perceiving brain system is able to "fill in" these areas using knowledge which is internally available.

*The work reviewed in this paper was partly supported by grants from the Swiss National Science Foundation, The SANDOZ Foundation, Basel, The Hartmann-Mueller Foundation, Zurich, and The EMDO Foundation, Zurich.

Experimentally one can demonstrate nicely that mental images of complete figures are automatically generated by the brain in many conditions where the incoming information clearly does not present complete or even correct information for the perceived figure. The KANIZSA-triangle (Figure 1) is a basic example of such "illusory figures" [2, 3], where crucial missing portions of the borders are automatically and convincingly filled in, and the perceptually unimportant but physically dominating disks are largely disregarded for the perceived image of the triangle. Even more, the disks of the figure are relegated into a background against which the physically non-existing triangle is contrasted with heightened intensity. The percept of the figure is not accessible to voluntary control, it cannot willfully be made to "go away." Similarly, a random-dot stereogram figure [4] cannot be made to perceptually disappear by willful decision, once the viewer has learned to perceive it.

The perception of meaningful images which are not completely available in external reality is thus a general function of the visual system, and one might consider that all visual situations with partially hidden contours demonstrate this "illusory figure" perception. Gestalt psychology has spoken of "figure closure" or "good figures" in related cases. Indeed, the context-driven "fill-in" tendency in the construction of the perceived image can easily be observed by everybody. Upon closing one eye, there is the "blind spot" in the visual field of the seeing eye, but the viewer is not readily able to perceive this–only when a known visual target is moved into the blind area can the target's perceptual absence be realized. A similar "fill-in" tendency can be observed in patients with retinal visual field defects (scotomata), where the functionally blind area is perceived as content-continuous with the surround, not as "missing" and never as "black." For instance, when overlooking a large audience, the patient has the feeling that heads are present even in the blind area.

Visual perception thus is a dynamic, context-directed, top-down process. A model of the suspected or expected experience serves as a guideline for processing the available external and internal information, and the memorial availability of models of complex experiences governs the actual results of the process: Accordingly, strategies available in memory and recallable repertoires of images play a major role in the process. The consciously perceived end-result of this process may contain many or few features that have entered the process as internally available information. Later discussion will show that state-dependent access to processing strategies and memory materials is a key point in these dynamic processes–dream generation being an extreme case in point.

The model-driven property of perception of course is a general characteristic for all sensory modalities. An example from the auditory modality might illustrate this: an encounter between two people, one of whom (A) expects the other one (B) to speak in a foreign language which A is certain not to be able to understand. If B quite unexpectedly speaks in A's natural language, A might not be able to understand immediately what has been said–a short time of readjustment

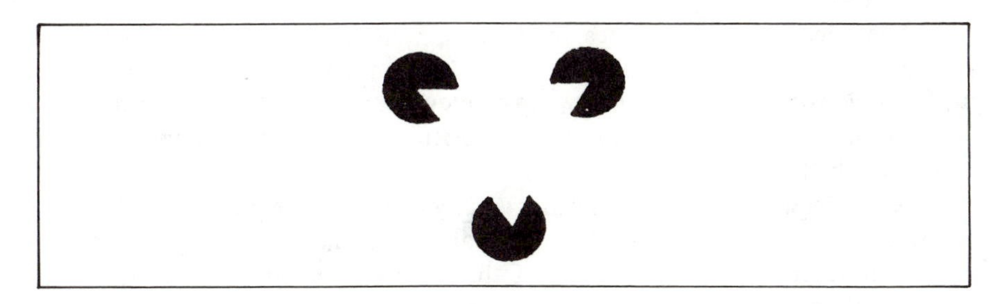

Figure 1. Triangle with illusory contours after Kanisza [2]. Only portions of the contours are really present, but the triangle is a compelling percept. The triangle shares its surface structure with its surround; nevertheless, the perceived triangle appears whiter than the surround.

to the corrected expectation is necessary. On the other hand, if the spoken message is expected but is badly distorted, it might still be understandable thanks to the expectations and contextual information. The example also illustrates that input-driven sensory feature extraction mechanisms in the brain [5] are successful only within restricted tasks. Accordingly it is conceivable that attempts for a general model covering all brain functions are unrealistic; it appears more likely that the brain chooses a particular "expert system" from a large number of such tools for processing information. (Expert systems diagnose and solve problems within a very constrained situation; classics in this branch of artificial intelligence are e.g. "visiting a restaurant," and "cubes on the desk"). The selection of the expert system depends on the momentary functional state with its particular goals, and on the outcome of the first step of information processing.

There are many other examples of the healthy and diseased brain's power to perceive whole visual images which are more or less unrelated to the momentary external visual information; in short, very different brain conditions might be associated with visual imagery [6]. Healthy people report voluntary recall of image-based information such as faces, imagery in spontaneous daydreaming, hypnagogic/hypnopompic hallucinations at sleep onset and termination, and visual imaging during sensory deprivation. Under abnormal conditions, people report drug-induced hallucinations, visual experiences during migraine attacks ("fortification figures"), visual experiences during *deja vue* episodes and during epileptic seizures, visual imagery induced by space-occupying brain lesions, and visual imagery induced by electric stimulation of higher brain areas. Contrary to the latter reports, it is of interest that stimulation of the cortical input areas in the visual system (area 17 and 18 of the visual cortex) did not result in percepts other than star-like light dots [7]. No percepts of patterns, not even of the theoretically expected lines or corners, were elicited. It is further noteworthy that, despite the predominance of visual imagery in most conditions, the hallucinations in schizophrenia are most frequent in the auditory modality, and if visual, are accompanied by auditory experiences—similar to the few reports on conversive hallucinations [8].

The vividness of visual images varies greatly across different people and different situations. There is a well-known age gradient in visual imagery. Many children have eidetic capabilities [9, 10], but there are few eidetic adults. Moreover, the ability to visualize (and to mentally manipulate visual information) differs across adults [11-13], just as the ease of perceiving "hidden figures" differs. The tendency to vividly experience visual imagery (during sleep onset, under Cannabis, and under Psilocybin) is systematically correlated with EEG measures present before the imagery-inducing treatment is started [14, 15].

This chapter is based on models of human information processing and discusses psychophysiological mechanisms underlying dream formation as a mental state where visual imagery is prominent. It utilizes knowledge-driven and state-dependent brain mechanisms. It is suggested that there is a common principal mechanism, pre-attentive processing, which subserves all mental processes, including imagery phenomena as reviewed above and dream experiences. The psychophysiological characteristics which distinguish imagery from vision-derived symbolic processes and from other mental strategies depend on the brain's functional state during processing.

THE HUMAN BRAIN AS AN INFORMATION PROCESSING SYSTEM

From the perspective of information theory, humans are in a continuous and selective interaction with their internal and external environment [16]. The internal environment includes memories, goals, motives, feelings, emotions, hormonal and metabolic conditions, etc. The interaction between the two environments is coordinated by the brain, using multiple feedback loops. Behavior is the measurable manifestation of this interaction. Thus, behavior is the end product of mental operations (brain functions) through which humans readjust their way of functioning, continuously, as a result of the messages which come from the external and internal reality. The aim of this readjustment is to maintain the functional well-being of the individual as a living, goal-oriented, adaptively functioning biological system.

Basic elements of the human information processing system are stored in three memory categories: first, information (multi-modal representations of past experience including both its physical characteristics coded in the verbal and symbolic languages of the brain and its emotional aspects coded in the emotional languages of the brain) [17, 18, see also 19]; second, developed skills (fixed or automated responses to specific incoming information) [20]; and third, developed strategies (cognitive-emotional strategies for confronting complex or new information, and for pursuing long-term goals) [21].

Thus, human memory can be defined as the sum of stored information about the symbolic and emotional aspects of internal and external events, the context in which they occurred, and the cognitive and emotional strategies and behavioral responses which were developed to deal with them [22]. With experience, these memory stores develop, and their utilization becomes more quick and efficient [20, 23-25]. At a given moment in time, only a part of the total memory storage is accessible for current information processing ("working memory" [26]). Memory is state-dependent.

Functional States of the Brain and State-Dependent Information Processing

The type of execution of all brain work depends on the momentary global functional state of the brain, and in turn is reflected by this momentary state. An example is that the momentarily accessible memory store is defined by the momentary functional state, i.e. that memory retrieval is state-dependent as noted above, and that the treatment of the processed material is reflected by the state. The brain's global functional state is conceived as a mosaic of many local functional states. Viewing the succession of global functional states over time, gross states such as sleep or wakefulness are seen as consisting of temporal sequences of global micro-states, i.e. of "atoms of thought."

The brain functional state depends on the momentary external and internal information, on the momentary thoughts, emotions, goals, motives, feelings, etc. Possible functional states are constrained by maturational age, internal clocks, metabolic and hormonal conditions, drugs, and diseases.

The brain functional states are manifest in various dimensions: biochemical measures, electrical measures, behavioral data and subjective experiences. The brain's electrical activity, which is recordable as scalp EEG, is a sensitive indicator of the brain's functional state. We have reviewed experimental evidence in electrophysiology, experimental and developmental psychology, and psychopharmacology which suggests that the momentary EEG state reflects the "dimension" of the accessible portions of the memory store at a given moment in time, in other words, the part of the activated knowledge which is available for the organization of momentary behavior [27]. Different functional states of the brain accordingly are reflected by different EEG characteristics, have access to different memory stores, and are associated with cognitive-emotional strategies which are state-innate or have been acquired during the same state. The complexity of the strategies reflect the complexity of the state.

The state-dependency of learning and retrieval was originally shown in experiments with centrally active drugs [28, 29]. Behavior learned during the

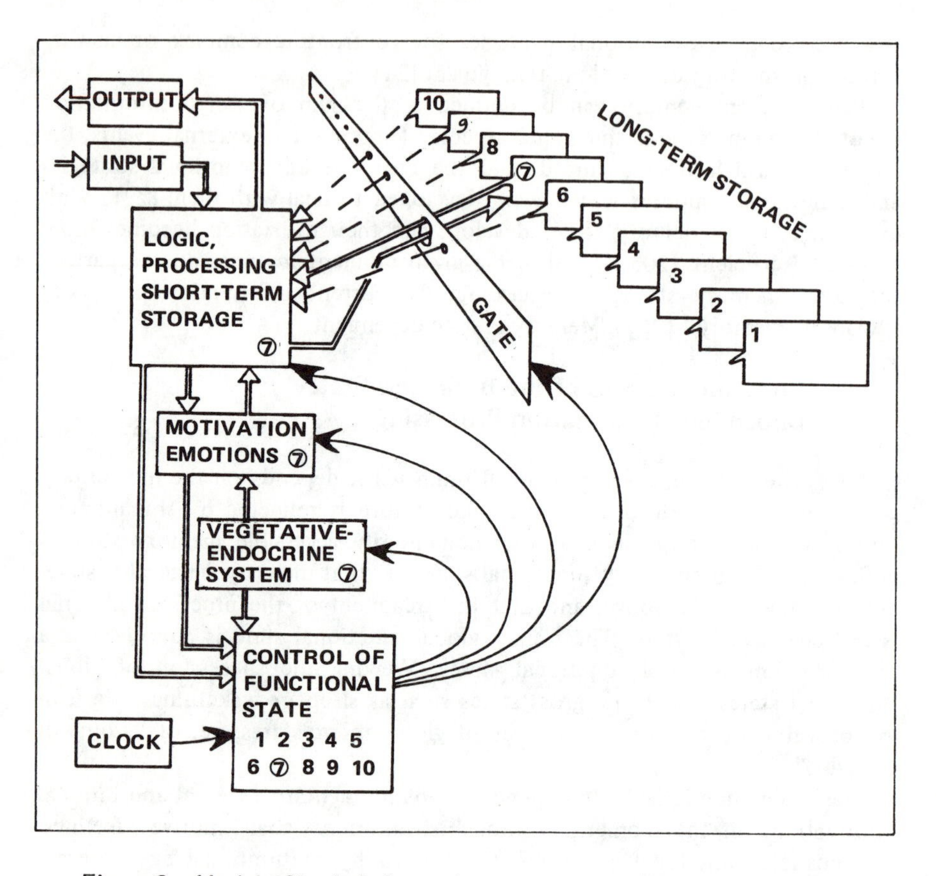

Figure 2. Model of brain information processing functions. Double lines indicate open information channels, dashed lines partially open channels, solid lines with black arrowheads control channels. The functional state of the brain (illustrated is a state called "7") is adjusted by the control system according to clock input and input received as result of the preattentive processing from the logic/processing (analysis) system with its short-term working memory and from the motivation/emotion system, and input from the vegetative system. The control system adjusts the function of the logic/processing and motivation and vegetative systems to the momentary functional state, and opens the access gate to the associated long-term memory storage for deposit and recall of informations and strategies (in the illustration, storage space 7). Memory of higher levels (8 to 10) can be accessed partially; of the lower levels, only the next neighbor storage (space 6) is partially open for recall. Shifts of functional state put different memory storages and processing strategies into use. The Figure illustrates functions, not anatomical structures. (From [27]).

effect of a drug is recalled better during the same drug state than during a drug-free state [30; see also 22, 31]. The phenomenon has also been reported in mood states [32], in hormonal states [33], and in mental disease [34]. Thus, operationally for each functional state of the brain, only a part of the total memory is accessible. Storage of new information is optimal in the state-associated memory store. Read-out of stored information is asymmetric: For a given functional state, read-out is also possible out of storages associated with higher, more complexly organized states, but not out of storages of lower states. Higher states are, e.g., non-drug states or more developed states or more vigilant states. Thus, the functional state of the brain permits and restricts access to certain parts of the memory (illustrated in Figure 2).

An illustrative example of state dependency in memory and behavior functions is human sleep walking, which occurs during human slow wave sleep [35]. Sleep walkers react to the surround (albeit slowly) and conduct goal directed acts (go to the fridge, eat) drawing on past experiences; but after awakening, during fast wakeful EEG, there is typically very little recall of the sleep walking experiences.

Examples of state dependent thinking are the gross functional states of wakefulness and sleep in adults, or wakefulness in childhood and adulthood. Wakeful thinking and feeling in early childhood (with its slow EEG frequencies) and in adults (with its faster EEG frequencies) follow different strategies [36, 37], and it is well known that wakeful adult thinking and feeling are different from adult dreaming. Spontaneous state changes occur as a function of time, in principle governed by internal clocks (life cycle, circadian rhythms, 90-minute cycle, 5 sec periods of variations of attention, 10 Hz periodicity of human brain electric activity, etc.). These basic internal periodicities can be strongly influenced, reset, and interrupted by readjustments of state. EEG studies showed that changes of brain state occur at split-second intervals, as discussed below in the section on micro states.

The functional state is readjusted continuously (within constraints given by developmental age and currently existing state) to the demands made on the organism by the externally or internally generated information, including newly formed thoughts, emotions, and goals. The readjustment is the result of pre-attentive processing, and is executed via the orienting reaction. The mechanisms which mediate the interaction of these factors are illustrated in Figure 2.

The Pre-Attentive Processes

According to models of human information processing [16, 20, 24], the information processing mechanisms of pre-attentive processing work continuously and in parallel for all input channels and during all levels of consciousness. Such mechanisms accomplish very rapidly an automatic, preliminary, and relatively complex identification of two properties of the information; momentary familiarity and momentary significance of the information for the organism. For research on the level of human behavioral organization, the sequential stages of the pre-attentive processes can be summarized as 1) encoding of the physical characteristics of the information which is transmitted to the brain into the verbal, symbolic, and emotional languages of the receiving brain, and 2) comparing of the thus molded multi-dimensional information with the momentarily accessible portion of memory.

Thus, pre-attentive processing interacts closely with the accessible memory. The result of pre-attentive processing is an estimate of the subsequent processing required, and a selection of the characteristic answer of the organism. Specifically, it leads to the following processes: 1) selection and initiation of the information processing mode (automatic or/and controlled) for the further analysis and interpretation of the information (cognitive analysis); 2) separation of currently new and important information from currently unimportant or familiar information; and 3), selection and initiation of the answer.

The basic assumption is that an answer is selected for all complex information which reaches the human information processing system. An answer is a change or a "no change" of the level of functioning of the organism, as compared to the level just prior to the start of the processing of the information [18, 38]. The answer is installed via the orienting reaction. The answer is subjectively perceivable in cognitive and emotional aspects, and is objectively measurable in various realms, in particular as behavior, and as vegetative and EEG data. Thus, the type and magnitude of the response of the brain's functional state is executed as the EEG component of the "orienting reaction," or as its "habituation" [18, 39].

An information processing analysis of the mechanisms underlying the orienting reaction indicates that these are identical with mechanisms underlying the pre-attentive processes [18, 38, 40, 41]. There is strong evidence that the information processing sequences of the pre-attentive processes operate with automatic access to the activated memory stores. Accordingly, pre-attentive processing operates within the automatic information processing mode, and relies heavily on practice or past knowledge [20, 24, 42]. Numerous parallel processing channels are always available to the automatic processing mode.

If the pre-attentive processes recognize the information as momentarily unimportant or as information for which an established (automated) response is available in the accessible memory store, the answer consists of "no change of state," and if applicable, the available automatic response is executed. That means that the automatic information processing mode is also used for the further analysis of this information. But if the information was recognized as important (emotion arousing) or new, an appropriate change of state (with an EEG change to more arousal) is implemented in order to deal optimally with the information; this change of state not only makes accessible different memory stores and processing strategies, but also shuts off access to lower-order stores and strategies. This call for more analysis in the case of very important or completely unknown information gives the information access to the limited-capacity channel of conscious information processing, which utilizes the "controlled processing mode" [20] for the following step of "cognitive processing" [43]. Within this processing mode, analysis and decision making is slow but very adaptive, and the available range of selectable response behavior is very large [23].

The form, strength and topography of event-induced EEG changes reflect the functional adaptation of the brain to the demands made by the event on the organism [44, 45] as estimated by the pre-attentive processes. The functional adaptation is installed as the central component of the orienting reaction, manifested as change or no change ("habituation") of the EEG [18, 38-41, 46, 47]. It initiates the brain's next functional state and, thereby, its access to the particular memory stores within which further analysis and interpretation of the event will occur.

TEMPORALLY DEFINED EEG STATES AND COGNITIVE-EMOTIONAL STYLE

Frequent changes of functional state are detectable in the scalp-recorded electric activity (EEG) of the human brain. Conventional EEG recordings display the time-dependent changes of potential differences between two electrode locations as EEG tracings. These tracings show patterns of quasi-periodic voltage fluctuations with varying "wave" frequencies which manifest gross functional states. The dominant frequency of the EEG patterns changes as a function of age and as a function of vigilance: from infancy to adulthood, there is a systematic increase in the dominant frequency of the wakeful EEG [e.g. 48] and an increased reality orientation in thinking; on the other hand, sleep is typically associated with slower EEG frequencies, wakefulness with faster EEG frequencies, paralleled respectively by reality-remote dreaming and by reality-close wakeful thinking. Thus, there is a general EEG similarity between the child's wakeful developmental stages and the adult's lowered vigilance stages, which is mirrored by cognitive styles.

Sleep in the human consists of "stages" which re-occur in cycles of about 90 minutes characterized by the dominant EEG frequencies. There is EEG slowing at sleep onset, and while sleep becomes deeper (while the arousal threshold becomes higher), more and more slow waves appear ("sleep stages 2 to 4"), finally to give way to a somewhat faster, sleep-onset-related EEG pattern which is associated with rapid eye movements ("stage REM sleep") and which is followed by another sleep cycle with slower waves. Summing up, the EEG evidence indicates similarities of functional organization of brain electric activity between sleep EEG patterns in adults, and wakeful states during earlier stages of development. The variety of different sequential EEG stages in sleep suggests that an adult goes through repeated functional regressions to earlier developmental stages during sleep [27]. The gross EEG sleep stages, and the EEG's from different developmental stages can be classed by eye-inspection of chart tracings.

Relations between EEG and dream experiences have traditionally been based on such "eyeballing" assessment of the EEG, typically considering the data in multiples of 30-sec-chuncks. It has often been reported that dream reports are more frequent when the subject is awakened out of REM-sleep than out of Non-REM sleep, but it needs to be emphasized that "non-REM dreams" are by no means rare, and that full-fledged dream reports can be recalled out of awakenings long before the first REM epoch [49, 50]. The right hemisphere with its hypothetical "holistic" processing strategies has been proposed as "dream generator" based on reported absence of dreaming in (split brain) patients after surgical dissection of the interhemispheric connections [51] and on selective EEG studies of REM epochs suggesting right hemisphere activation in normals [52]. However, statistics on dream recall in patients with localized brain lesions showed that disturbances in either posterior brain quadrant interfered with dream recall, unlike disturbances in the anterior quadrants [53]. The problem of hypothetical localizations of the "dream generator" cannot be discussed here; however, complex brain functions assumedly require information processing which involves different and extended brain areas. Studies on brain areas involved in dreaming need to distinguish between different aspects: sensory modality of the experience, reality testing, consciousness level, ability to recall, and ability to verbalize.

At closer scrutiny, the EEG patterns during wakefulness and during sleep show many pattern changes within short time epochs. It appears reasonable to assume that at least each homogeneous EEG wave train represents a particular brain state [54]. This implies that within a few seconds, many different functional states follow each other in rapid succession within the gross state of wakefulness and within the different stages of sleep. Sometimes, the changes are accounted for by an externally triggered "orienting reaction," i.e. the organism's behavioral response to new or important information, which is associated with a typical change to faster EEG frequencies. Such reaction can be graded; i.e., a minor shift towards faster frequencies might occur in sleep following the presentation of a soft sound, whereas a loud noise might be followed by wakeful EEG patterns. Often there is no external information, but internally generated information such as body sensations or newly formed thoughts or retrieved memories might cause the "orienting reaction" with its associated EEG change.

Numerical computer-assisted analysis has been able to describe very many ruleful correspondences between EEG data viewed as short time series, and behavioral parameters or introspective experiences which show that the EEG is a very sensitive state indicator. Various relationships between brain states defined by EEG patterns and different types or classes of cognitive and emotional processing have been repeatedly reported, using EEG data epochs lasting from

16 seconds to a few minutes. The reports are inhomogeneous as there is a great variety of different EEG analysis methods; however, many apparent discrepancies in the literature might originate from the utilization of differing experimental conditions and analysis strategies, and there are converging lines of evidence when the conditions are taken into account. In the following, selected findings pertaining to visual imagery and to dreaming will illustrate the direction of work and of possible findings.

Wakeful recall of information presented during sleep depended on the EEG frequency spectra immediately after presentation; more wakeful patterns were related to superior recall quality [55]. EEG frequency spectra during the 20 sec immediately before awakening were significantly related to probability of dream recall in REM awakenings [56].

Concerning EEG correlates of visual imagery, we found predominant EEG activation over the right occipital area during visual imagery in normals [57-59]. In these experiments, completely spontaneous and unconstrained thoughts were collected during a "no task" situation, and 16 sec of EEG immediately before the thought reports were analyzed. (Similar strategies have been generally used in studies of dreaming, but typically only with "eyeballing" of the EEG; sleep onset studies relating the qualities of mentation and the EEG, using computer analysis, showed promising results) [60]. Other designs have used tasks of more or less constraining types: For example, when the subjects were asked to execute mental tasks chosen from a pre-agreed, restricted set, no right/left hemispheric difference was found in visual imagery conditions [61, 62]. Still more constraining are tasks where in addition to input-driven tasks there is a request for a motor response [63]. We suggest that the brain requires powerful routines for volitional task re-focussing and compliant task execution, and even more powerful routines for selection, preparation and execution of motor acts whose manifestations are present in the brain electric activity [64]. Under such conditions, the EEG manifestation of other aspects of information processing might become very difficult to detect. In addition, in many experimental designs there is provision for training in task execution [63]. This might well be counter-productive for the detection of manifestations of specific processes, as training automates task execution and thereby reduces the demand on specific brain mechanisms to a minimum [18].

Shorter EEG epochs in the range of few seconds also show correlations with functions. The typical "alpha" rhythm (about 9 Hz) in relaxed human adults shows fluctuations of amplitude in the range of seconds which are related to fluctuations of sensitivity in visual perception [65, 66], and fluctuations of the wave pattern in the same range of seconds which are related to fluctuations of choice reaction time [67]. However, classical EEG phenomena such as the "K complex" (which occurs as electric response to external information during sleep), and studies of event-related brain potentials have made it likely that much shorter epochs might be functionally identifiable in the EEG, eventually down to the "single waves," electric manifestations in the one-tenth of a second range.

SPATIALLY DEFINED EEG MICRO STATES AND INFORMATION PROCESSING

Studies of the micro structure of the EEG and its functional and introspective correlates show that very brief states can be clearly distinguished. For this study of micro states, brain electric activity is not viewed as waveforms but as a continuous series of instantaneous electric landscapes, i.e. as momentary maps of the brain electric field at a rate of, say, 128 per second. This leads to the description of momentary states of brain activity as reflected by the pattern of the momentary spatial distribution of electric potential. At each moment in time, there is a particular spatial pattern or "landscape" of brain electric activity. A given landscape of activity can be assumed to represent a particular step or mode or content of information processing [68]; a change of the landscape must mean that a different configuration of brain activity exists which in all likeliness manifests a different step or mode of processing. Over a certain time, a given landscape remains stable in its configuration, but periodically changes in polarity, which gives rise to the temporal patterns visible in the conventional waveform tracings. As long as the spatial configuration or landscape remains stable, the processing mode or step might be assumed to continue. When it changes, a new step or mode begins, regardless of the local waveform.

We have analyzed human adult EEG's as to the durations of stationary brain electric landscapes (the duration of micro states), using a space-oriented procedure for adaptive temporal segmentation of multichannel EEG data. We found over six subjects that the mean segment duration in the alpha EEG band was 210 msec; 50 percent of all time was covered by segments longer than 323 msec [69]. These segments or functional micro-states are suggested to represent the "atoms of thought," and their durations might reflect the probability that the particular brain processing step finds access to the consciousness channel, considering the putative minimal "consciousness time" [64]. We hypothesize that each change of micro state reflects a completed result of pre-attentive processing.

The functional significance of these micro states was examined in experiments on choice reaction time, and with the collection of spontaneous, subjective experiences. The results, which are briefly reviewed below, indicate that it is possible to identify momentary micro states of brain electric activity with performance quality and with the mode of subjective experiences, supporting the functional significance of the EEG micro states.

Randomly presented auditory stimuli were processed with significantly different motor reaction times depending on the momentary brain electric (EEG) landscape which existed at the moment of stimulus delivery; the results were similar in eight subjects using 323 stimuli per subject [69].

In experiments with B. A. Kofmel and C. Michel, we studied mode of spontaneous mentation and EEG momentary-potential landscapes in twenty healthy right handed volunteers. About thirty short reports of private experiences were collected from each subject, spoken into an audio recorder when prompted by a gentle tone at about 3 minute intervals. The momentary EEG maps immediately preceding the prompt were searched for the maximally "hilly landscape," i.e. the last map with maximal voltage between potential peaks and troughs which on the average occurred 50 msec before the prompt. This map was searched for the locations of the peak and trough voltages (the locations of the "extreme potentials"). The subject's reports were rated as to "visually imaged" and "non-visual" thoughts. Two or more reports of either type occurred in sixteen subjects; in the average subject, there were 10.3 imagery and 8.6 non-visual cases. For each subject and for the two types of thoughts, the map locations of the extreme potentials were accumulated, and median locations were computed. The hemispheric locations across the subjects' medians for the imaged thoughts and for the non-visual thoughts were compared: these hemispheric locations across subjects were significantly ($p > 0.005$) more to the right for the imaged than for the non-visual thoughts.

Summarizing we see that the mode (visually imaged thoughts vs non-visual thoughts) of a subjective experience is manifest in the configuration ("landscape") of the momentary brain electric field measured immediately before the subject is asked to report the experience. The brain micro state reflects the mode of information processing. Imagery mode and non-visual mode of processing are associated with brain field distributions of differing lateralization.

Images and Thoughts: Developmental Aspects

General hypothesizing about mental development in humans reasonably assumes that the primordial, innate, experiential qualities in a newborn might well be on the axis pleasant/unpleasant, as one might indeed also suppose for less complex creatures. These qualities would suffice for simple decisions and might serve initially to classify and encode sensory input, including visual input, for storage. As the visual system in sheer number of incoming fibers is larger than the other sensory systems, its perceptual predominance in the subjective experience of sighted individuals appears reasonable. Motoric-sensoric interactive experiences lead to identification and recognition of objects, connections between them, and hence, to scenes that are predominantly available for recall as visual images in the young child, much more so than in the adult. The general "eidetic" talent of young children, which is largely lost during adolescence, suggests this. With the build-up of a repertoire of memory-stored material, conceptual generalizations become possible, and eventually abstractions (symbolizations) and concatenations between symbols [70]. Children's mental manipulations of concrete, generalized or abstract items recalled from memory might primarily be done as manipulations of images, as suggested by Premack (personal communication) for thought processes in apes. In fact, even in adult thinking, it is not easy to avoid completely visual associations when thinking about abstractions. Present theorizing about human information processing considers specific image-handling routes [71, 72], such as in Paivio's dual encoding theory [73].

On the other hand, perception of visual images by an individual must be learned via motor-sensory interactive operations in early developmental stages. This is shown not only by the deprivation studies in kittens where the absence of specific visual information (e.g., horizontal bar patterns) at an early developmental stage makes it impossible for the adult animal to "see" this type of information, but also by observations of formerly blind people who obtained the ability to see late in life and were unable to handle the newly available visual information [74].

Parallel to the modern technological developments which provided the possibilities for information transfer, storage and retrieval as high-grade images in massive quantity, social acceptance has developed for images as respectable carriers of serious information beyond emotionally appealing or entertaining art products. From large scale 19th century reproductions of printed images, to blue prints for designs, to journals, to TV and finally to the present avalanche of image-oriented presentation of information, images have gained stature. New ideas have appeared suggesting that images might be useful in themselves in information processing, and that there might be ways to manipulate images and concepts in the form of images on a high level without the need to dissect them into formal, meaning-deprived fragments. The current practical and theoretical interest in pattern recognition techniques reflect this, including the tendency to investigate the results of the systematic development of certain mathematical formalisms as images (MANDELBROT-figure, LORENTZ-figure). In parallel, purely intellectual, emotion-free, abstract reasoning has lost popularity. Volitional and spontaneous imagery has even found some acceptance in therapeutic settings [75, 76].

Neural network theories and practical implementations have shown that emergent, higher order, functional properties appear in systems which are made up of identical elements, once they have been exposed to structured input such as visual figures, but without having been supervised during the implied learning period. In other words, the acquisition of pattern recognition capabilities in an adequately designed system does not require an all informed central agent. This is related to the capability of interconnected arrays of individual, active elements to spontaneously generate distinct patterns of activity (self organizing systems) in response to a disturbance [77]. Hence, these systems show what might be called goal-directed behavior, although no goal has been preprogrammed. The final pattern of achieved activity is an emergent property of its connectivity. The model of dream generation to be discussed below includes related features which make an all-knowing and detail-recognizing agent unnecessary when accounting for such psychological aspects of dreams as "repression," "distortion," "condensation," "displacement," etc.

Subjective Acceptance of Imagery as External Information

Acceptance of the experienced image as external reality does not necessarily depend on the vividness of the imagery, even though more vivid images might be more persuasive. Examples are Cannabis-induced hallucinations which are very vivid for some people, but hardly ever misinterpreted as reality, or the vivid mental images one can conjure up in wakefulness when trying to remember the where-abouts of a missing item. On the other hand, LSD-induced hallucinations not infrequently are perceived as external reality, particularly when higher doses are used. Dream imagery typically is not recognized as such (i.e. as not real) until after awakening. Levels of subjective acceptance have been proposed for classifying hallucinations ("true vs pseudo-hallucinations"), but this is of little clinical diagnostic usefulness (a schizophrenic patient might report some hallucinations as compelling thoughts, others as external voices) although it can have practical implications since imagery accepted as reality might lead to severe behavioral consequences.

In general, states of decreased clarity of consciousness and reflective self-awareness tend to be associated with increased subjective acceptance of experienced imagery as external reality (Kunzendorf [78] calls this "unmonitored images"). Although imagery is possible during high and low attention and consciousness states, a change of functional state triggered by new or important information (i.e. an orienting reaction) tends to discontinue ongoing imagery. This is so for spontaneous normal imagery (daydreaming, dreaming) and for drug-induced and spontaneous pathological imagery (schizophrenic imagery). Imagery, and in particular reality-remote imagery, typically does not persist during attention to externally generated information (people tend to close their eyes when trying to visualize something), nor during the associated brain state change which implies a shift to higher levels of vigilance and to increased reality orientation.

From the viewpoint of ontogenetic development of the organism's information processing strategies, we note that the ability to distinguish between internally and externally generated information develops over time. The learning of contingency between volitional motor acts and tactile sensory feedback (and associated visual and auditory experiences) leads to the interpretational strategy to "project" experiences into the outside world, thus laying the foundations for the demarkation between self and the external surround. As soon as this projection strategy is established, it becomes necessary to learn that its indiscriminant application (PAVLOV's "generalization") is not always effective when dealing with reality: Internally generated thoughts and emotions, or simply material retrieved from memory, should not be ascribed to external sources for successful planning of future actions. Experience makes it evident that behavioral acts often are not successful when based on the assumption that internally generated concepts are identical with external reality. However, the complexity of the world might delay this insight, as neurotic behavior shows [79]. Thus, mature interaction with reality requires successful distinction between internally and externally generated information, even though in both cases top-down strategies play a major role.

When considering mechanisms of dream generation as well, it appears to be useful to distinguish between the two phenomena, the experience of visual imagery and the subjective acceptance of the experience as external reality. Brain functional states associated with lack of reality testing and brain functional states associated with imagery need not be identical, although the likeliness of imaginal processing increases within states of lower functional complexity. The tendency during drowsiness to transform symbolic, abstract thoughts into perceptual images, combined with the lack of reality testing, leads to the "literal translations" which sometimes badly cloud the original, contextual meaning (as Silberer [80] so elegantly described it).

The EEG parameter associated with reality-remote strategies and acceptance of thoughts as external reality is the lowered temporal frequency of the polarity reversals of the brain electric field, detectable in short epochs in time. An example is the systematic slowing of the EEG wave frequency during periods of hypnagogic hallucinations, within sleep onset, as compared with pre-sleep periods of reality-oriented thoughts [27]. Visual imagery vs non-visual thoughts appear to be reflected spatially in the EEG, as the local state in the occipital areas discussed above—detectable even in the momentary brain field map.

Dream Generation

Reported dreams are the recall of cognitions and emotions, which means private aspects of brain information processing which was done during sleep. The change from waking to sleeping does not interrupt the communication of the individual with its internal and external environment. The pre-attentive information processing sequences function equally well during wakefulness and during sleep. This implies that information is transmitted to the brain and/or retrieved from memory, and its meaning is evaluated using the accessible memory stores. This is supported by behavioral, evoked potential data and EEG reactivity measurements [81-83].

A theory of dream generation has to account for several major characteristics of dream experiences: no reference to momentary external reality, strong tendency to imagery, typically no reflective self-awareness (the dreamer is not aware he is dreaming), difficulty of wakeful recall of the dream, inadequacy of dream emotions, and the discontinuity of dream narratives.

A general psychobiological theory of dream generation also must not be based on physiological features which are particular to REM sleep stages, as complete dream reports can be obtained before the occurrence of a first REM stage [49]: "Dreams," i.e. cognitive-emotional experiences occur during all sleep stages [50]. Likewise, incoming information is processed and recognized during all sleep stages, and conveniently might lead to possible awakenings by alarm clocks or partners. On the other hand, the probability that dream experiences are recalled in subsequent wakefulness varies over sleep stages, which indicates that there is a state-dependent function of retrieval.

We suggest that consideration of the general state-dependency of brain functions (see Figure 2), and of the "functional asymmetry" of the state dependent retrieval of memory material can account for the observed phenomena in dreams [27]. In general, dreams are the internal and subjective aspects of some state-dependent types of human information processing, using as material almost exclusively the state-dependent portions of memory. On the other hand, for the evaluation of the momentary significance of the processed internal and external information, all the knowledge of the individual can be used because of the functional asymmetry of the memory retrieval process.

Based on similarities in EEG patterns, we have proposed that many of the functional states of the adult brain during different sleep stages correspond to functional states of the awake brain during earlier phases of development [27]. Thus, sleep implies physiological regressions to earlier functional stages of development. This suggests that during sleep, both memories and cognitive-emotional processing strategies of earlier developmental stages become available for information processing. Accordingly dreams, being the result of a regression in information processing strategy, show properties which are common for cognition in earlier developmental stages: a high propensity of visual images and reality-remote strategies, which imply content-inadequate emotional associations.

On the other hand, information processing during sleep cannot be expected to show (and does not show) characteristics which are not available to the system in wakeful states or which were not available to the system in earlier stages. Cases in point are the dreams of children, which vary stylistically in accordance with the developmental age [84], and the dreams of blind people which do not include visual experiences [85]. In the same vein, the question why most imagery, including dreams, is visual in healthy people has the parsimonious answer that this is so because the visual system is physically (in terms of afferent nerve fibers) much larger in size than other sensory systems.

Changes of state are frequent during sleep, as manifest in the quickly changing EEG patterns. These changes can be caused by spontaneous state changes (time-dependent sleep stages) or as a result of recognition of signal information. The recognition leads to a smaller or larger shift of functional state, which implies access to different storages for information processing and inaccessability of others. Signal information can originate from associations between material of the accessible memory store, or from incoming internal or external information. Thus, very different portions of previously stored material and very different treatment strategies are available in quick succession, and are used for recombinations and variations of the material which result in newly formed thoughts and conclusions. The result is a sequence of events which is concatenation of material and strategies from different levels. This concatenation accounts for the typical discontinuity or originality of the dream narrative.

The poor recall of dream products in subsequent wakefulness is accounted for by the asymmetry of state-dependent recall. There is effective recall from higher to lower-organized/developed states (good recognition in sleep for material learned in wakefulness, such as names), but ineffective recall from lower to higher-organized/developed states (poor recognition in wakefulness for material presented during sleep) [55, 86]. Accordingly, a shift in functional state (an arousal reaction) due to recognition of some alarming feature in momentarily processed material during dreaming might change the momentary state in such a way that recall of it in the newly attained higher state is very difficult. This self-organizing feature which uses an unspecific "new information" or "alarming information" label for installation of a state change can be viewed as a goal directed mechanism: This appears to be the action of an all-contents-recognizing agent (FREUD's censor of dream content).

The model suggests a psychophysiological significance of sleep and sleep mentation: specifically, that information processing during sleep provides renewed access to memory stores of earlier developmental stages, with the goal to compare (and, if necessary, to assimilate) old engrams and processing strategies with new ones (see also [87, 88]). This re-opening of access to earlier memory stores and cognitive-emotional strategies, and the general possibility of shifts to other states with other stores and strategies, means that the individual has a wider spectrum of problem solutions available during sleep for exploratory application to new materials and problems.

REFERENCES

1. R. M. Jones, *The New Psychology of Dreaming*, Grune and Stratton, New York, 1970.
2. G. Kanizsa, *Organization in Vision*, Praeger, New York, 1979.
3. S. Petry and G. E. Meyer, (eds.), *The Perception of Illusory Contours*, Springer, Heidelberg, 1987.
4. B. Julesz, *Foundations of Cyclopean Perception*, University of Chicago Press, Chicago, 1971.

5. D. Marr, Early Processing of Visual Information, *Philosophical Transactions of the Royal Society of London*, Series B., 275, pp. 483-524, 1976.
6. L. J. West (ed.), *Hallucinations*, Grune and Stratton, New York, 1962.
7. G. S. Brindley, Sensory Effects of Electrical Stimulation of the Visual and Paravisual Cortex in Man, H. Autrum, R. Jung, W. R. Loewenstein, D. M. MacKay, and H. L. Teuber (eds), in *Handbook of Sensory Physiology*, vol. VII/3, R. Jung (ed.), Visual Centers in the Brain, Springer, Heidelberg, pp. 583-594, 1973.
8. P. Sirota and B. Spivac, Conversive Hallucinations, *British Journal of Psychiatry, 151*, pp. 844-846, 1987.
9. M. F. Weiner, Hallucinations in Children, *Archives of General Psychiatry, 5*, pp. 544-553, 1961.
10. A. Rothstein, Hallucinatory Phenomena in Childhood, *Journal of the American Academy of Child Psychiatry, 20*, pp. 623-635, 1981.
11. D. Marks, Imagery and Consciousness: A Theoretical Review from an Individual Differences Perspective, *Journal of Mental Imagery, 2*, pp. 275-290, 1977.
12. A. Dittrich, Aetiologie-unabhängige Strukturen veränderter Wachbewusstseinszustände, Enke, Stuttgart, 1985.
13. S. M. Kosslyn, J. Brunn, K. R. Cave and R. W. Wallach, Individual Differences in Mental Imagery Ability—A Computational Analysis, in *Visual Cognition*, S. Pinker (ed.), MIT Press, Cambridge, Massachusetts, pp. 195-244, 1985.
14. M. Koukkou and D. Lehmann, Human EEG Spectra Before and During Cannabis Hallucinations, *Biological Psychiatry, 11*, pp. 663-677, 1976.
15. M. Koukkou and D. Lehmann, EEG Spectra Indicates Predisposition to Visual Hallucinations Under Psilocybin, Cannabis, Hypnagogic and Day Dream Conditions, *Electroencephalography and Clinical Neurophysiology, 43*, pp. 499-500, 1977.
16. U. Neisser, *Cognition and Reality*, Freeman, San Francisco, 1976.
17. G. H. Bower, Mood and Memory, *American Psychologist, 36*, pp. 129-148, 1981.
18. M. Koukkou and D. Lehmann, An Information-Processing Perspective of Psychophysiological Measurements, *Journal of Psychophysiology, 1*, pp. 109-112, 1987.
19. H. Leventhal and A. J. Tomarken, Emotion: Today's Problem, *Annual Review of Psychology, 37*, pp. 565-610, 1986.
20. R. M. Shiffrin and W. Schneider, Controlled and Automatic Human Information Processing: II, Perceptual Learning, Automatic Attending, and a General Theory, *Psychological Review, 84*, pp. 127-190, 1977.
21. S. Grossberg, (ed.), *The Adaptive Brain, I: Cognition, Learning, Reinforcement and Rhythm*, Elsevier, Amsterdam, 1987.
22. D. L. Horton and C. B. Mils, Human Learning and Memory, *Annual Review of Psychology, 35*, pp. 361-394, 1984.
23. O. Neumann, Automatic Processing: A Review of Recent Findings and a Plea for an Old Theory, in *Cognition and Motor Processes*, W. Prinz and A. F. Sanders, (eds.), Springer, Heidelberg, 1984.

24. D. A. Norman, Reflections on Cognition and Parallel Distributed Processing, in *Parallel Distributed Processing, Vol. 2: Psychological and Biological Models*, J. L. McClelland, D. E. Rumelhart and the PDP Research Group, (eds.), MIT Press, Cambridge, Massachusetts, 1986.
25. J. Morton and D. Bekerian, Three Ways of Looking at Memory, in *Advances in Cognitive Science 1*, N. E. Sharkey (ed.), Ellis Horwood, Chichester, pp. 43-71, 1986.
26. A. D. Baddeley, Domains of Recollection, *Psychological Review, 89*, pp. 708-729, 1982.
27. M. Koukkou and D. Lehmann, Dreaming: The Functional State-Shift Hypothesis, a Neuropsychophysiological Model, *British Journal of Psychiatry, 142*, pp. 221-231, 1983.
28. H. Weingartner, State-dependent Learning, in *Drug Discrimination and State Dependent Learning*, B. T. Ho, D. W. Richards and D. L. Chute (eds.), Academic Press, New York, New York, pp. 361-380, 1978.
29. P. K. Oltman, D. R. Goodenough, D. Koulack, E. Maclin, H. R. Schroeder and M. J. Flannagan, Short-term Memory During Stage 2-Sleep, *Psychophysiology, 14*, pp. 439-444, 1977.
30. D. A. Overton, Major Theories of State-dependent Learning, in *Drug-Discrimination and State-Dependent Learning*, B. T. Ho, D. W. Richards and D. L. Chute (eds.), Academic Press, New York, New York, pp. 283-318, 1978.
31. J. E. Eich, The Cue-dependent Nature of State-dependent Retrieval, *Memory and Cognition, 8*, pp. 157-173, 1980.
32. J. D. Teasdale and M. L. Russel, Differential Effects of Induced Mood on Recall of Positive Negative and Neutral Words, *British Journal of Clinical Psychology, 58*, pp. 138-146, 1985.
33. J. L. McGaugh, Hormonal Influences on Memory, *Annual Review of Psychology, 34*, pp. 297-324, 1983.
34. V. T. Reus, H. Weingartner and R. M. Post, Clinical Implications of State-dependent Learning, *American Journal of Psychiatry, 136*, pp. 927-931, 1979.
35. A. Jacobson, A. Kales, D. Lehmann and J. Zweizig, Somnambulism: All Night Electroencephalographic Studies, *Science, 148*, pp. 975-977, 1965.
36. J. Piaget, *Play, Dreams and Imitation in Childhood*, Routledge and Kegan, London, 1962.
37. H. W. Reese, The Development of Memory: Life-span Perspectives, in *Advances in Child Development and Behavior*, H. W. Reese (ed.), Academic Press, New York, New York, pp. 208-240, 1976.
38. M. Koukkou-Lehmann, Hirnmechanismen normalen und schizophrenen Denkens, Springer, Heidelberg and New York, 1987.
39. J. W. Rohrbaugh, The Orienting Reflex: Performance and Central Nervous System Manifestations, in *Varieties of Attention*, R. Parasuraman and D. R. Davies (eds.), Academic Press, New York, New York, pp. 323-373, 1984.
40. A. Ohman, The Orienting Response, Attention, and Learning: An Information Processing Perspective, in *The Orienting Reflex in Humans*, H. D. Kimmel, E. H. von Olst and J. F. Orlebeke (eds.), Erlbaum, Hillsdale, New Jersey, pp. 443-471, 1979.

41. M. Koukkou and D. Lehmann, A Reply to R. C. Howard's Commentary on Our Paper: An Information Processing Perspective of Psychophysiological Measurements, *Journal of Psychophysiology, 1,* pp. 219–220, 1987.
42. D. Kahneman and A. Treisman, Changing Views of Attention and Automaticity, in *Varieties of Attention*, R. Parasuraman and D. R. Davies (eds.), Academic Press, New York, pp. 29-61, 1984.
43. F. I. M. Craik, Human Memory, *Annual Review of Psychology, 30*, pp. 63–102, 1979.
44. M. Koukkou, EEC Reactivity in Acute Schizophrenics Reflects Deviant (Ectropic) State Changes During Information Processing, in *Functional States of the Brain: Their Determinants*, M. Koukkou, D. Lehmann and J. Angst (eds.), Elsevier, Amsterdam, pp. 265–290, 1980.
45. ————, EEG Reactivity and Psychopathology: A Psychophysiological Information Processing Approach, *Advances in Biological Psychiatry, 13*, pp. 43–48, 1983.
46. N. Loveless, The Orienting Response and Evoked Potentials in Man, in *Orienting and Habituation: Perspectives in Human Research*, D. Siddle (ed.), Wiley, New York, pp. 71–108, 1983.
47. W. van Winsum, G. Segreant and R. Geuze, The Functional Significance of Event-related Desynchronization of Alpha Rhythm in Attentional and Activating Tasks, *Electroencephalography and Clinical Neurophysiology, 58*, pp. 519–524, 1984.
48. A. Katada, H. Ozaki, H. Suzuki and K. Suhara, Developmental Characteristics of Normal and Mentally Retarded Children's EEG, *Electroencephalography and Clinical Neurophysiology, 52*, pp. 192–201, 1981.
49. W. Kuhlo and D. Lehmann, Das Einschlaferleben und Seine Neurophysiologischen Korrelate, *Archiv für Psychiatrie und Zeitschrift für Nervenkrankheiten, 205*, pp. 687–716, 1964.
50. D. Foulkes, *The Psychology of Sleep*, Scribner, New York, 1966.
51. J. E. Bogen, The Other Side of the Brain II: An Appositional Mind, *Bulletin of the Los Angeles Neurological Societies, 34*, pp. 73–105, 1969.
52. L. Goldstein, Is Cerebral Laterality a Myth? *Research Communications in Psychology, Psychiatry and Behaviour, 5*, pp. 291–301, 1980.
53. L. Murri, R. Arena, G. Siciliano, R. Mazotta, and A. Muratorio, Dream Recall in Patients with Focal Cerebral Lesions, *Archives of Neurology, 41*, pp. 183–185, 1984.
54. D. Lehmann, Fluctuations of Functional State: EEG Patterns and Perceptual and Cognitive Strategies, in *Functional States of the Brain: Their Determinants*, M. Koukkou, D. Lehmann and J. Angst (eds.), Elsevier, Amsterdam, pp. 189–202, 1980.
55. D. Lehmann and M. Koukkou, Computer Analysis of EEG Wakefulness-sleep Patterns During Learning of Novel and Familiar Sentences, *Electroencephalography and Clinical Neurophysiology, 37,* pp. 73–84, 1974.
56. D. Lehmann, G. Dumermuth, B. Lange and C. A. Meier, Dream Recall Related to EEG Spectral Power during REM Periods, *Sleep Research, 10*, p. 151, 1981.

57. M. Koukkou, A. Andreae and D. Lehmann, EEG States and Classes of Day Dreaming Mentation, *Electroencephalography and Clinical Neurophysiology, 52*, p. 60, 1981.
58. M. Koukkou, D. Lehmann and A. Andreae, Information Processing and Hemispheric Electrical States: Studies with Normals, Acute Schizophrenics, and Neurotics, in *Biological Psychiatry*, C. Perris, G. Struwe and B. Janson, (eds.), Elsevier, Amsterdam, pp. 199–202, 1981.
59. D. Lehmann, M. Koukkou and A. Andreae, Classes of Day-dream Mentation and EEG Power Spectra, *Sleep Research, 10*, pp. 152, 1981.
60. D. Lehmann, B. Meier, C. A. Meier, T. Mita and W. Skrandies, Sleep Onset Mentation Related to Short Epoch EEG Spectra, *Sleep Research, 12*, p. 80, 1983.
61. H. Erlichman and M. S. Wiener, EEG Asymmetry During Covert Mental Activity, *Psychophysiology, 17*, pp. 228–235, 1980.
62. H. Ehrlichman and J. Barett, Right Hemisphere Specialization for Mental Imagery: A Review of the Evidence, *Brain and Cognition, 2*, pp. 55–76, 1983.
63. A. S. Gevins, G. M. Zeitlin, J. C. Doyle, C. D. Yingling, R. E. Schaffer, E. Callaway and C. L. Yeager, Electroencephalogram Correlates of Higher Cortical Functions, *Science, 213*, pp. 918–922, 1979.
64. B. Libet, C. A. Gleason, E. W. Wright and D. K. Pearl, Time of Conscious Intention to Act in Relation to Onset of Cerebral Activities (Readiness Potential); The Unconscious Initiation of a Freely Voluntary Act, *Brain, 106*, pp. 623–642, 1983.
65. D. Lehmann, G. W. Beeler and D. H. Fender, Changes in Pattern of the Human Electroencephalogram During Fluctuations of Perception of Stabilized Retinal Images, *Electroencephalography and Clinical Neurophysiology, 19*, pp. 336–343, 1965.
66. U. T. Keesey and D. J. Nichols, Changes Induced in Stabilized Image Visibility by Experimental Alteration of the Ongoing EEG, *Electroencephalography and Clinical Neurophysiology, 27*, pp. 248–257, 1969.
67. I. Gath, E. Bar-On and D. Lehmann, Fuzzy Clustering of EEG Signal and Vigilance Performance, *International Journal of Neurosciences, 20*, pp. 303–312, 1985.
68. D. Brandeis and D. Lehmann, Event-related Potentials of the Brain and Cognitive Processes: Approaches and Applications, *Neuropsychologia, 24*, pp. 151–168, 1986.
69. D. Lehmann, H. Ozaki and I. Pal, EEG Alpha Map Series: Brain Micro-states by Space Oriented Adaptive Segmentation, *Electroencephalography and Clinical Neurophysiology, 67*, pp. 271–288, 1987.
70. E. L. Moerk, Object, Percept, Concept, Word, in *Sensory Experience, Adaptation, and Perception*, L. Spillman and B. R. Wooten (eds.), Erlbaum, Hillsdale, New Jersey, pp. 143–167, 1984.
71. M. A. McDaniel and M. Pressley, (eds.), *Imagery and Related Mnemonic Processes*, Springer, Heidelberg, 1987.
72. R. N. Shepart, The Mental Image, *American Psychologist, 33*, pp. 125–137, 1978.

73. A. Paivio, *Mental Representation: A Dual Encoding Approach*, Oxford University Press, New York, 1986.
74. R. L. Gregory, *Eye and Brain*, McGraw Hill, New York, 1966.
75. A. A. Sheikh and C. S. Jordan, Clinical Use of Mental Imagery, in *Imagery –Current Theory, Research, and Application*, Wiley, New York, New York, 1983.
76. J. Shorr, *Psychotherapy through Imagery*, Thieme-Stratton, New York, New York, 1983.
77. H. Haken, *Advanced Synergetics*, Springer, Heidelberg, 1983.
78. R. G. Kunzendorf, Self-consciousness as the Monitoring of Cognitive States: A Theoretical perspective, *Imagination, Cognition and Personality, 7*, pp. 3-22, 1987.
79. M. Koukkou and D. Lehmann, A Psychophysiological Model of Dreaming with Implications for the Therapeutic Effect of Dream Interpretation, in *Research on Psychotherapeutic Approaches, Vol. 2*, W. R. Minsel and W. Herff (eds.), Peter Lang, Frankfurt, pp. 27–34, 1983.
80. H. Silberer, *Der Traum*, Enke, Stuttgart, 1919.
81. I. Oswald, A. M. Taylor and M. Treisman, Discrimination Responses to Stimulation during Human Sleep, *Brain, 83*, pp. 440–453, 1960.
82. H. L. Williams, Information Processing during Sleep, in *Sleep*, W. P. Koella and P. Levin (eds.), Karger, Basel, pp. 36–43, 1973.
83. D. G. McDonald, W. W. Schicht, R. E. Frazier, H. D. Schellenberger and D. J. Edwards, Studies in Information Processing in Sleep, *Psychophysiology, 12*, pp. 624-629, 1975.
84. D. Foulkes, *Children's Dreams*, Wiley, New York, 1982.
85. D. D. Kirtley, *The Psychology of Blindness*, Nelson-Hall, Chicago, 1975.
86. A. Moffit, R. Hoffmann, R. Wells, R. Armitage, R. Pigeau and J. Shearer, Individual Differences between Pre- and Post-awakening EEG Correlates of Dream Reports Following Arousals from Different Stages of Sleep, *Psychiatric Journal of the University Ottowa, 7*, pp. 111–125, 1982.
87. S. R. Palombo, *Dreaming and Memory: A New Information-Processing Model*, Basic Books, New York, New York, 1978.
88. C. A. Pearlman, The Adaptive Function of Dreaming, *International Psychiatric Clinics, 7*, pp. 329–334, 1970.

CHAPTER 6
Psychophysiology of Hypnotic Hallucinations

DAVID SPIEGEL AND ARREED F. BARABASZ

INTRODUCTION

Perceptual alteration has long been considered a core hypnotic phenomenon [1], and most hypnotizability scales include a measure of the ability to produce hallucinations [2-4] or alterations in perception [5]. The hypnotic state has been described as "imaginative involvement" [6], "believed-in imaginings" [7], "absorption" [8], and an "addiction" to fantasy [9]. The hypnotizable and hypnotized individual affiliates intensely with a metaphor, suspending critical judgment about it as he maximizes focal attention [5]. This makes alterations in perception which might simply be imagined in other states seem real in hypnosis. The imagined object is not merely thought of or visualized, but rather hallucinated. While the subject may be aware that the hallucinated object is not really there, he ignores or dissociates that awareness, which intensifies the hallucinatory experience.

Early Studies

While event-related potentials (ERP) research appears to show the greatest promise in quantifying the psychophysiology of hypnotic hallucinations, several alternative approaches have been attempted over the past thirty years. The theoretical bases are varied, and methodologies have been quite creative. Examples of some of the most interesting studies are reviewed, highlighting a range of dependent variables and research design control issues. In 1954, Malmo, Boag and Roginsky conducted the first electromyographic study of hypnotic deafness induced as a negative hallucination [10]. Although no standardized test of hypnotizability was used, two experimental subjects were chosen from thirty-six volunteers "on the basis of their marked suggestibility and ease with which hypnotic deafness was induced during the first trial session." During a six-week period these subjects were exposed to several hypnotic inductions designed to maximize hypnotizability. Two control subjects were employed. The first, apparently considered low in hypnotizability, was not asked to simulate hypnosis, but rather to "try on a conscious basis not to react to stimulation." The second control subject was completely deaf on an organic basis.

Electromyographic potentials were obtained by surface electrodes placed at the chin, sternomastoid, and neck. Eye-blink was also recorded electrically. Auditory stimuli (700 Hz tones, 90 db above normal auditory threshold) were of 3 seconds duration and considered by the experimenters to be "sharp on effect." Stimuli were given in both non-hypnosis and hypnosis exposure conditions. EMG data recorded in microvolts were considered reliable. The major results showed significantly reduced EMG levels (exclusive of eye-blink potentials) to strong auditory stimulation during the hypnotic deaf state negative hallucination for the two experimental subjects in hypnosis.

The findings of the Malmo et al. study may have been confounded by problems in obtaining EMG baselines, hypnotic-state effects, auditory habituation, extremely small *N*, nonequivalent pre-experimental hypnosis trials for experimental versus control subjects, and the fact that the researchers were not blind with respect to subjects' hypnotizability [10]. This pioneering effort must, however, be applauded for the clever introduction of psychophysiological measures, the attempt to differentiate high hypnotizables from a large sample group, and the efforts made to maximize or plateau subjects' hypnotic performance (anticipating Shor and Cobb [11]) long before these issues were fully appreciated as important research considerations.

In 1968, Serafetinides measured EEG, EKG, respiratory rate, and "galvanic skin response" employing a single subject believed to be highly hypnotizable [12]. Both auditory ("fairly loud randomly intermittent sounds of various auditory frequencies") and visual stimuli ("stroboscopic flashing at rapidly alternating frequencies of flashes per second") were presented in hypnotic and non-hypnotic state conditions. The negative hypnotic hallucination consisted only of a suggestion to "ignore" the stimuli. While "no appreciable differences" were found between hypnotic and non-hypnotic state conditions, increases in breathing, heart rate, and galvanic skin responses appeared to occur during hypnosis.

As another pioneering effort, the Serafetinides study introduced the use of multiple psychophysiological measures [12]. Unfortunately, the single-subject, A–B design, without any attempt to measure hypnotizability or to compare results with low or non-hypnotizable subjects serving as controls, makes the apparent findings difficult to assess. It is not surprising to find "no appreciable differences" between hypnotic and non-hypnotic conditions given a cuing suggestion to "ignore" stimuli, which is paradoxical. Also, scoring EEG data only by "visuomanual" inspection makes the data analysis impressionistic at best.

Gray, Bowers and Fenz [13], in 1970, set new standards of experimental control in their study of heart rate activity in anticipation of and during an hypnotically induced negative visual hallucination. Using an experimental paradigm developed by Orne in 1959 [1], ten highly hypnotizable subjects (controls) simulating hypnosis were presented with the same hypnotic inductions and were instructed by an experimenter who was unaware of their group membership. The blind hypnotist asked all subjects to perform identical hypnotic tasks. The high and low hypnotizability subjects were chosen from 300 volunteers on the basis of their performance on three standardized tests: the Harvard Group Scale of Hypnotic Susceptibility, Form A by Shor and Orne, 1962 [14]; the Stanford Hypnotic Susceptibility Scale, Form C by Weitzenhoffer and Hilgard, 1962 [3]; and the Stanford Profile Scale of Hypnotic Susceptibility, Form I, by Weitzenhoffer and Hilgard, 1963 [15]. After the first two scales were administered, subjects identified as controls (extremely low hypnotizability) were instructed to simulate or fake hypnosis throughout all remaining sessions.

Heart rate recordings were taken during the experiment in four 45-second periods, including preinduction, postinduction, immediate prehallucination and during the hallucination. The experimental hypnotic function and all subsequent suggestions were administered by tape to assure consistency and exact replicability. All subjects were told they would see three red dots projected on the wall. The ten high and ten low hypnotizable groups were further subdivided into treatment groups of five each. The first group, labeled the "Hypnotic 4" group, was actually shown four dots on the wall. Their task was to negatively hallucinate, not see one of the dots. The second group, labeled the "Hypnotic 3" group was shown only the three dots. The remaining groups, labeled "Control 4" and "Control 3" groups, simulating hypnosis, were treated in the same manner as the two hypnotizable groups. During the experiment, all subjects were asked "Do you see the three red dots?" Fifteen seconds later they were asked "Do you see anything else?"

The Gray, et al. study demonstrated individual heart rates records to be extremely consistent with their respective group patterns [13]. Highly hypnotizable subjects, trained in hypnosis, responded with significant heart rate acceleration in anticipation of a negative visual hallucination. Low hypnotizables responded with significant heart rate deceleration during the same period. This very carefully done study set a new standard for this type of research, emphasizing a simulator design, standardized hypnotizability testing, adequate numbers of experimental and control subjects, blind experimenters, and taped inductions to assure replicability. Since the study was not conceptualized to test a specific theory, the exciting findings are open to alternative explanations.

Brady and Levitt, in 1966, attempted to ascertain whether or not a hypnotized subject experiences hallucinations in a way which is similar to a real percept [16]. This intriguing investigation tested the veridicality of hynotically induced hallucinations using optokinetic nystagmus (a reflexive pattern of eye movements) as a criterion measure of a cognitive event. Optokinetic nystagmus occurs when repetitive stimuli, such as watching passing telephone poles from a moving train, traverse the field of vision. This apparently reflexive response includes an initial slow, smooth pursuit followed by a fast saccadic movement in the opposite direction. Brady and Levitt found that four of their nine deeply hypnotized subjects showed optokinetic nystagmus eye movements while hallucinating either a rotating striped drum or telephone poles flashing by as they imagined a train ride [16]. Optokinetic nystagmus movements were apparent with eyes open and closed in hypnosis. In the non-hypnotic condition, subjects were unable to duplicate these eye movements by conscious volition, imagining the rotating drum, the train ride, practicing or after watching the eye movements of a technician looking at the spinning drum. Since the investigators recognized that hypnotized subjects may suppress non-hypnotic performance to protect the integrity of their hypnotic performance, additional subjects not involved in hypnosis research were also tested. Despite several alternative attempts, these later subjects were unable to produce optokinetic nystagmus.

In 1972, Evans, Reich and Orne [17] challenged the conclusion of the Brady and Levitt [16] study on a methodological basis. Evans et al. emphasized that subjects' preconceived ideas and expectations about hypnosis may affect hypnotic and non-hypnotic performance, particularly when subjects are aware they are serving as their own controls [17]. In 1959, Orne developed the use of simulator controls to aid in recognition of responses, if any, that were due to hypnosis, as opposed to those that were the result of subjects' prior knowledge, expectations, and experimental demand characteristics [1]. The Orne simulator quasi-control group design adds subjects who are essentially not hypnotizable [1]. These control subjects are asked to pretend that they are hypnotized when faced with an independent investigator who is blind with respect to the identity of the highly hypnotizable and simulator subjects. Since, in the context of the experiment the investigator typically cannot detect which subjects are stimulating, it is assumed that he or she treats all subjects alike. This procedure was employed by Evans et al. [17] to evaluate their contention that the apparently involuntary optical nystagmus movements of the Brady and Levitt [16] high hypnotizables may be brought under voluntary control. Evans et al. found that some deeply hypnotized subjects hallucinating an adequate stimulus produced optokinetic nystagmus in the absence of an actual stimulus [17]. However, optokinetic nystagmus appeared to be ruled out as an objective physiological criterion for hypnosis because both unhypnotizable subjects simulating hypnosis and highly motivated subjects while not hypnotized were able to produce optokinetic nystagmus by conscious volitional effort.

In summary, the early studies introduced a variety of creative approaches. The studies ranged from essentially clinical single-subject A–B methodologies to the introduction of multiple controls with established samples of high and low hypnotizable subjects in simulator control group designs. The investigations were highlighted by lack of sensitivity in measurement, such as simplistic visual inspections of EEG data, paradoxical instructions to subjects, confounding on a variety of bases and failure to replicate. The failures and methodological problems, however, served to set the stage for modern measurement approaches applied in highly controlled sophisticated designs.

Cortical Event-Related Potentials

Cortical event-related potentials (ERPs) have been productively employed in the study of attentional processes. The amplitude of the early components of the evoked response are related to stimulus intensity and perceptual channel selection [18, 19], while the later components are affected by changes in information processing strategy elicited by such variables as task relevance and surprise [20, 21]. The psychophysiological study of attention lends itself well to the examination of hypnotic alterations in perception. The intention of this portion of the chapter is to examine recent research on the relationship between changes in event-related potentials and the subjective experience of hypnotic perceptual alteration.

Findings in this area have been conflicting. Some have shown reduction in the amplitude of the evoked response during a hypnotic instruction that the stimulus be perceived as attenuated [23-26], but a number of other studies have failed to demonstrate any differences [12, 27-32].

Negative Studies

As noted above, early studies of the effects of hypnotic hallucination on cortical ERPs were anything but encouraging. Halliday and Mason, in 1964, failed to find any significant modification of the somatosensory evoked response in eight subjects, despite the fact that six of them were able to produce hypnotic anesthesia [31]. Further, there was no significant increase in ERP amplitude when these subjects were instructed to pay more attention to the stimulus. The same absence of ERP differences, this time auditory, was observed among four subjects, three of whom were able to experience hypnotic deafness. Amadeo and Yanovski [27] failed to obtain differences in auditory and somatosensory ERPs among a group of five experienced hypnotic subjects in response to hypnotic suggestions of inability to hear or feel the stimuli or that the stimuli would be more intense. They noted that the hypnotizable subjects may have undergone some nonspecific cortical arousal, making it difficult to demonstrate differences among conditions. They postulated that high hypnotizability may be an important intervening variable, but employed no standardized measure of hypnotizability.

Beck and Barolin and Beck, Dustman and Beier found small but significant changes in ERP amplitude correlated with changes in the real stimulus intensity of a visual signal [29-30]. However, they also found that a hypnotic suggestion that a signal of fixed brightness would be either brighter or dimmer had no effect on the ERP amplitude. While this paradigm is clear and at first makes sense, it has one limitation. It requires a different kind of mental process to alter the intensity of a stimulus than it does to inattend to one as a result of hallucinating another. If anything, one needs to pay more attention to a stimulus to diminish its brightness. Thus a condition expected to result in a decrease in ERP amplitude could theoretically lead to an amplitude increase. More recently, in 1981, Zakrzewski and Szelenberger reported no changes in the early ERP components but an apparent decrease in N_{250} amplitudes after a hypnotic suggestion of blindness [32]. However, they were appropriately cautious in interpreting the results since the ERP amplitude obtained during the hypnotic blindness condition was not significantly different from a non-hypnotic control condition among the same subjects. Their testing of hypnotizability was informal, and they used no low hypnotizable control subjects.

Positive Studies

Effects of hypnotic hallucination on ERPs have, however, been reported. Hernandez-Peon and Denoso utilized electrodes implanted in the occipital lobes of two "suggestible" patients, although no formal testing of hypnotizability was reported [25]. Suggestions that a visual stimulus would be brighter resulted in greater ERP amplitudes, while the opposite suggestion resulted in an amplitude decrease. The authors speculated that these hypnotic alterations in perception might work by modifying afferent transmission on sensory pathways at subcortical levels. These two patients obviously had concomitant neurological problems requiring craniotomy. However, the study employed a similar paradigm to that utilized by Beck and Barolin and Beck, Dustman and Beier [29-30] but yielded a significant association between hypnotic alteration in perception and ERP amplitude.

In a study with similar methodology, Guerrero-Figueroa and Heath implanted subdural and subcortical electrodes and reported a reduction in the amplitude of primary and secondary elements of the ERP to constant photic stimulation in response to suggestion that the stimulus would be less bright [24]. The opposite suggestion resulted in an increase in all components of the evoked response. These changes were obtained in the optic tract, the reticular formation, and the visual cortex. A similar inhibition of auditory evoked potentials was noted when the subject was preoccupied and calculating. However, these findings were obtained in only one patient. Clynes et al. [22] reported that one subject who was scored as deeply hypnotizable on the Davis-Husband [31] scale was able to eliminate ERP peaks in the range of 200-500 msec when given a suggestion that she would look at a ruler just below the monitor and see nothing else. The tracings which resulted were different from normal tracings with the same photic stimulation. However, the authors noted that they were unable to obtain similar results with a second subject classified as moderately hypnotizable. Further, he observed that differences in the first subject could have been due to defocusing, since she was asked to look below the monitor. Defocusing reduces ERP amplitude and increases latency [34]. The stimuli could also have hit a less densely populated portion of the retina below the macula.

Galbraith et al. [23] employed a more sophisticated design in that they compared the ERPs of high versus low hypnotizable subjects as measured by scores on the Harvard Group Scale of Hypnotic Susceptibility [14]. They used a crossover attention task, providing visual and auditory stimuli and instructing subjects to count either clicks or flashes. ERPs were analyzed from Cz only, and a crude averaged amplitude between 100 and 300 msec was obtained. High hypnotizables did what they were told, i.e., they had higher amplitudes to flashes than clicks when counting flashes, and conversely. Low hypnotizables did the opposite: they had higher amplitudes to the supposedly inattended stimulus. While this was a study of ERP correlates of hypnotic attention rather than hallucination, it is important in that it illustrates the sensitivity of high hypnotizables to instruction and their ability to intensify or diminish ERP response. The suppression of the inattended stimuli was accomplished because it was secondary to the primary task, which was attending to another set of stimuli. Had they been told simply to diminish response to one perceptual channel, they would likely not have shown reduced amplitudes. Also, low hypnotizables showed themselves to be unable to eliminate distractors. Their response amplitudes were increased to the supposedly ignored channel, i.e. their focal attention on one set of stimuli did not allow them to reduce cortical response to another set.

Barabasz and Lonsdale reported amplitude increases in the olfactory ERP of four high hypnotizables experiencing anosmia compared to five low hypnotizables attempting to simulate the response [35]. Subjects were given the anosmia instruction contained in item 9 of the Stanford Hypnotic Susceptibility Scale: Form C [3], which is "You can no longer smell anything at all" [4]. High hypnotizables showed significant increased P_{300} amplitudes to both weak and strong odors, but not in a no-odor air puff control condition. In addition, high hypnotizable subjects had significantly higher P_{300} amplitudes in hypnosis as compared to waking conditions for weak and strong odors. Recordings were made at T_3 and T_4. Barabasz and Lonsdale concluded that the findings may have represented a state of "increased cortical arousal during the attentional redirection of filtering out incoming messages that are not to be admitted to full awareness" [35, 522]. The results were consistent with a pilot study by Barabasz and Gregson showing increased temporal region olfactory evoked potentials (OEPs) during hypnosis [36]. Subsequently, cerebral blood flow research has also demonstrated hypnotically induced increases in temporal activity [37, 38]. Spiegel et al. demonstrated the opposite effect, the suppression of P_{300} amplitude among six high hypnotizables experiencing an obstructive hallucination, an imagined cardboard box blocking view of the stimulus generator

Recordings were made at Fz, Cz, Pz, O_1 and O_2. There was significant suppression of the P_{300} component of the visual ERP throughout the cortex, and of N_{200} as well as P_{300} in the occipital region. Further, the suppression was greater in the right as compared with the left occipital cortex, suggesting greater involvement of the right hemisphere in generating the hallucinated image and reducing perception of the visual stimulus. Six low hypnotizable controls attempting to simulate the hallucination showed no difference in their evoked response amplitudes, and the suppression effect was also significantly greater than differences observed among six other non-hypnotized controls instructed to attend actively (button press) and passively (no button pressing). High hypnotizables reported that they could not see the stimulus, and pressed to only five percent of the stimuli, compared to 96 percent for the low hypnotizable controls. Thus their subjective experience of attending to the hallucinated box rather than the stimulus was confirmed by the suppression of N_{200} and P_{300} amplitude.

This difference in findings was likely related to a surprise effect [40] in the Barabasz and Lonsdale study [35]. In it subjects were told "You can no longer smell anything at all." When the obstructing hallucination was less than perfect, they were surprised by the smell, and novelty of a stimulus is usually associated with an increase in the P_{300} amplitude [20, 21]. Indeed, Barabasz and Lonsdale observed that when high hypnotizable subjects were in a condition in which they were told they would smell something, but instead were offered a puff of air, they showed an increase in P_{300} amplitudes, and were surprised at the absence of a smell [40]. The nature of the hypnotic instruction meant that any smell at all was a flat contradiction, causing conflict about whether the paradigm or their perception was primary. Given that high hypnotizables focus intently and are desirous of pleasing, they may have been especially surprised that their anosmia was less than perfect, hence the increase in P_{300} amplitude. The surprise effect explanation seems further supported by the increased P_{300} amplitudes demonstrated by the low hypnotizables for the no odor air puff condition only. The low hypnotizables, who were only simulating being hypnotized, were smelling odors throughout both hypnotic and waking conditions. These subjects, expecting an odor with each air puff, demonstrated a P_{300} surprise effect increase when no odor was presented with the air puff. The findings closely resemble those of the pilot study [36]. The later ERP response components seem to reflect increasingly complex levels of psychological processing. Hassett studied subjects asked to listen to a series of tones spaced at regular intervals, with a tone randomly omitted from the series [41]. When ERPs were computed for the omitted stimuli (averaged from the point where the stimulus should have occurred), the surprise was registered by an increase in the amplitude of the P_{450} wave. In the Barabasz and Lonsdale study ERPs were determined from the range of 300-450 msec [35].

By contrast, in the Spiegel et al. study, subjects were instructed to focus on an image of a cardboard box which by inference would block the view of the TV monitor generating the stimuli [39]. The fact of obstructed view was therefore a secondary consequence of the hallucination, not a primary instruction, such as ("You will no longer see anything at all on the screen"). This means that in the 5 percent of cases in which the high hypnotizables did see something, they were not surprised or distracted from the primary task. Rather they simply saw something through the box, something which was incongruous but not impossible. Their absorption in the hallucination experience was not disrupted by their perceptual experience [40].

More recently, the finding of a link between hallucinatory experience and ERP amplitude has been replicated and extended using somatosensory stimulation [42]. In this study, ten high and ten low hypnotizable subjects were instructed to develop hypnotic anesthesia to sensation in the wrist receiving pulsed electrical stimulation. The anesthesia instruction involved developing a sense of cool, tingling numbness which would filter out other perceptions. High hypnotizables, but not lows, demonstrated significant reductions of somatosensory ERP amplitude at both P_{100} and P_{300}, confirming the association between ERP amplitude and obstructive hallucination observed in the visual system [39] but extending it by finding strong effects at P_{100} as well as P_{300}. In addition, subjects in this study were given an hypnotic enhancement instruction, in which the stimulus was to be experienced as especially intense and pleasant. High hypnotizables showed a significant increase of P_{100} amplitude in this condition, while low hypnotizables did not. Thus, the highs were able to show bidirectional task-related changes in ERP amplitude, both reducing and enhancing the amplitude of their response. Thus, these and previous studies suggest that hypnotic perceptual alteration among high hypnotizables is associated with changes in ERP amplitude.

Interpreting Results

Confounding variables are always a problem in such research. Attention, habituation, and learning may have an effect on the size and waveform of the ERP. Later components (after 200 msec) are especially affected by these attentional or information processing variables [21]. The ERP amplitude has been shown to diminish with inattention or habituation and increase with attention, especially when the stimulus is unexpected, intrusive, and defined as task relevant [19]. The amplitude of the early components such as P_{100} and N_{100} primarily reflects channel selection rather than attention [18-19]. These findings on the one hand are a reminder that even demonstrated differences could be accounted for by mechanisms other than hypnosis. On the other hand, they provide a body of data which could be helpful in interpreting the meaning of any differences observed using hypnosis to alter perception.

Significant findings of alteration in ERPs during hypnotic hallucination have occurred in the later (N_{200}-P_{300}) rather than earlier portions of the waveform.

Suppression of early somatosensory ERP positive peaks such as P_{60} has been shown to be associated with cognitive dissonance about a painful stimulus which motivates subjects to suppress it [43], while analgesic drugs tend to suppress later components such as N_{150} and P_{200} [44]. The distinction between detection of a signal and its meaning or response criterion has been investigated usefully in this regard. Davis et al. found that schizophrenics had lower P_{100}, N_{120}, and P_{200} amplitudes than did normals to marginally painful stimuli [45]. The between group differences in signal detection were reversed by administration of naloxone, while the response criterion differences (rating the signal as painful) were not. This finding is of interest because hypnotic analgesia has been found not to be reversed by the administration of naloxone [46]. Thus hypnotic alteration of perception would seem to operate not at the level of sensitivity in signal detection, but rather by altering the response criterion to the stimulus.

CONCLUSIONS

There is evidence that the experience of hypnotic hallucination is associated with changes in the amplitude of event-related potentials. Studies have shown that hypnotic attention to a stimulus may enhance the amplitude of ERP response, and that hallucinating an obstructing object diminishes the amplitude of later components of cortical response, especially P_{300}. High hypnotizables who are surprised by the failure of an obstructive hallucination likewise show an increase in P_{300} amplitude. Several variables may account for inconsistencies in the research literature:

1. *Hypnotic Instruction*. There is a world of difference between altering perception of a stimulus by attending to it and diminishing its intensity and experiencing a hallucination which by inference reduces perception of the stimulus. Attending to a stimulus will increase ERP amplitudes, especially P_{300}, regardless of the type of perceptual transformation, as will surprise at the failure of an instruction to eliminate all perception of a stimulus.
2. *Hypnotizability*. It is crucial that a standardized measure of hypnotizability be employed. Simply giving hypnotic instructions to a non-hypnotizable subject will not result in hypnotic phenomena. All studies with positive results found them only among highly, not moderately hypnotizable individuals.
3. *Comparative hypnotizability*. Good design involves comparing the performance of suitably tested high and low hypnotizable individuals undertaking identical tasks. Only significant differences between these groups on identical tasks establish a hypnotic hallucination effect. Even better, the experimenter administering the hypnotic instructions should be blind to subjects' hypnotizability scores, as has been done so far only in two ERP studies [35, 42].
4. *Subject selection*. Normal subjects unencumbered by neurological or psychiatric disease should be studied. Many papers have been little more than case reports. Adequate numbers of subjects should be employed to allow for meaningful between and within group comparisons.
5. *Data analysis*. Standard methods for peak selection within established latency windows or principal components analysis should be utilized. This will allow comparison of findings with the large literature on ERPs. Statistical analysis of amplitude and latency differences should be employed.

6. *Cognitive tasks.* Each group must be studied in a number of conditions which provide controls for variance in baseline ERP amplitude, attention, surprise, task relevance, defocusing, and arousal. All of these have independent effects on ERP amplitude, and thus must be controlled before any statement can be made about the cortical electrophysiological effect of hypnotic hallucination.

REFERENCES

1. M. T. Orne, The Nature of Hypnosis: Artifact and Essence, *Journal of Abnormal and Social Psychology, 58*, pp. 277-299, 1959.
2. A. M. Weitzenhoffer and E. R. Hilgard, *Stanford Hypnotic Susceptibility Scale: Forms A and B.* Consulting Psychologists Press, Palo Alto, California, 1959.
3. A. M. Weitzenhoffer and E. R. Hilgard, *Stanford Hypnotic Susceptibility Scale: Form C*, Consulting Psychologists Press, Palo Alto, California, 1962.
4. E. R. Hilgard, *Hypnotic Susceptibility*, Harcourt, Brace and World, New York, 1965.
5. H. Spiegel and D. Spiegel, *Trance and Treatment: Clinical Uses of Hypnosis*, Basic Books, New York, 1978.
6. J. R. Hilgard, *Personality and Hypnosis: A Study of Imaginative Involvement*, University of Chicago Press, Chicago, 1970.
7. T. R. Sarbin and W. C. Coe, *Hypnosis: A Social Psychological Analysis of Influence Communication*, Holt, Rinehart, and Winston, New York, 1972.
8. A. Tellegen and G. Atkinson, Openness to Absorbing and Self-altering Experiences ("Absorption"), a Trait Related to Hypnotic Susceptibility, *Journal of Abnormal Psychology, 83*, pp. 268-277, 1974.
9. S. C. Wilson and T. X. Barber, The Fantasy-prone Personality: Implications for Understanding Imagery, Hypnosis and Parapsychological Phenomena, in *Imagery: Current Theory, Research, and Application*, Anees A. Sheikh (ed.), Wiley, New York, 1983.
10. R. B. Malmo, T. F. Boag and B. B. Raginsky, Electromyographic Study of Hypnotic Deafness, *Journal of Clinical and Experimental Hypnosis, 2*, pp. 305-317, 1954.
11. R. E. Shor and J. C. Cobb, An Exploratory Study of Hypnotic Training Using the Concept of Plateau Responsiveness as a Referent, *American Journal of Clinical Hypnosis, 10*, pp. 178-193, 1968.
12. E. A. Serafetinides, Electrophysiological Responses to Sensory Stimulation Under Hypnosis, *American Journal of Psychiatry, 125*, pp. 112-113, 1968.
13. A. L. Gray, K. S. Bowers, and W. D. Fenz, Heart Rate Anticipation of and During a Negative Visual Hallucination, *International Journal of Clinical and Experimental Hypnosis, 18*, pp. 41-51, 1970.
14. R. E. Shor and E. C. Orne, *Harvard Group Scale of Hypnotic Susceptibility, Form A*, Consulting Psychologists Press, Palo Alto, California, 1962.
15. A. M. Weitzenhoffer and E. R. Hilgard, *Stanford Profile Scales of Hypnotic Susceptibility, Forms I and II*, Consulting Psychologists Press, Palo Alto, California, 1963.
16. J. P. Brady and E. E. Levitt, Hypnotically-induced Visual Hallucinations, *Psychosomatic Medicine, 28*, pp. 351-363, 1966.

17. F. J. Evans, L. H. Reich, and M. T. Orne, Optokinetic Nystagmus, Eye Movements and Hypnotically Induced Hallucinations, *Journal of Nervous and Mental Disease, 154*, pp. 419–431, 1972.
18. J. M. Ford, W. T. Roth, S. J. Dirk, and B. S. Kopell, Evoked Potential Correlates of Signal Recognition Between and Within Modalities, *Science, 181*, pp. 465–466, 1978.
19. S. A. Hillyard and T. W. Picton, Event-Related Brain Potentials and Selective Information Processing in Man, in *Progress in Clinical Neurophysiology*, J. E. Desmedt (ed.), Karger, Basel, Vol. 6, pp. 1-52, 1979.
20. S. A. Hillyard, T. W. Picton and D. Regan, Sensation, Perception, and Attention: Analysis Using ERPs, in *Event-Related Brain Potentials in Man*, E. Callaway, P. Tueting and S. H. Koslow (eds.), Academic Press, New York, 1978.
21. J. Baribeau-Braun, T. W. Picton and J. U. Gosselin, A Neurophysiological Evaluation of Abnormal Information Processing, *Science 219*, pp. 874–876, 1983.
22. M. Clynes, M. Kohn, and K. Lifshitz, Dynamics and Spatial Behavior of Light-Evoked Potentials, Their Modification under Hypnosis, and On-line Correlation in Relation to Rhythmic Components, *Annals of the New York Academy of Sciences, 112*, pp. 468–509, 1964.
23. G. C. Galbraith, L. M. Cooper and P. London, Hypnotic Susceptibility and the Sensory Evoked Response, *Journal of Comparative and Physiological Psychology, 80*, pp. 509–514, 1972.
24. R. Guerrero-Figueroa and R. G. Heath, Evoked Responses and Changes during Attentive Factors in Man, *Archives of Neurology, 10*, pp. 74–84, 1964.
25. R. Hernandez-Peon and M. Donoso, Influence of Attention and Suggestion upon Subcortical Evoked Electric Activity in the Human Brain, in *First International Congress of Neurological Sciences*, L. Van Bogaert and J. Radermecker (eds.), Pergamon Press, London, Vol. 3, pp. 385–396, 1959.
26. N. J. Wilson, Neurophysiologic Alterations with Hypnosis, *Diseases of the Nervous System, 29*, pp. 618–620, 1968.
27. M. Amadeo and A. Yanovski, Evoked Potentials and Selective Attention in Subjects Capable of Hypnotic Analgesia, *International Journal of Clinical and Experimental Hypnosis, 23*, pp. 200–210, 1975.
28. J. L. Andreassi, B. Balinsky, J. A. Gallichio, J. J. De Simone and B. W. Mellers, Hypnotic Suggestion of Stimulus Change and Visual Cortical Evoked Potential, *Perceptual and Motor Skills, 42*, pp. 371–378, 1976.
29. E. C. Beck and G. S. Barolin, The Effect of Hypnotic Suggestion on Evoked Potentials, *Journal of Nervous and Mental Disease, 140*, pp. 154–161, 1965.
30. E. D. Beck, R. D. Dustman and E. G. Beier, Hypnotic Suggestions and Visually Evoked Potentials, *Electroencephalography and Clinical Neurophysiology, 20*, pp. 397-400, 1966.
31. A. M. Halliday and A. A. Mason, Cortical-Evoked Potentials during Hypnotic Anaesthesia, *Electroencephalography and Clinical Neurophysiology, 16*, pp. 312–314, 1964.

32. K. Zakrewski and W. Szelenberger, Visual Evoked Potentials in Hypnosis: A Longitudinal Approach, *International Journal of Clinical and Experimental Hypnosis, 29*, pp. 77–86, 1981.
33. L. W. Davis and R. W. Husband, A Study of Hypnotic Susceptibility in Relation to Personality Traits, *Journal of Abnormal and Social Psychology, 26*, pp. 175–183, 1931.
34. C. Schulman-Galambos and R. Galambos, Cortical Responses from Adults and Infants to Complex Visual Stimuli, *Electroencephalography and Clinical Neurophysiology, 45*, pp. 425–435, 1978.
35. A. F. Barabasz and C. Lonsdale, Effects of Hypnosis on P_{300} Olfactory-Evoked Potential Amplitudes, *Journal of Abnormal Psychology, 92*, pp. 520–523, 1983.
36. A. F. Barabasz and R. Gregson, Antarctic Wintering-Over, Suggestion and Transient Olfactory Stimulation: EEG Evoked Potentials and Electrodermal Responses, *Biological Psychology, 9*, pp. 285–295, 1979.
37. L. Baer, R. Ackerman, O. Surmon, J. Correia, J. Griffith, N. Alpert, and T. Hackett, PET Studies during Hypnosis and Hypnotic Suggestion, in *Psychiatry: The State of the Art, Biological Psychiatry, Higher Nervous Activity*, P. Berner (ed.), Plenum. New York, pp. 293–298, 1985.
38. H. Crawford, B. Skolnick, D. Benson, R. E. Gur, and R. C. Gur, Regional Cerebral Blood Flow in Hypnosis and Hypnotic Analgesia, Paper presented at the 10th International Congress of Hypnosis and Psychosomatic Medicine, Toronto, Canada, August, 1985.
39. D. Spiegel, S. Cutcomb, C. Ren, and K. Pribram, Hypnotic Hallucination Alters Evoked Potentials, *Journal of Abnormal Psychology, 94*, pp. 249–255, 1985.
40. D. Spiegel and A. F. Barabasz, Effects of Hypnotic Instructions on P_{300} Event-Related Potential Amplitudes: Research and Clinical Implications, *American Journal of Clinical Hypnosis, 31*, pp. 11–17, 1988.
41. J. Hassett, *A Primer of Psychophysiology*, Freeman, San Francisco, p. 122, 1978.
42. D. Spiegel, P. Bierre, and J. Rootenberg, Hypnotic Alteration of Somatosensory Perception, *American Journal of Psychiatry, 146*, pp. 749–754, 1989.
43. G. Schechter and M. Buchsbaum, Cognitive Dissonance Modifies Somatosensory Evoked Potentials to Experimental Pain, *Society for Psychophysiological Research Abstracts, 22*, p. 612, 1985.
44. M. S. Buchsbaum and G. C. Davis, Application of Somatosensory Event-Related Potentials to Experimental Pain and the Pharmacology of Analgesia, in *Human Evoked Potentials: Applications and Problems*, D. Lehmann and E. Callaway (eds.), Plenum, New York, 1979.
45. G. C. Davis, M. D. Buchsbaum, D. P. van Kammen and W. E. Bunney, Jr., Analgesia to Pain Stimuli in Schizophrenics and Its Reversal by Naltrexone, *Psychiatry Research, 1*, pp. 61–69, 1979.
46. D. Spiegel and L. Albert, Naloxone Fails to Reverse Hypnotic Alleviation to Chronic Pain, *Psychopharmacology, 81*, pp. 140–143, 1983.

CHAPTER 7

Schizophrenic Hallucinations in the Context of Psychophysiological Studies of Schizophrenia

PIERRE FLOR-HENRY

In the light of recent experimental psychopathological research into the cerebral determinants of hallucinations, two observations at the turn of the century have proved, retrospectively, of prophetic importance. Kandinskii [1] was the first to emphasize a definite relationship between verbal hallucinations and inner speech [2]. The neuroanatomical substrate for this assumption was provided by Southard [3] who was the director of the Psychopathic Department of the Boston State Hospital and Professor of Neuropathology at Harvard University. He studied the topography of cortical lesions in twenty-five cases of dementia praecox and found that the lesions were unilateral on the left side in 25 percent of the cases and diffuse in all the others, except for a single one which was unilateral, right-sided. Further in the comparison of nine cases with hallucinations against the sixteen patients without hallucinations it was found that temporal lobe lesions were present in eight of the nine with hallucinations whereas cases without hallucinations had diffuse lesions or intact temporal lobes. In cases with hallucinations the left hemisphere was implicated unilaterally in five, bilaterally in two and affecting the right temporal lobe in one. In the single patient with hallucinations and intact temporal lobes there was atrophy of the left supramarginal gyrus and of the left Sylvian fissure. In his informative "Anatomy of Hallucinations" Johnson reviews some historical aspects of the question [4]. Baillarger had distinguished between psychosensorial and psychic hallucinations [5], the former perceived through the ears as coming from outside, the latter "produced in the interior of the soul" and he concluded that such patients "hear not voices but thoughts." Maudlsey [6] pointed out that the insane "do not always hear the voices as distinct, articulated utterances. . . . they are in his head and are interior voices, thoughts which he hears rather than words actually heard with his ears. They are distinctly apprehended and clearly understood even when they come . . . mysteriously from great distances. . . ." Parish noted that ". . . auditory hallucinations consist merely in the unnoticed articulation of one's thoughts, which become audible and take the form of an auditory hallucination . . . it would appear that the greater number of the 'voices,' if not all, are caused by the automatic speech on the part of the participant" [7]. Modell emphasized that the most essential feature of hallucinatory experiences is the process by which one's own thoughts are attributed to voices and considered verbal hallucinations, to be in fact *hallucinations of inner speech* [8]. Drawing from his profound knowledge of the phenomenology of schizophrenic mentation Bleuler viewed their acoustic hallucinations in the following way: "the voices are unlike spoken voices but are as if thoughts" [9, 10]. Similar are the opinions of Ey who considers that verbal hallucinations are a disturbance of internal speech [11]; of Janet who discusses "hallucinations psychomotrices verbales" [12, 13]; of Lhermitte who states that hallucinations are disorders of thought and of inner language [14, 15]. Thus, as Johnson concludes "the evidence (is) that hallucinations of inner speech are the most important features of auditory hallucinations" [4].

It is clear that in the period between 1900 and 1950 the clinical and phenomenological evidence led to a very general agreement in that, underlying auditory hallucinations, there was an activation of those neural systems relating to inner speech. The much more limited neuropathological data implied an association, in dementia praecox, between auditory hallucinations and cortical lesions of the temporal lobes, particularly of the left temporal regions. Hoffman in a detailed and persuasive "cognitive processing model of schizophrenia hallucinations" re-examines these issues in the context of modern experimental studies [16]. He notes—*inter alia*—that in schizophrenia the severity of (formal, linguistic) discourse disorganization correlates with the presence of verbal hallucinations and thus is consistent with the notion that disruptions in discourse planning cause disorganized speech as well as experientially unintended verbal imagery. Noteworthy also is the fact that whereas in normals pseudo-hallucinations increase as the subject passes from wakefulness to somnolence; the opposite is true in schizophrenia. Hoffman remarks on the not uncommon automatic utterance in schizophrenic patients which intrudes and interrupts the flow of their normal speech—and *of which they are totally unaware.* Hoffman's model links speech disorganization and verbal hallucinations. It emphasizes that the sensory properties of hallucinations are those of ordinary verbal imagery but are accompanied by a feeling of unintendedness (because of disruptions of language planning processes) and for this reason are nonconcordant with concurrent cognitive goals and are subjectively experienced as being of non-self origin . . . i.e. internally or externally hallucinated.

Gould investigated hallucinating patients by auscultation of the larynx in order to determine if subvocal speech occurred during hallucinations [17]. Subvocal speech is defined as "organically articulated but not voiced or whispered."

Electronic amplification of the laryngeal musculature showed that all episodes of hallucinations were associated with subvocal speech; that the subvocal speech was of whispering type, incoherent and about twice the speed of her normal speech and that it was produced during both inspiratory and expiratory phases of respiration. Electromyography of the vocal musculature showed increased neuromuscular activity during hallucinations and associated subvocal speech. Overall, Gould confirmed in the study of eighty-four patients with auditory hallucinations that verbal hallucinosis was the expression of automatic speech, and drew attention to the frequency with which hallucinating subjects are aware of talking to themselves; of hearing their own thoughts; identify thinking with talking; experience the voices as originating in their throats before moving to their ears, or show clear evidence of soft whispering (of which they are unaware) when hallucinating [17]. Of interest is the observation that in one patient hallucinating two voices, the one emerges during inspiration and the other during expiration.

Given the above evidence some mention must be made of the organization of the laryngeal muscles in man. The definitive study is that of Faaborg-Anderson [18]. The intrinsic laryngeal muscles move the vocal cords; the extrinsic move or fix the larynx as a whole. The former are of relevance in this context and consist of seven muscles: crico-thyroid, vocal, thyro-arytenoid, transverse arytenoid, oblique arytenoid, lateral crico-arytenoid and posterior crico-arytenoid. Of interest is the fact that all except one are adductor. The only intrinsic muscle whose contraction produces abduction is the posterior crico-arytenoid. The supply of the whole group is mediated via the inferior and superior laryngeal nerves, terminal branches of the recurrent laryngeal nerve, itself a branch of the vagus. Electromyographic studies showed that the posterior crico-arytenoid muscle is active in the absence of phonation and becomes silent with phonation. Conversely during phonation activity in all the adductors (except vocal and thyro-arytenoid) occurs. During whispers there is increased activity in the crico-thyroid muscle while during silent speech the rate and amplitudes of the action potentials increase in the crico-thyroid and vocal muscles. Faaborg-Andersen and Edfeldt were able to confirm in ten healthy adults that silent speech is associated with increased myogenic activity in the posterior crico-arytenoid [19].

Given the neurophysiological evidence that "silent" or "inner" speech activates the laryngeal musculature the observations of Gould, together with their more elaborate, cognitive expression as outlined by Hoffman, take on considerable significance. Indeed the pioneering studies of Gould have been confirmed by numerous authors, including Cerny [20, 21], McGuigan [22], Inouye and Shimizu [23], Johnson [24, 25], and Green and Preston [26]. McGuigan confirmed in the study of a single case what he calls the "amazing finding" of Gould, namely that auditory hallucinations are produced by a person's own speech behavior [22]. Measuring the action potentials of the tongue and chin with laryngeal amplification and with monitoring of breathing amplitude, it was found that all these measures increased immediately before the report of hallucinations. Further soft whispering was detected significantly often prior to the hallucinatory experience. In a more precise investigation of the relationship existing between EMG activity of the speech musculature and verbal hallucinations Inouye and Shimizu studied nine schizophrenic patients, all of whom were actively hallucinating at the time. With a number of technical improvements over previous work in this field, i.e. the use of stainless steel electrodes and the study of the temporal relation between increased muscle tension and verbal hallucinosis Inouye and Shimizu [23] found that, in almost 50 percent of instances, hallucinations were associated with increased EMG activity of the speech musculature, notably the orbicularis oris. The duration of verbal hallucinations was significantly and positively correlated with the EMG increase; as was the loudness of the hallucination. A contact microphone attached to the subjects' throats showed that the increased EMG activity, which occurred either prior, or during the hallucination, demonstrated the presence of subvocal speech during the episodes. The authors conclude that their results suggest that "the hallucination is an expression of subvocal speech as part of inner speech." Green and Preston studied the vocal correlates of auditory hallucinations with two throat microphones attached to each side of the larynx [26]. The amplified whispers corresponded with the content of the hallucinations and occurred independently of the normal speech of the patient. These were taped and fed back to the patient, thus allowing for a three-way conversation between the experimenter, the patient and his hallucinations (emanating from a "Miss Jones:" a complete transcript is provided as an appendix, a fascinating and often humorous three cornered 'dialogue.')

At the neurophysiological level pathological dysregulation of inner speech with consequent subliminal activation of the laryngeal musculature implies a disorganization in the neural networks mediating language, i.e. of the dominant fronto-temporal network. I have reviewed elsewhere the evidence derived from extremely varied experimental approaches which shows that the fundamental defect in schizophrenia relates to impaired dominant hemispheric functions [27-29]. If this is true, schizophrenia should be associated with formal abnormalities in the phonological and/or linguistic system since these functions are dependent on the integrity of neural systems in the dominant hemisphere. This is indeed the case. The study of language abnormality in schizophrenia in the last twenty years has shown that there is, in this syndrome, a defect in formal linguistic organization at the semantic and lexical level of discourse; a defect in speech comprehension; and a correspondence between thought disorder, statistical abnormalities in the relative frequency of certain linguistic elements, and motility abnormalities. In view of the fundamental importance of motility systems abnormality in psychopathology the demonstration by Manschreck [30] that language deviance and abnormal motor behavior in thought-disordered schizophrenia are significantly correlated is theoretically important. Subvocalizations can be viewed as an expression of disordered motility regulation. In addition, the so-called nonaphasic disturbances of language, neologisms, echolalia and paucity of speech are identical in chronic schizophrenia, in certain stages of dementia, and in neurological syndromes where the language regions of the dominant hemisphere are partially disconnected from the rest of the left hemisphere: it seems improbable that these relationships are chance events (see Flor-Henry for review [29, pp. 85-89]).

The investigations of Green [31-33] of speech comprehension in schizophrenics under monaural versus binaural listening conditions are of importance in the elucidation of the cerebral mechanisms responsible for auditory hallucinations. In the first report it was shown that there was a left ear and binaural disadvantage relative to the right ear in schizophrenics. Further the relative left ear disadvantage was significantly greater in female, compared to male schizophrenics. In normals the three conditions are equivalent. In the later reports it was found that, considering schizophrenia as a whole, 75 percent showed a left ear deficit while 25 percent showed a relative right ear deficit: the former group corresponding to acute, the latter to chronic forms of the schizophrenic syndrome. In depressive psychoses, the left ear deficit is characteristic whereas manic states are associated with a relative right ear defect in speech comprehension. In a small number of patients with intractable hallucinations an ear plug, usually in the ear with maximum deficit, leads to the immediate cessation of auditory hallucinations. I will give two clinical vignettes illustrating this remarkable phenomenon.

> Mrs. X was the youngest of twelve children, and only completed four or five grades of elementary eduction. Before her marriage, at the age of eighteen, she worked, variously, in restaurants, laundries, elevators and also as a ward aide in a general hospital. Menarche was at the age of fourteen, with regular menstruation, initially with dysmenorrhea. Until the onset of her illness at the age of thirty-one, she considered her marriage reasonably happy, except for the fact that her husband, a cook on the railways, was often away from home. She has had two children, a boy and a girl. The daughter committed suicide at the age of twenty when on holidays with a boy friend in the United States. The psychosis, which has been continuous for the last twenty years, was characterized in the early stages by hallucinations and delusions, she would hear voices, music and singing in her left ear, voices in her right ear calling her name and commenting on her actions. She had numerous persecutory delusions, feeling that heat from the T.V. and radio was affecting her health and would produce cancer.
>
> When I first encountered the patient she was then forty-nine years old. She continued to believe that her husband and son were trying to kill her, that she was electronically pregnant, that her husband was impregnating a number of young girls, that she was hypnotized by her brother-in-law and that she was controlled by a police

robot giving her constant instructions, which she heard exclusively in her left ear. Mood was suspicious but not subjectively depressed and objectively profoundly flat and blunted. Psychometrically (WAIS-R) the verbal I.Q. was 66, performance I.Q. 72 and full scale I.Q. 66. On the Auditory Comprehension Test [33] left ear and binaural comprehension were more impaired than the right ear (left ear 40% of right ear comprehension–right ear score 40% greater than the binaural score). Over the years, the delusional ideas and auditory hallucinations were never influenced by neuroleptic medications, which only produced non-specific tranquilization. *With a left ear plug, however, the hallucinations ceased, immediately*. After one week the patient removed the plug, because she missed the hallucinations which gave her a sense of importance; these returned! (diagnosis: chronic schizophrenia with positive symptomatology).

When first seen Mr. Y. was age twenty-four. His father, a successful businesman who owns his company, had been treated for depression. Patient is the eldest of three siblings. Succeeded easily at school, without effort and at University obtained a degree, Bachelor in electrical engineering. He had previously attempted an honors course in Physics, then in Mathematics and Computer Sciences, but found these subjects too difficult. His mother died when he was in the middle of his university studies, following which he failed all his exams. Later he took amphetamine during examinations, then dropped out for one year but finally obtained his degree with 8.6 average (Stanine system). Sexually promiscuous, having gone through some twenty heterosexual relationships, each lasting one or two months on average. Extremely athletic in the mid 1970s, excelling in Kung Fu, as a black belt and instructor. He described cyclothymic mood swings from the age of 16 and following the death of his mother attempted suicide. For two years prior to the first psychiatric hospitalization he had used Hashish excessively, daily for prolonged periods, spending some $400 a week on this habit. He was also prone to bouts of heavy drinking. He became involved in a bewildering variety of companies, corporations, etc., nine in number, losing $72,000 in the process. During the first hospitalization mood was euphoric and the mental state was dominated by grandiose delusions: he could speak seven languages, he was more intelligent than all men, a spirit was sending him on a mission to enlighten the peoples of the world and he was in the process of building a computer that would control the world. Six months earlier following a period of withdrawal and seclusion he became very energetic, started to spend money wildly, took flying lessons, travelled extensively and acquired many girl friends. He began to hear voices nine months previous, when on marijuana, but these hallucinations persisted when no longer on the drug and became continuous. Dexamethasone suppression test was positive on several occasions. Neuroleptics induced marked extrapyramidal side effects and had to be discontinued. Lithium induced hypothyroidism and was also discontinued. This was followed by depression but tricyclic antidepressants triggered thought-disordered hypomania. He became essentially asymptomatic on carbamazepine. Following his discharge he stopped his medication after about one month and slowly relapsed. When

> re-admitted nine months later he was irritable and euphoric, overactive and restless, thought that he and his girl friend were going to heaven, became unusually religious, praying and listening to God speaking to him. Over the four months of the second hospitalization the mental symptoms were difficult to control, but he was finally discharged on Carbamazepine, Modecate and Imipramine: mood was no longer depressed, the hallucinations were no longer present and there were no signs of overt psychosis although the affect was blunted. A few weeks later he committed suicide.
>
> Psychometrically (WAIS-R) the verbal I.Q. was 107; performance I.Q. 80 and full scale I.Q. 94. On the MMPI both the Depression and Mania scales showed significant elevation, as did the psychasthenia scale. On the Auditory Comprehension Test there was a clear right ear deficit, compared to the left ear score, with the binaural condition the most impaired. Neuropsychological testing indicated bilateral frontal dysfunction (left > right) and left temporal dysfunction. *With a plug in the right ear the voices disappeared altogether, returning within 1/2 hour of removing the plug* (diagnosis: bipolar affective psychosis).

Several communications have been published since 1983 confirming that, in certain instances, treatment refractory auditory hallucinations in schizophrenia could be abolished by applying an ear plug, sometimes in the ear with maximum deficit, sometimes in the ear with better comprehension, sometimes with equal benefit by plugging the ear with inferior, or superior comprehension [34-37].

In recent years a number of CT scan, cerebral circulation, acoustic and Positron Emission Tomography investigations have thrown some light on the locus of disorganization associated with auditory hallucinations in schizophrenia. Takahashi in the CT scan examination of 280 schizophrenics compared to 234 age and sex-matched controls found that cortical atrophy of the left temporal lobe was significantly and specifically associated with the presence of auditory hallucinations [38]. Uchino studied the correlations between CT scan measures and mental symptoms (PSE schedule) in forty schizophrenics during the first episode of their illness [39]. The presence of auditory hallucinations was significantly associated with enlargement of the left Sylvian fissure and with enlargement of the left anterior horn of the lateral ventricle. There is also evidence of structural abnormality of the left hemisphere in epileptic psychoses with hallucinations: Toone in a neuro-radiological study of the psychoses of epilepsy observed that when they compared cases with hallucinations to cases without hallucinations, there was a striking absence of right sided lesions in the hallucinated group [40]. Kurachi using the ^{1333}Xe inhalation technique for the measurement of regional cerebral blood flow note that schizophrenics with auditory hallucinations have significantly increased blood flow in the left temporal region, when compared to patients without hallucinations [41]. Uchino [42] correlated regional cerebral blood flow values and PSE mental symptoms [43] in fifty-four schizophrenics. Twenty-six patients exhibited the symptom 'of voices heard arguing in the third person,' associated with a significant decrease in left mid-temporal flow while 'voices speaking directly to the subject' had a significant increase in left fronto-temporal flow (25 subjects). In this study auditory hallucinations are clearly related to local changes in the left fronto-temporal regions.

A neurometabolic approach to the question of auditory hallucinations in schizophrenia also implicates the left temporal zone. DeLisi investigating twenty-one unmedicated schizophrenics and controls with PET (^{18}F Deoxy-glucose) found a significant degree of hypermetabolic activity in the left temporal lobe positively correlated with the intensity of verbal hallucinosis [44]. Left temporal lobe pathology also emerges as being central to the formation of auditory hallucinations in the acoustic threshold investigations of Bazhin [2]. Threshold is the lowest intensity of a signal tone heard by the subject at least three times. There is in normals a relationship between signal duration and threshold intensity: the latter increases as the signal (200-300 msec. at onset) decreases. The threshold increase in normals is symmetrical in the right and left ear under monaural testing and is of the order of 30 dB elevation as the sound duration decreases from 1000 to 1 msec. In schizophrenics with hallucinations there is a significant increase in right ear threshold, starting at 10 msec. tone duration and maximal at 1 msec. The average difference between the right and left ear thresholds was 5.3 dB. There were thirty patients, all dextrals: ten with 'genuine' auditory hallucinations; ten with auditory pseudo-hallucinations and ten with psychic hallucinations. The effect was strongest in the group with 'genuine' hallucinations and least in patients with 'psychic' hallucinations. Ten normals and twelve "schizophrenics with a paranoiac syndrome," i.e. without auditory hallucinations, had normal symmetrical threshold effects. Two additional patients, schizophrenics with hallucinations but who were sinistrals, showed a left ear threshold increase. The authors conclude that these results suggest a relationship between auditory hallucinations and the mechanisms of inner speech. The characteristic hallucinations in schizophrenia are acoustic; however, in some 30 percent of cases visual hallucinations are encountered as well. It is noteworthy that in the endogenous schizophrenias visual hallucinations are not found, in the absence of auditory hallucinations, whereas the auditory hallucinatory mode is the rule. Remarkably Bracha examined forty-four chronic schizophrenics with unequivocal visual hallucinations [45]. Of the twenty-six patients who were clearly left hemisphere dominant and dextral, thirteen reported that their hallucinations occurred in the right visual hemifield; only two in the left visual field, the remaining eleven without lateralization. Thus, very significantly ($p < 0.008$) visual hallucinations in schizophrenia are the result of abnormal left hemispheric events. In sinistral or ambidextrous patients with hallucinations ($n = 18$), seven saw their hallucinations in the left, four in the right visual field and seven did not lateralize. In seventeen dextral patients who were also experiencing auditory hallucinations at the time of the study the distribution of the spatial characteristics was, in fact, Gaussian: heard in the left ear in four subjects, no lateralization in nine and right ear in four. Curiously there is evidence that visual hallucinatory experiences may be generally determined by left hemispheric pathology–curiously, given the right hemispheric specialization for visuo-spatial processing. Takahashi, reporting on the relationship existing between various forms of psychic seizures and the laterality of the inter-ictal EEG focus in fifty-two patients, described twelve patients with visual-hallucinatory seizures: eleven with left hemisphere focus, one with bilateral foci [46]. The presence of visual hallucinations in the hemifield contralateral to the affected hemisphere is a well known neurological sign in migraine, epilepsy and in neurosurgery following electrical stimulation of the parieto-occipital regions. It is perhaps less widely appreciated that there is a comparable contralateral lateralization for complex auditory hallucinations, the result of local brain disease in the region of the superior temporal gyrus. Tanabe described in detail a single case of a sixty-four-year-old woman who, following a haemorrhagic infarct of the left superior temporal gyrus, developed for a two-week period verbal hallucinations in the right ear: two voices, that of a female TV announcer and, in a noisy background, that of her grandson [47]. During the period of right ear verbal hallucinosis "she heard her own spoken words inside her head" and the words of others entered her head and became confused with her own thoughts. Tanabe collected from the international literature seven other cases of unilateral complex auditory hallucinations in the ear contralateral to temporal lobe lesions. In all cases ($n = 6$) of left temporal pathology and right ear hallucinations the hallucinations were verbal (verbal + musical in 1 case) while in the two cases of right temporal lobe pathology with left ear hallucinations, these were musical in the first and verbal in the second.

In the telemetric EEG investigation of forty schizophrenics compared to twelve healthy controls Stevens [48] observed in the pooled power spectra of these patients that auditory hallucinations were associated with left temporal alpha power suppression, indicating therefore that left temporal activation was related to the emergence of verbal hallucinosis. In a later study with similar methodology Stevens and Livermore [49] noted that four of eight chronic paranoid schizophrenics with active auditory hallucinations exhibited left central parietal "ramps" spectra (a smooth decline in power from lowest to highest frequencies, which previous work by Stevens has correlated with abnormal sub-cortical activity). Further in the eighteen schizophrenic patients studied during hallucinatory states there was "a striking increase in left centro-parietal slow activity and more alpha activity." In the study of a single case Serafetinides noted that during non-verbal reporting of auditory hallucinations there is a systematic asymmetry in the anterior derivations with increase in high frequency power ($>$ 20 Hz) on the right and decrease power in the 16-20 Hz band on the left side [50]. Ishibashi [51] subjected seventeen chronic schizophrenics to craniotomy of the non-dominant side, exposing the temporal lobe cortex to which electrical stimulation was applied directly (Square waves, 100 Hz, 3 msec. duration, 4-8 volts intensity, repeated for 5 seconds). Elementary visual hallucinations resulted from stimulation of the deep temporal structures, but not from the temporal cortex and were related to the after discharges. Auditory hallucinations, on the other hand, only occurred on temporal cortex stimulation and were unrelated to after-discharges. Visual and auditory hallucinations were only elicited by stimulation of the superior temporal gyrus, over its whole length for visual, but only in the anterior portion for auditory phenomena. The induced auditory hallucinations were never identical to those spontaneously experienced, which indeed were suppressed for a period of three months in eight of eleven cases, after which, however, they recurred. The specific importance of the temporal lobe in the genesis of acoustic hallucinations is confirmed by the intracerebral electrical stimulation of a psychiatrically normal young woman with left temporal lobe epilepsy undertaken by Mahl [52]. Stimulation of the left temporal lobe induced auditory hallucinations, which tended to be contextually related to mental ideas that the subject was experiencing just prior to the stimulation–but never occurred after stimulation of the left frontal lobe.

Following focal lesions of the CNS visual and/or auditory hallucinations accompany pathology at various sites. The 'peduncular hallucinations' associated with upper brain stem lesions have been described by Lhermitte [15]. They are considered to be the consequence of 'release disinhibition' of hemispheric cortical systems by disruption of ascending brain stem reticular inhibitory pathways. The auditory and visual hallucinations, components of the aura of temporal lobe epilepsy (complex partial seizures), are well known. Peroutka described auditory and visual hallucinations present for two weeks after a right temporo-parietal-occipital infarct and, reviewing the literature, cited nine other cases where infarction of the right posterior hemisphere resulted in visual and auditory hallucinations, accompanied by constructional apraxia [53].

Asaad and Shapiro briefly reviewed biochemical approaches to hallucinations [54]–given the frequency with which hallucinations occur as a side effect of medications in nonpsychiatric medically ill patients. The key neurotransmitter involved is dopamine since L-Dopa induces a hallucinatory syndrome in Parkinsonism, as does d-amphetamine an indirect dopamine agonist, in normal subjects. Various hallucinogenic drugs such as Lysergic Acid (LSD) and mescaline block central serotoninergic receptors, and the former in addition slows intracerebral serotonin turn-over. Further, poisoning with anti-cholinergic agents also provokes hallucinations. It should be noted that in the light of the series of reciprocal relationships linking the principal neurotransmitters in a bilaterally asymmetrical functional dynamic (see [55] for review), diminished activity of both serotoninergic and cholinergic systems leads to a state of functional dopaminergic predominance, with a left hemisphere emphasis. Bromocriptine, an amide of Lysergic Acid, is a dopamine agonist and also induces hallucinations [56].

The evidence is clear that disruption of critical cortical neuronal systems in the anterior parts of the superior temporal gyrus–in effect Heschl's gyrus, the cortical center for hearing–provokes auditory hallucinations, which in the case of localized lesions, are perceived in the contralateral ear. Dopaminergic systems are implicated as shown by the pharmacological evidence. Visual hallucinations are evoked by disruption of deeper and more extensive structures involving the whole of the superior temporal gyrus and the parieto-occipital junction. In the special case of acoustic hallucinations in schizophrenia the anatomical evidence (CT scan and post-mortem neuropathological analysis), the neurophysiological evidence (cerebral circulation, neurometabolic studies and EEG findings) as well as acoustic research (right ear threshold changes) are all convergent and indicate that the primary locus is in the dominant temporal lobe.

Certain aspects of the question need to be considered further. Given the dominant temporal origin of auditory hallucinations in schizophrenia, why are these generally perceived bilaterally and not unilaterally in the contralateral right ear? Why in a small proportion of cases are they unilateral hallucinations? Why in some cases of treatment are refractory hallucinations abolished by preventing afferent acoustic impulses from reaching the right or the left hemisphere, depending on the case?

Gruzelier has shown that the schizophrenic syndrome is dichotomous in terms of the directionality of electrodermal amplitude asymmetry [57]. Acute schizophrenia with florid symptomatology is characterized by EDA asymmetry (right < left) while the chronic deficit negative symptomatology syndrome exhibits the opposite asymmetry (left < right). In other words the acute (hallucinatory) syndrome corresponds to a brain state with relative left hemispheric preponderance and the chronic deficit syndrome to a brain state of relative right hemispheric preponderance. To the extent that in schizophrenia auditory hallucinations are associated with the acute rather than with the chronic syndrome, there are acoustic studies which indirectly confirm the Gruzelier model. Takahashi with verbal type dichotic tests finds that, comparing hallucinating with non-hallucinating schizophrenics, the hallucinatory group has a very significant relative right ear advantage compared to non-hallucinating patients or controls [58]. (This is due to a very poor left ear performance in the hallucinators with near normal right ear scores.) Thus hallucinating schizophrenics display dysfunctional overactivation of the left hemisphere associated with right hemisphere hypofunction. Related observations were made by Alpert [59] utilizing a monaural semantic integration test. Non-hallucinators made most errors, discriminating better from the left ear input (rather than the right ear as in normals or hallucinators) thus consistent with a state of relative right hemisphere preponderance in the non-hallucinators and left brain preponderance in hallucinators. Recent neurometabolic investigations indicate that the positive symptomatology syndrome (i.e. hallucinatory) is hypermetabolic (left > right) while the chronic deficit syndrome is hypometabolic (left > right) so that this dimension has to be superimposed on the hemispheric imbalance model (see [60] for review). Thus in schizophrenia hallucinatory forms are hypermetabolic with left hemisphere preponderance while the deficit syndrome is hypometabolic with right hemisphere preponderance. Keeping in mind these complex interactions a fascinating observation of Machiyama [61] might explain why an ear plug would, under certain circumstances, abolish auditory hallucinations. He found in the study of the topographic relationships of auditory evoked potentials to right and left monaural stimulation that in schizophrenics left ear stimulation reduced parallel latencies bilaterally while right ear stimulation increased latencies bilaterally. (In normals right hemisphere latencies are reduced on left ear stimulation.) A reduction of EP latencies implies increased cerebral activation, a prolongation, increased cerebral inhibition. Thus in the hypermetabolic state blocking afferent acoustic impulses from the right ear would normalize the pre-existing cerebral instability while blocking the left ear would normalize the hypometabolic syndrome. It must be remembered that, even if auditory hallucinations are generally related to acute positive-symptomatology schizophrenia (the so called paranoid form of the Anglo-Saxon nomenclature), hallucinations are present in some 50 percent of chronic deficit-symptomatology schizophrenias. Finally let us examine the question of the subjectively bilateral perception of acoustic hallucinations in schizophrenia, this in spite of the fact that their cerebral origin is left temporal. Here we have to consider certain aspects of callosal functions as proposed by Normal Cook [62] in a brilliant and original exposition. Briefly the major points of relevance in our context are the following:

1. most of the cortex (except the primary somatosensory, auditory and visual areas) receive and send callosal fibres;
2. the number of callosal fibres is of the order of 200-250 million;
3. there are approximately 125 million cortical columns per hemisphere: the fundamental functional units of the cortex which, when activated, inhibit adjacent columnar units by surround inhibition;
4. thus the approximate ratio of two callosal fibres for each cortical column implies that a topographical relationship between the hemispheres is anatomically feasible;
5. because in brain evolution, as the corpus callosum increases in size, there is a corresponding massive increase in functional brain asymmetry, the fundamental action of callosal transmission must be inhibitory, rather than excitatory;
6. this is confirmed by physiological experiments which indicate that stimulation of the corpus callosum produces a brief excitation followed by prolonged inhibition at the termination of the callosal fibres—which originate and end in layers 3 and 4 of the cortex;
7. 75 percent of callosal fibres form homotopic projections; the others are symmetrically heterotopic or project into the limbic system;
8. subcortical brain-stem ascending monoaminergic (arousal) pathways are bilaterally symmetrical in their neocortical projections;
9. thus in the above system cortical activation leads to a mirror-image negative relationship between the cerebral hemispheres, given the inhibitory function of the corpus callosum;

10. it must be emphasized that contralateral inhibition does not imply the absence of information transfer but leads to the possibility of higher order subordinate constructs, through the disinhibition of adjacent columns.

It follows immediately from the above representation of the mechanisms regulating information transfer between hemispheres that auditory hallucinations in schizophrenia would be perceived (as a rule) bilaterally, since the dysregulation of the association cortex (auditory) in the left hemisphere would trigger a perturbation in the contralateral auditory association neurones through inhibitory disinhibition, thus accounting for the fact that the voices heard, in schizophrenia are multiple. Considering our two personal cases of unilateral acoustic hallucinations, abolished by an ear plug applied to the affected ear, a few points arise leading towards a possible explanation of the unilateral hallucinosis. The first case Mrs. X was the last born of twelve children and was sinistral (mixed, left handed on the Annett [63] classification). This suggests a birth trauma effect, implicating the dominant hemisphere, with compensatory sinistrality. (This is consistent with the report of Mary Seeman [64] which showed that early onset poor prognosis schizophrenia in women was significantly associated with an excess of birth trauma and sinistrality when compared with late onset, remitting schizophrenic women.) The hallucinations were in the left ear. In the second case, Mr. Y, who on neuropsychological testing with an extensive battery showed frontal dysfunction (left > right) and left temporal dysfunction, had a performance I.Q., 27 points lower than the verbal, a very significant verbal/performance I.Q. discrepancy revealing profound hypofunction of the right hemisphere. The hallucinations were heard in the right ear. Thus in cases of massive dysfunction predominantly of one hemisphere the hallucinations appear to originate from the contralateral hemisphere (? contralateral disinhibition). Swinburne utilized a perceptual asymmetry design to study male schizophrenic patients, divided into two groups, one with a predominance of hallucinations, the other with a predominance of delusions [65]. A healthy control group was also investigated. Words and pictures were used alternately as probes and the WAIS Similarities, Vocabulary and Block Design subtests were also administered. Only hallucinating subjects showed significant asymmetry in hemisphere functioning with the right hemisphere responding more quickly but the left hemisphere more accurately. Patients with delusions were quicker and more accurate to word probes whereas hallucinating subjects reacted faster to picture probes but more accurately to word probes. Swinburne interprets these results as being in favor of a hemispheric disconnection hypothesis in hallucinating schizophrenics.

In conclusion the evidence indicates that in schizophrenia auditory hallucinations are the consequence of local dysregulation of the central and anterior parts of the dominant superior temporal gyrus which produce a subliminal activation of the laryngeal apparatus and consequent subvocalizations. In general the hallucinations are subjectively perceived as bilateral on account of the homotopic, mirror-image negative nature of callosal transmission. Exceptionally in schizophrenia the acoustic hallucinations are unilateral; however unilateral hallucinations heard in the ear contralateral to lesioned superior temporal gyrus is the rule in neurological disorders. Visual hallucinations are determined by dysregulation of deeper and more extensive neural systems in the superior temporal gyrus and parieto-occipital regions and, in schizophrenia, occur significantly more often in the right visual hemifield. Biochemically the major neurotransmitter implicated in the genesis of hallucinosis is dopamine; serotoninergic and cholinergic transmission also play a role, in a manner which would, indirectly, also exercise a hyperdopaminergic effect.

REFERENCES

1. W. Ch. Kandinskii, *Psewdogallucinaciyach*, Petersburg, 1890.
2. E. F. Bazhin, L. I. Wasserman and I. M. Tonkonogii, Auditory Hallucinations and Left Temporal Lobe Pathology, *Neuropsychologia, 13*, pp. 481–487, 1975.
3. A. H. Southard, On Topographical Distribution of Cortex Lesions and Anomalies in Dementia Praecox, with Some Account of Their Functional Significance, *American Journal of Insanity, 71*, pp. 603–671, 1960.
4. F. H. Johnson, *The Anatomy of Hallucinations*, Nelson-Hall, Inc., Chicago, 1978.
5. J. Baillarger, *Des Hallucinations*, J. B. Bailliere, Paris, 1846.
6. H. Maudsley, *Natural Causes and Supernatural Seemings*, Kegan Paul, Trench and Co., London, 1886.
7. E. Parish, *Hallucinations and Illusions*, Walter Scott, London, 1897.
8. A. H. Modell, An Approach to the Nature of Auditory Hallucinations in Schizophrenia, *Archives of General Psychiatry, 3*, pp. 259–266, 1960.
9. E. Bleuler, *Dementia Praecox or the Group of Schizophrenias. Aschaffenberg's Handbuch*, 1950 Translation. International Universities Press, New York, 1911.
10. E. Bleuler, *Textbook of Psychiatry*, A. A. Brill (Translation) Macmillan, New York, 1930.
11. H. Ey, *Hallucinations et delire, Les formes hallucinatoires de l'automatisme verbale*, Alcan, Paris, 1934.
12. P. Janet, *Major Symptoms of Hysteria*, McMillan, New York, 1906, 1929.
13. ————, Le language interieur dans l'hallucination psychique, *Annales Medicopsychologiques, 2*, pp. 377–386, 1936.
14. J. Lhermitte, Comment comprendre les hallucinations, *Gazette Medicale de France, Paris, 56*, pp. 345–351, 1949.
15. ————, *Les Hallucinations, Clinique et Physiopathologie*, G. Doin, Paris, 1951.

16. R. E. Hoffman, Verbal Hallucinations and Language Production Processes in Schizophrenia, *The Behavioral and Brain Sciences, 9,* pp. 503–548, 1986.
17. L. N. Gould, Verbal Hallucinations as Automatic Speech, The Reactivation of Dormant Speech Habit, *American Journal of Psychiatry, 107*, pp. 110–119, 1950.
18. K. Faaborg-Andersen, *Electromyographic Investigation of Intrinsic Laryngeal Muscles in Humans*, S. L. Mollers Bogtrykkeri, Copenhagen, 1957.
19. K. Faaborg-Andersen and A. W. Edfeldt, Electromyography of Intrinsic and Extrinsic Laryngeal Muscles during Silent Speech: Correlation with Reading Activity, *Acta Otolaryngologia, 49*, pp. 478–482, 1958.
20. M. Cerny, Electrophysiological Study of Verbal Hallucinations, *Activitas Nervosa Superior (Praha), 6*, pp. 94–95, 1964.
21. M. Cerny, On Neurophysiological Mechanisms in Verbal Hallucinations: An Electrophysiological Study, *Activitas Hervosa Suprior (Praha), 7*, pp. 197–198, 1965.
22. F. J. McGuigan, Covert Oral Behaviour and Auditory Hallucinations, *Psychophysiology, 3*:1, pp. 73–80, 1966.
23. T. Inouye and A. Shimizu, The Electromyographic Study of Verbal Hallucination, *The Journal of Nervous and Mental Disease, 151*:6, pp. 415–422, 1970.
24. F. H. Johnson, Auditory Hallucinations as Interpreted by Means of Recorders, *Anatomical Record, 130*, pp. 321, 1958.
25. F. H. Johnson, Neurophysiological Disuse of Inner Speech as Used in Thinking in Schizophrenia, *Anatomical Record, 157*, pp. 366, 1967.
26. P. Green and M. Preston, Reinforcement of Vocal Correlates of Auditory Hallucinations by Auditory Feedback: A Case Study, *British Journal of Psychiatry, 139*, pp. 204–208, 1981.
27. P. Flor-Henry, Psychosis and Temporal Lobe Epilepsy, *Epilepsia 10*, pp. 363–365, 1969.
28. ————, Commentary and Synthesis, in *Laterality and Psychopathology*, P. Flor-Henry and J. Gruzelier (eds.), Elsevier/North Holland Biomedical Press, Amsterdam/New York/Oxford, pp. 1–18, 1983.
29. ————, *Cerebral Basis of Psychopathology*, Wright. PSG, Inc., Boston/Bristol/London, 1983.
30. T. C. Manschreck, B. A. Maher, and D. N. Ader, Formal Thought Disorder, the Type-Token Ration, and Distributed Voluntary Motor Movement in Schizophrenia, *British Journal of Psychiatry, 139*, pp. 7–15, 1981.
31. P. Green and V. Kotenko, Superior Speech Comprehension in Schizophrenia Under Monaural versus Binaural Listening Conditions, *Journal of Abnormal Psychology, 89*:3, pp. 399–408, 1980.
32. P. Green, S. Hallett and M. Hunter, Abnormal Inter-hemispheric Integration and Hemispheric Specialization in Schizophrenics and High-risk Children, in *Laterality and Psychopathology*, P. Flor-Henry and J. Gruzelier, Elsevier/North Holland Biomedical Press, Amsterdam/New York/Oxford, pp. 443–469, 1983.

33. P. Green, Interference Between the Two Ears in Speech Comprehension and the Effect of an Earplug in Psychiatric and Cerebral-lesioned Patients, in *Cerebral Dynamics, Laterality and Psychopathology*, R. Takahashi, P. Flor-Henry, J. Gruzelier, S-I. Niwa (eds.), Elsevier Science Publishers BV, Amsterdam, pp. 287–298, 1987.
34. D. A. E. James, The Experimental Treatment of Two Cases of Auditory Hallucinations, *British Journal of Psychiatry, 143*, pp. 515–516, 1983.
35. D. J. Done, C. D. Frith and D. C. Owens, Reducing Persistent Auditory Hallucinations by Wearing an Ear Plug, *British Journal of Clinical Psychology, 25*, pp. 151–152, 1986.
36. S. E. Levick and E. Peselow, Unilateral Auditory Occlusions and Auditory Hallucinations, *British Journal of Psychiatry, 148*, pp. 747–748, 1986.
37. M. Birchwood, Control of Auditory Hallucinations Through Occlusion of Monaural Auditory Input, *British Journal of Psychiatry, 149*, pp. 104–107, 1986.
38. R. Takahashi, Y. Inaba, Y. Inanaga, N. Kato, H. Kumashiro, T. Nishimura, T. Okuma, S. Otsuki, T. Sakai, T. Sata and Y. Shimazono, CT Scanning and the Investigation of Schizophrenia. Third World Congress of Biological Psychiatry, Stockholm, (S 371), 1981.
39. J. Uchino, K. Araki, Y. Kominaga, H. Niwa, I. Nakama, S. Michitsuji, M. Ishizawa, Y. Ohta, Y. Nakane, and R. Takahashi, Correlation Between CT Findings of Schizophrenics and Their Clinical Symptoms (2): Using Discrimatory Analysis and Chi-square Test, *Folia Psychiatrica et Neurologia Japonica, 38*, 2, pp. 179, 1984.
40. B. K. Toone, J. Dawson, and M. V. Driver, Psychoses of Epilepsy: A Radiological Evaluation, *British Journal of Psychiatry, 140*, pp. 244–248, 1982.
41. M. Kurachi, K. Kobayashi, M. Suzuki, H. Hiramatsui, N. Yamaguchi, H. Matsuda, K. Hisada and F. Momonoi, Front-temporal Blood Flow in Schizophrenic Disorders, *Folia Psychiatrica et Neurologia Japonica, 39*, 1, pp. 102, 1985.
42. J. Uchino, K. Araki, Y. Tominaga, I. Nakama, Y. Ohta, Y. Nakane, S. Michitsuji, N. Hirota, H. Mori, and H. Yonekura, The Correlation between the Regional Cerebral Blood Flow and PSE Findings in the Patients with Schizophrenia, *The Japanese Journal of Psychiatry and Neurology, 40*, 1, pp. 133, 1986.
43. J. K. Wing, J. E. Cooper and N. Sartorius, *The Measurement and Classification of Psychiatric Symptoms*, Cambridge University Press, London, 1974.
44. L. E. DeLisi, M. S. Buchsbaum, H. H. Holcomb, K. C. Langston, A. C. King, R. Kessler, D. Pickar, W. Carpenter, J. M. Morihisa, R. Morgolin, D. R. Weinberger and R. Cohen, Increased Temporal Lobe Glucose Use in Chronic Schizophrenic Patients. *Biological Psychiatry, 25*, pp. 835–851, 1989.
45. H. S. Bracha, F. J. Cabrera, C. N. Karson and L. B. Bigelow, Lateralization of Visual Hallucinations in Chronic Schizophrenia, *Biological Psychiatry, 20*, pp. 1132–1136, 1985.
46. Y. Takahashi, F. Yokoyama, Y. Yashima, and H. Kumashiro, Relationship Between Psychic Seizure and Laterality of Electroencephalographic Abnormality, *Folia Psychiatrica et Neurologia Japonica, 39*, 1, pp. 105–106, 1985.

47. H. Tanabe, T. Sawada, H. Asai, J. Okuda, and J. Shiraishi, Lateralization Phenomenon of Complex Auditory Hallucinations, *Acta Psychiatrica Scandinavica, 74*, pp. 178–182, 1986.
48. J. R. Stevens, L. Bigelow, D. Denney, J. Lipkin, A. H. Livermore, F. Rauscher and R. J. Wyatt, Telemetered EEG-EOG During Psychotic Behaviors of Schizophrenia, *Archives of General Psychiatry, 36,* pp. 251–262, 1979.
49. J. R. Stevens and A. Livermore, Telemetered EEG in Schizophrenia: Spectral Analysis during Abnormal Behaviour Episodes, *Journal of Neurology, Neurosurgery and Psychiatry, 45*, pp. 385–395, 1982.
50. E. A. Serafetinides, R. W. Coger and J. Martin, Different Methods of Observation Affect EEG Measures Associated with Auditory Hallucinations, *Psychiatry Research, 17*, pp. 73–74, 1986.
51. T. Ishibashi, H. Hori, K. Endo and T. Sato, Hallucinations Produced by Electrical Stimulation of the Temporal Lobes in Schizophrenic Patients, *Tohoku Journal of Experimental Medicine, 82*, pp. 124–139, 1964.
52. G. F. Mahl, A. Rothenberg, J. M. R. Delgado and H. Hamlin, Psychological Responses in the Human to Intracerebral Electrical Stimulation, *Psychosomatic Medicine, xxvi*, 4, pp. 337–368, 1964.
53. S. J. Peroutka, B. H. L. Sohmer, A. J. Kumar, M. Folstein and R. G. Robinson, Hallucinations and Delusions Following a Right Temporoparietooccipital Infarction, *The Johns Hopkins Medical Journal, 151*, pp. 181–185, 1982.
54. G. Asaad and B. Shapiro, Hallucinations: Theoretical and Clinical Overview, *American Journal of Psychiatry, 143*, 9, pp. 1088–1097, 1986.
55. P. Flor-Henry, Observations, Reflections and Speculations on the Cerebral Determinants of Mood and on the Bilaterally Asymmetrical Distributions of the Major Neurotransmitter Systems, *Acta Neurologica Scandinavica, 74* (suppl. 109), pp. 75–89, 1986.
56. D. A. Goodkin, Mechanisms of Bromocriptine-induced Hallucinations, *New England Journal of Medicine, 302*, pp. 1479, 1980.
57. J. H. Gruzelier, Hemisphere Imbalance Masquerading as Paranoid and Unparanoid Syndromes? *Schizophrenia Bulletin, 7*, pp. 662–673, 1981.
58. Y. Takahashi, Y. Yashima, S. Ochiai, F. Takamatsu, M. Kanno, H. Kumashiro and M. Sugishita, Responses to Dichotic Listening Tasks by Schizophrenic Patients, in *Cerebral Dynamics, Laterality and Psychopathology*, R. Takahashi, P. Flor-Henry, J. Gruzelier, S-I. Niwa (eds.), Elsevier Science Publishers BV, Amsterdam, pp. 307–312, 1987.
59. M. Alpert, H. Rubinstein and M. Kesselman, Asymmetry of Information Processing in Hallucinators and Non-hallucinators, *The Journal of Nervous and Mental Disease, 162*, 4, pp. 258–265, 1976.
60. P. Flor-Henry, Cerebral Dynamics, Laterality and Psychopathology: A Commentary, in *Cerebral Dynamics, Laterality and Psychopathology*, R. Takahashi, P. Flor-Henry, J. Gruzelier, S-I. Niwa (eds.), Elsevier Science Publishers BV, Amsterdam, pp. 3–21, 1987.
61. Y. Machiyama, Y. Shiihara and F. Kubota, Topographic and Temporal Aspects of Information Processing Abnormalities in Schizophrenia, in *Cerebral*

Dynamics, Laterality and Psychopathology, Elsevier Science Publishers BV, Amsterdam, pp. 211–220, 1987.

62. N. D. Cook, *The Brain Code: Mechanisms of Information Transfer and the Role of the Corpus Callosum*, Methuen & Co., London and New York, 1986.
63. M. Annett, A Classification of Hand Preferences by Association Analysis, *British Journal of Psychiatry, 61*, pp. 303–321, 1970.
64. M. V. Seeman, Sex and Schizophrenia, *Canadian Journal of Psychiatry, 30*, 5, pp. 313–315, 1985.
65. W. J. Swinburne, Hallucinations and Functional Brain Asymmetry in Schizophrenia, *Dissertation Abstracts International, 42*, 1, pp. 393-B, 1981.

PART III

Applications of Psychophysiological Methods and Principles: Mental and Physical Health

CHAPTER 8

Neuropsychological Concepts of Mood, Imagery, and Performance

JENNIFER LANGHINRICHSEN AND DON M. TUCKER

Mental imagery is said to alleviate depression, facilitate creativity, and enhance athletic performance. Writers in the popular press suggest that by exercising the imagery skills of the right hemisphere people can excel in work or sports [1]. Complex movements used in sports are difficult to describe with words, and seem to involve the arrangement and manipulation of mental images [2]. Successful performance is thus thought to require the ability to draw on the right hemisphere's imaginative capacities. Porter and Foster suggest that the mind's inner pictures can be powerful factors in setting goals for performance and preparing for competition emotionally [3]. In contrast to this optimism expressed by the popular press, a number of recent scientific approaches to imagery have questioned whether it is indeed the province of the right hemisphere [4, 5]. In this chapter we will consider specific capabilities of the brain which are thought to be manifestations of functional hemispheric asymmetries. Specifically, we will address whether emotion is right lateralized. Then we will consider possible links between emotion and imagery and how these may be relevant to the literature on the laterality of imagery. Neurophysiological models may help explain the interaction between imagery and emotion, and they may suggest how imagery can facilitate performance.

IS THERE HEMISPHERIC SPECIALIZATION FOR EMOTION?

Neuropsychologists have begun to clarify the neural substrate of elementary emotional functioning in humans. Primitive emotional functions are regulated by the hypothalamus, amygdala, hippocampus, and prefrontal cortex. The link between emotional mechanisms and cognition has been associated with limbic connections to the temporal lobe [6]. Evidence that emotional functions are lateralized is drawn from studies of brain lesioned patients, EEG data, and experiments designed to show how normal people recognize and communicate affect (for reviews see [7-9]). The most striking initial finding of lateral differences in emotional orientation was observed in patients with brain lesions. Lesions to the left hemisphere often produce a depressive-catastrophic reaction, while lesions to the right hemisphere may produce anosognosia or denial of illness [10]. Specifically, right hemisphere lesions may result in denial of the existence of a gross impairment, inappropriate optimism, or an indifference to misfortune [11]. In 1964, Terzian reported similar observations of emotional differences following unilateral sedation of the hemispheres [12]. These results have generally been interpreted to conclude that the left hemisphere in normal persons contributes a positive emotional orientation, and the right hemisphere a negative one [10].

Tucker however, proposed a disinhibition explanation for the observed emotional responses [8]. He based this interpretation on a classical neurological principle that a cortical lesion may disinhibit subcortical processes. A depressive-catastrophic reaction to a left hemisphere lesion could represent a disinhibition of the negative affect of the left side of the brain, rather than a release of the right hemisphere. Thus, a hemisphere lesion would be observed to exaggerate the emotional contribution of that hemisphere.

Researchers who have studied nonverbal cognitive operations of the right hemisphere also postulate its importance to normal emotional communication. The evidence for this assertion includes the finding that understanding emotion in facial expression or in tone of voice seems to require an intact right hemisphere [13] and a greater reliance on right hemisphere processing for emotional communication [14]. It is currently a matter of debate whether these asymmetries reflect facilitation by the right hemisphere or inhibition of emotion by the left hemisphere [15].

Recently, there have been attempts to resolve the controversy in the lateralization literature by increasing the complexity of the theoretical explanations. For example, human emotion may not be categorized appropriately on a unidimensional positive-negative axis. Furthermore, it may be necessary to move beyond a model based on unidimensional quantitative increases or decreases in arousal for each hemisphere. Instead, it seems likely that brain regulation involves specific systems producing qualitative changes in neural function.

Pribram and McGuinness postulated two main systems that increment brain activity: the activation and arousal systems [16]. The arousal system is primarily a perceptual orienting system which is particularly important to habituation processes. The activation system is linked to motor readiness and may apply a redundancy bias to ongoing neural operations [17]. Tucker and Williamson propose that the redundancy bias would allow a focusing of attention that may be particularly important to the cognitive skills of the left hemisphere [17]. Similarly, they suggest that the habituation bias may lead the brain to respond to novel events and may thus be particularly important in the holistic and expansive thinking characteristic of the right hemisphere.

Similarly, Tucker, Vannatta, and Rothlind theorize that the unilateral lesion evidence and the evidence suggesting the right hemisphere's role in emotional communication may both be explained using a two dimensional model [19]. They postulate that one underlying emotional dimension important to the right hemisphere's level of activity and function is mood, varying from depression to elation. The mood level is thought to modulate the organism's cognitive appraisal of incoming affective stimuli. Isen has published findings which indicate that a positive mood state changes memory access by facilitating access of emotionally and semantically related events [19]. Isen also reports qualitative changes in specific types of cognitive processing. For example, in subjects induced into a positive emotional state, she found a greater use of an intuitive heuristic than a logical strategy. It seems that the elated mood state is facilitating the more creative and expansive thinking long associated with the right hemisphere and can be readily linked to the search for novelty that is a characteristic of Pribram and McGuinness's phasic arousal system.

Tucker et al's second dimension ranges from relaxation to anxiety [18]. At high levels of anxiety, a person's memory and attention are focused on potentially threatening events. In addition, the redundancy bias of the tonic activation system restricts the range of unique information held in working memory and consequently restricts the range of access to long-term memory. Thus, excessive anxiety can result in obsessive, pathologically redundant behavior [20, 21]. Tucker et al. theorize that the emotional dimension of relaxation-anxiety is primarily associated with the left hemisphere.

Bear summarized several formulations of the hemispheres' specialized cognitive processing abilities [6]. Many researchers have described the right hemisphere as affective and emotional, while the left is seen as cognitive and neural. Moreover, in its cognitive function, the right hemisphere shows a preference for spatial, simultaneous, and holistic thinking. Temporal, sequential, and analytic cognitive functions are ascribed to the left brain. While these characteristics are fairly consistent with clinical observations, they fail to lead directly to explanations of the asymmetries in terms of mechanism, anatomy, or evolution. Like Tucker and Williamson [17], Bear suggested that we increase the complexity of the explanation [6]. In particular, he stressed the importance of the cortical sensory connections to and from the limbic system. He postulated the existence of hemispheric asymmetries in these connections. Specifically, Bear presents evidence, largely from animal work, for two separate and complementary cortico-visual systems with independent limbic connections. One is the ventral or temporofrontal system, and the other is the dorsal or parietofrontal system.

The ventral pathway is a foveal system designed to recognize objects by processing multiple attributes independent of the object's exact position in the visual field. Bear suggested that the ventral pathway is crucial for appropriate drive response and new stimulus-response learning. Consequently, ventral lesions of the temporal lobe or the orbital prefrontal cortex might prevent access to previously learned emotional associations as well as learned social norms and restraints. Thus, the ventral lesion could produce a "transient, reflexive release of, e.g., sexual or aggressive responses to environmental stimuli, without consideration of learned (delayed) consequences " [6].

In contrast, the dorsal pathway involves polysynaptic projections from the striate cortex to the inferior parietal lobule. The inferior parietal lobule is thought to be implicated in detection and spatial localization of drive-relevant stimuli. Bear posits that lesions to the dorsal limbic route might alter the organism's surveillance, orientation, and emotional arousal [6]. The interference could result in neglect and emotional apathy.

Bear suggested that the lateral asymmetries in the dorsal and ventral systems may account for the contrasts in hemispheric dominance in both emotional functions and cognitive domains [6]. For example, dreaming has often been considered an emotional experience. While dreaming, the individual may experience rapid eye movements and autonomic responses. The dreaming state is often characterized by intense visual images, many of which seem to carry an affective charge. Bear suggests that dreaming is a nocturnal activation of the dorsal emotional surveillance circuits not specialized in the right hemisphere.

These neuropsychological approaches to emotion have developed theoretical frameworks that go beyond lateralization to consider other dimensions of brain organization. Tucker and Williamson [17] suggested that left hemisphere processes in emotion have emerged from its more fundamental role in motor control, whereas right hemisphere specialization for many emotional functions reflect its specialization for coordinating perceptual orienting mechanisms of the posterior brain. Bear similarly looks for hemispheric specialization in the more fundamental dimension of dorsal versus ventral pathways [6]. Thus, in the area of emotion research, earlier concepts of simple hemispheric dichotomies, such as characterizing the right hemisphere as emotional and left hemisphere as non-emotional, have given way to more complex formulations of lateralization. This has also been the case in approaches to mental imagery.

NEUROPSYCHOLOGICAL CONCEPTS OF MENTAL IMAGERY

The importance of the right hemisphere to the process of mental imagery has been an implicit assumption in the literature on functional hemispheric asymmetries [22]. The logic of the assumption seems to be that imagery and spatial ability are linked; spatial ability and the right hemisphere are linked; therefore, imagery is likely to be a right hemisphere phenomenon. This assumption has persisted despite the fact that reviewers of hemispheric specialization such as Levy [23], Springer and Deutsch [24], and Bradshaw and Nettleton [25] do not mention imagery as a lateralization function. However, in the lateralization of emotion literature, the proposed link between emotion, imagery, and the right hemisphere has been assumed, as in Tucker, Stenslie, Roth, and Shearer's [26] interpretation that a negative correlation between self-reported depression and self-reported vividness of imagery may indicate decreased right hemisphere function in depression.

Ehrlichman and Barrett however, questioned right hemisphere specialization for mental imagery [22]. They reviewed studies of brain lesioned patients and commissurotomized subjects, EEG studies, lateral eye movement studies, and behavioral studies of non-brain injured people and concluded, "there is, presently, insufficient empirical basis for considering imagery a right hemisphere function."

While the indeterminate conclusion of this review may be discouraging for theorists who assumed a right hemisphere basis for mental imagery, again the evidence seems to require a greater complexity of explanation. Studies of brain lesioned patients who report a loss of imagery have shown that the loss is not contingent on damage to the right hemisphere. In fact, damage in the posterior areas of the left hemisphere seems more likely to cause patients to report a loss of imagery. Farah used a componential analysis of thirty-seven cases of loss of imagery in the English literature [4]. She concluded that "examination of the lesion sites in this subset of patients implicated a region in the posterior left hemisphere as critical for the image generation process."

There are several potential interpretations of Farah's work. The most obvious would be that imagery is left-lateralized. However, a left hemisphere lesion could also produce a disconnection syndrome, whereby visual imagery is cut off from the language system [27]. Ehrlichman and Barrett have suggested that there is an inherent ambiguity in using verbal tasks to study imagery, since individuals with left hemisphere lesions are almost certain to show poor performance as a result of linguistic-verbal deficits [22]. They propose that specific components of imagery tasks can be either ascribed to the right hemisphere or may require bilaterally shared functioning.

A consideration of neuropsychological models of emotion may offer a potential integration of Farah's [4] left hemisphere results with previous models. Perhaps the right hemisphere and the left hemisphere have qualitatively different modes of experiencing and elaborating imagery. For example, consistent with notions of left hemisphere function, left hemisphere imagery might be detail-oriented, subvocally or verbally mediated, and connected to motor systems. Perhaps this left hemisphere imagery is related to the anxiety-relaxation dimension. In contrast, right hemisphere imagery may appear as a holistic or global display. It may well be past-oriented and unconnected to any perception of threat or anxiety. Right hemisphere imagery may be aligned with the mood dimension ranging from elation to depression. The right hemisphere may use imagery to facilitate access to affectively valanced long term memory.

A recent neuropsychological model of imagery proposed by Kosslyn [5] is not entirely inconsistent with these speculations. Kosslyn considers the tasks faced by an image analysis system. These include the need to recognize object qualities as separate from spatial location, plus the need to accurately perceive spatial relations in the perceiver's visual field. Kosslyn suggests that the mechanisms used in higher perceptual processes can serve as important guides to the mechanisms used in imager generation and manipulation. He proposes that because it is specialized for controlling output functions, such as fine motor control, the left hemisphere emerges early in life with a specialization for production skills. In addition, given its exercise of categorical processing due to its language skills, the left hemisphere may serve to process imaginal data, in a categorical fashion. Kosslyn argues that many of the neuropsychological findings reviewed by Farah, as well as tachistoscopic studies he reports with a split-brain patient, may be understood as reflecting the left hemisphere's skill in generation of images that have a categorical nature.

In contrast, the right hemisphere's imagery skills are particularly important to spatial relations within a coordinate system [5]. Kosslyn points to the superiority of the right hemisphere in orienting mechanisms, and in visual search processes. He suggests that early in life these innate superiorities predispose the right hemisphere toward spatial skills. This predisposition leads to hemispheric specialization for spatial skills on the right side, and Kosslyn proposes that it will be only those imagery tasks which draw on spatial skills that will show strong right-lateralization.

Kosslyn's model provides some interesting ways of considering how each hemisphere's specialized cognitive and perceptual skills may suggest unique modes of handling imagery. Yet how are the hemisphere's emotional functions integrated with these differing kinds of imagery manipulations?

In an influential paper, Galin proposed that psychoanalytic concepts of primary and secondary mental processes describe the emotional characteristics of the right and left hemispheres respectively [28]. McLaughlin also theorized that primary process thinking can be characterized by an affective motivation of psychic energy to seek pleasure and avoid pain [29]. McLaughlin described primary processes as thinking dominated by emotion; utilizing a fluid and loose cognition; emphasizing "thing-representations based on visual imagery and the tonal, rhythmic components of the auditory sphere, along with concrete tactile, kinesthetic and olfactory images and qualities of affect, all combined in gestalt or engrammatic form" [29]. This is distinct from secondary process thinking, which is logical, involved with mediating between the inner self and the pressures of the outside world, and primarily embedded in the verbal lexical mode. McLaughlin postulates that secondary process thinking is focused on functions of categorizing and organizing. This kind of thinking has capabilities of inhibition and censorship in order "to enhance a kind of linear, logical scanning of memory traces." The ideas of McLaughlin and Galin [28, 29] on primary and secondary process thinking would be congruent with a model that relates the right hemisphere's role in emotion to primary process mentation oriented toward wish-fulfillment and hedonism. Imagery drawing on right hemisphere mechanisms might be particularly oriented to self-regulation by depression and elation. This kind of imagery draws on gestalt processes and is holistic in nature. It might be particularly important to wish-fulfillment. Perhaps this kind of imagery plays a prominent role in encoding affective events and enhancing current mood state.

In contrast, if the left hemisphere's role in emotion relates to secondary process mentation, this would involve a mediation between the needs of the self and the demands of the environment. We speculate that imagery drawing on the left hemisphere is likely to be influenced by the individual's position on the relaxation-anxiety dimension. This type of imagery may be used to fix attention on future events as well as to determine drive relevant behavior. Given the left hemisphere's focal attention, this imagery may be very detail oriented and may have a strong connection to the motor system.

RESEARCH ON COGNITION, EMOTION, AND HEMISPHERE ROLES IN IMAGERY

An EEG study by Robbins and McAdams supports the idea that specific types of imagery might be lateralized [30]. Robbins and McAdams measured interhemispheric alpha activity while subjects were covertly engaged in imaging familiar picture postcards [30]. Alpha suppression was used to determine which hemisphere was engaged during the activity. There were three conditions. One group of subjects was asked to image the material in terms of its shapes and colors, to form a mind picture. Another group was asked to imagine the scene in terms of its colors and shapes while subvocally describing it. The third group was instructed to subvocally describe the scene. They found that subjects who were asked to imagine the scene visual-spatially showed the greater alpha suppression over the right hemisphere. Alpha suppression over the left hemisphere was observed in the group engaged in imagining in linguistic terms. Ley proposes that if imagery is seen as involving visual-spatial skills, then right hemisphere processing is essential [31].

The connection between the right hemisphere and imagery has also found support in tachistoscopic studies. Stimuli presented to the left visual field are processed initially by the right hemisphere and those presented to the right visual field are processed by the left hemisphere. This paradigm was initially used to determine that verbal stimuli seem to be more quickly and accurately reported if presented to the right visual field or the left hemisphere. Most nonverbal stimuli are reported more quickly and accurately if presented to the left visual half field or right hemisphere [32]. Researchers have interpreted the results as indicating differential specialization for verbal and nonverbal/perceptual performance despite the fact that the mechanisms underlying visual field superiority are poorly understood [33].

Seamon and Gazzaniga used a variation of the visual field paradigm to study whether there were hemispheric differences in coding processes, rather than physical characteristics of the stimuli itself, that could be responsible for the observed laterality effect [34]. They recorded reaction times for a same/different discrimination task. A pair of words was presented in a central position so that it was given access to both hemispheres. The pair of words was followed by a picture presented either to the right or left visual half field. The picture was either a representation of one of the two prior presented words or was unrelated to them. The design included two conditions with six subjects in each. In one condition the subjects were told to subvocally rehearse the two words prior to the presentation of the picture. In the second condition the subjects were told to use the two referent words to construct a visual image. Faster same/different judgments were found when the subjects subvocally rehearsed the referents and the picture was presented to the right visual field. The judgments were faster from the left visual field, indicating right hemisphere involvement, when the subject was asked to construct visual images of the preceding words.

Critics of the Seamon and Gazzaniga study have pointed out that of the two attempts to replicate in the literature only one attempt was successful [34]. Also, some, like Ehrlichman and Barrett, conclude that although the Seamon and Gazzaniga results are consistent with the hypothesis that the right hemisphere is specialized for imagery, the results can also be interpreted as supporting a bilateral representation of imagery [22].

EMOTION AND IMAGERY

As we have seen, a neuropsychological model might hold that only certain kinds of imagery are localized in the right hemisphere. For example, as was previously noted, visuospatial tasks, such as those requiring mental rotation of an object, seem quite clearly to call upon right hemisphere skills. Other imagery, such as the visual imagery of the Seamon and Gazzaniga study, may also be facilitated by right hemisphere processes. Moreover, our theoretical model would predict that affective imagery would also be predominantly a right-lateralized function. What is the evidence that imagery and affect are connected?

Davidson and Schwartz designed a study to vary modes of imagery and affect [35]. They had subjects self-induce covert affective and non-affective states using either a verbal or visual strategy. They used EEG to measure the activation of the right or left hemisphere during the task. For the affective trials, subjects were told to "relive the feeling" of scenes from their past that they had previously rated as intense. The affective-verbal trial involved writing a letter to a friend describing the situation. Nonemotional trials involved imaging activities of a particular day. They found self-generation of affective imagery to have significantly greater right hemisphere involvement than self-generation of non-affective imagery. They also reported a nonsignificant difference between the verbal and the visual imagery modes, although the effect, as predicted, was in the direction of greater right hemisphere activity during imagery. There are several possible reasons for the failure of the modality condition. One might be that the visual imagery mode involved writing a letter to a friend which might activate a subvocal function more likely associated with the left hemisphere than with the right. Secondly, the scenes chosen for the affective imagery mode were designed to reproduce feelings of relaxation or anger. Both of these emotional states might be more characteristic of the tonic activation system which may restrict the range of unique information in working memory. It may be that visualizing this type of affective scene to describe it to a friend and reliving the emotions of the scene both utilize the left hemisphere to some extent, thereby diminishing the effect. Ley suggests that the failure may result from the inextricability of affect and image [31]. A majority of the subjects in the study spontaneously reported that it was difficult to perform the verbal-emotional trials which involved reliving a scene from memory without utilizing some kind of visual imagery.

Although these modes, the visual and verbal, were separated during the Robbins and McAdams same-different reaction time task with picture post-cards, the task was fairly nonemotional in nature. The intensely personal affective component of the Davidson and Schwartz [35] stimuli seems to have washed out the expected lateral differences between the verbal and the visual modes of processing. Ley suggests that much of the evidence for the laterality of emotion might even be an inadvertent by-product of the covariation of imagery and affect [31].

Tucker, Stenslie, Roth, and Shearer found that students undergoing a depressed mood induction showed impaired imagery and an auditory attentional bias [26]. The subjects' performance on an arithmetic task was unaffected by the mood induction. The selective impairment of imagery suggests that decrements in the vividness of imagery may accompany transient periods of depression. The auditory attentional bias indicated a relative shift in attention toward the right ear in the depression condition. The shift suggested a change in hemisphere activation during the depressed mood. The change could be a result of a decrease of right hemisphere activation during depression, or it could reflect greater activation of the left hemisphere. A second study was conducted to use EEG alpha desynchrony indices to determine whether the depressed mood resulted in a decrease in right hemisphere activation. The data indicated that, when compared to the euphoria condition, the depression condition resulted in less activation of the left frontal lobe and greater activation of the right frontal lobe. Tucker et al., theorized that the frontal activity in the right hemisphere may represent some sort of inhibitory function that serves to suppress the information processing operations of the right hemisphere during depressive emotion [26]. Perhaps the most important feature of these results is the association that is indicated between hemispheric activation, performance effects, vividness of imagery, and a transient affective state in individuals who are clearly neurologically intact.

Another line of evidence that has been used to support the connection between imagery and affect has involved studying conjugate lateral eye movements (LEMS). The assumption underlying this type of research is based on the contralateral innervation of the human body. Therefore, eye movements to the left are presumed to reflect an activation of the right hemisphere and vice versa. Tucker, Roth, Arenson, and Buckingham found significantly greater left LEMS to emotional questions than to nonemotional questions [36]. They also found an increase of the left LEMS under a stress condition. They interpreted this finding as an increased likelihood of right hemisphere activation with emotional arousal. It was an assumption of this study that instructions to "visualize your father's face" would elicit both affect and imagery.

Other researchers have used a conjugate lateral eye movement paradigm to further support the association between imagery and the right hemisphere. Here the results have been more ambiguous. For example, some research has attempted to classify people as either "left lookers" or "right lookers" based on their immediate eye movement after being given a question to ponder. Left lookers have been found to use more imagery and rate their imagery as more clear than subjects who looked to the right [37]. However, other published studies have failed to support this association [38]. Moreover, there has been substantial criticism of the basic assumptions underlying the lateral eye movement research. A review of Ehrlichman and Weinberger raised doubts about whether eye movements necessarily reflect asymmetrical hemisphere involvement [39].

Unlike the lateral eye movement research, EEG studies seem to provide more direct evidence of hemispheric activation. Ratio or difference scores are commonly used as indices of left and right hemisphere activation. Typically the results have supported the proposed functions ascribed to the two hemispheres with relatively more left hemisphere activation (or less right hemisphere activation) noted during verbal tasks. Likewise, increased right hemisphere activation has been noted during visuospatial tasks [40].

In a review of the EEG studies on the laterality of imagery, Ehrlichman and Barrett [22] point out that few have monitored EEG asymmetry during visual imagery in the absence of visual stimuli. Furthermore, in a number of studies subjects were not required to make any overt response. The lack of an imagery manipulation check makes it impossible to ascertain the extent of imagery occurring or to adequately determine that the imagery questions were eliciting more imagery than the baseline condition. In addition, Ehrlichman and Weiner [41] found a negative correlation between their subjects' verbal and imagery ratings, suggesting that mental tasks that are primarily verbal are relatively free of imagery and mental tasks heavily saturated with imagery are relatively free of verbal thinking. Thus, changes in either verbal or imaginal task content could result in the observed differences in EEG asymmetry.

Ehrlichman and Weiner used multiple regression analysis to determine whether the observed EEG asymmetry could result because engaging imaginal processes tends to inhibit or disengage verbal functions [41]. They found that imagery contributed little to the explained variance of the EEG index. It was suggested that the moderate correlation found between the EEG asymmetry and imagery ratings was a result of a decrease in verbal thinking during imagery, and not evidence for the laterality of imagery.

Several recent studies have attempted to separate the independent contributions of verbal thought and imagery processes from EEG asymmetry. One study had subjects recall sentences that they had memorized [42]. The sentences were either high or low in imagery. EEG readings were made during the recall process. The researchers found no differences in alpha asymmetry in the two types of sentences. Other results reported by Ehrlichman and Barrett also reported the difference in the balance of hemispheric activation between high and low imagery questions using EEG asymmetry as an index [22].

DISCUSSION

For many readers, the introduction of more complex neuropsychological concepts into the imagery, emotion, and laterality literature will seem to have muddied the waters. However, it may be possible to clarify some of the issues by applying neuropsychological concepts of emotion, laterality, and imagery to practical situations where imagery is used therapeutically.

The evidence is strong that much of emotional communication is right lateralized [9]. We suggest it is even more important to consider the nature of the neurophysiological and neurochemical mechanisms which the brain uses to self-regulate its level of activity [17]. Each control system seems to modulate neural activity in a qualitative fashion. Two of the primary systems that work to augment brain function are the noradrenergic and dopaminergic pathways. The dopaminergic pathway seems to be integral to the activation or motor readiness system. An increase of dopamine serves to restrict range of behavior and increase repetition of a limited set of behaviors. In contrast, the noradrenergic pathway is linked to the arousal system. The arousal system operates by allowing the brain to become saturated with novel events or stimuli. It has been linked to a unique and expansive perception of the environment. There is evidence that the noradrenergic pathways are right-lateralized [43].

Can these lateralized forms of attention control be related to differing hemispheric contributions to imagery? Might it be the case that in its specialization for output functions and production skills the left hemisphere's contribution to categorical image generation [5] may draw on the constancy and focused attention provided by the redundancy bias of the activation system? As it integrates diverse forms of information into a coherent apprehension of the spatial location of elements in the visual array, does the right hemisphere draw on the holistic attentional modes provided by the perceptual orienting system?

IMAGERY, AFFECT AND PERFORMANCE

Imagery techniques are employed in a variety of therapeutic and educational settings. Imagery is a major component in systematic desensitization. In this technique, the phobic individual imagines closer and closer approximations of the phobic object and event. During the imagining process, the subject is taught to remain relaxed while simultaneously experiencing a realistic vivid image of the feared object. Although using imagery is not as effective as actual controlled exposure to the feared object, using imagery may be an effective way to reduce or eliminate phobias. As a result of the moderate correlations often reported between self-reported imagery and hypnotic susceptibility [44] it has been theorized that *in vivo* emotive imagery has a strong potential for enabling people to deal with inescapable, discomforting situations. Disabling, discomforting situations would include the experience of turbulence while being airborne, a trip to the dentist, and the process of giving birth, to name a few examples.

In a preliminary study of the effects of *in vivo* emotive imagery on the experience of dental discomfort, twenty-seven female subjects were exposed to three treatments in a counter-balanced order. The three treatment groups consisted of a relaxation imagery group, a neutral imagery group, and a blank tape control group. Positive differences in self-reported discomfort were reported between relaxation imagery and both of the two control conditions [45]. While the study could have been methodologically stronger with a between-subjects design, multiple physiologic indices, and an *a priori* check of the effectiveness of the materials, this finding does support previous work by Horan and Farr which suggests that imagery is an effective way of reducing noxious stimulation and dealing with inescapable discomfort.

Imagery has also been used therapeutically with depression. Depression is commonly accompanied by a diminished sense of self-worth. The depressed mood can occur when external sources of esteem-boosting input are removed or when, as is often the case, an individual reads negative meanings into neutral comments or constructive criticism. Imagery is one technique used to reduce the negative impact of intrusive, self-deprecatory thoughts by developing a conscious, systematic habit of dismissing the thoughts quickly and replacing them with positive thoughts and mental images [46].

Imagery has also been developed as a tool to facilitate performances in many arenas including the work environment and the athletic field. Sports psychologists such as Porter and Foster [3] have taught athletes to visualize their success prior to its actual occurrence. A runner who would like to break forty minutes in a 10 km road race is helped to image the course and his or her reactions at different points in the race. Each athlete chooses certain words and phrases that bring to mind the type of performance that is desired. For example, a gymnast might visualize herself on the uneven bars and think, "I am strong and powerful. I feel calm and solid." For another gymnast a light and graceful image might be more appropriate [3]. Interviews with successful athletes show that many intuitively visualize themselves as winners. Similar techniques can be applied to any high pressure performance situation, including public speaking and business presentations.

It has been suggested that imagery is a prominent means of structuring our universe [47]. Imagery may provide us with a world view, a location in time and space. Some propose imagery as the modality through which we attach meaning to behavior and relate emotional reactions to events [48]. It may be that successful performers in any domain have learned to attach positive and useful emotional reactions to particular situations. Teaching people to use imaginal modes may help engender optimal emotional reactions and thereby facilitate performance.

Ley relates the process of psychotherapy to the right hemisphere [31]. He begins with a "working assumption" that most therapeutic strategies including psychoanalytic, gestalt, and behavioral, are attempts to communicate with the non-dominant or right hemisphere. A strategy attempting to gain access to a right hemispheric repository of experience could be based on developmental reasoning. Evidence has shown that the right hemisphere develops more rapidly than the left hemisphere during the first year [49, 50]. It is at that point that the left hemispheric differentiation of language begins in earnest [51]. These maturational differences may result in early childhood experiences being stored in the right hemisphere. Moreover, the predominant experience of the young child's life is emotional in tone. It consists of sounds, pictures, feelings, and images, all of which may be primarily processed by the right hemisphere in the early years of life [52]. Using verbal, logical, and sequential strategies in therapy might only engage the left hemisphere. Techniques such as the free association characteristic of psychoanalysis may have developed to engage the right hemisphere and facilitate recall of emotional experiences stored primarily through its unconscious, imaginal representation.

Ley theorizes that differences in therapeutic strategies are all efforts to increase right hemisphere mentation and facilitate the mode of right hemisphere experience [31]. He partitions the right hemisphere environment of therapy into three primary features: the therapeutic setting, the therapeutic words, and the therapeutic task. Psychoanalysis provides a classic example of a therapeutic setting designed to facilitate right hemisphere thought and experience. The patient is given little tactile or verbal stimulation with eyes closed or while staring at a blank ceiling. This is essentially akin to sensory deprivation experiences which have been shown to facilitate imagic or hallucinatory experiences. Other therapeutic settings which are experiential or meditative, such as relaxation training, would also facilitate intuitive, expansive, and holistic thought, characteristic of the right hemisphere.

Another aspect of the therapeutic setting may contribute to qualitative differences in thought processes. Specifically, research has indicated that the patient's posture significantly changes the nature and flow of the thought process. Some have even gone so far as to conclude that one of Freud's greatest contributions to psychology was his recognition of the importance of the couch [53]. Ley theorizes that the prone position may activate right hemisphere material, including imagic and emotional experiences [31].

Although words and the left hemisphere are typically linked, Ley suggests that the therapeutic discourse is quite distinct from ordinary, every-day language patterns. Talk therapies tend to use more emotional and image-laden expressions than is common in normal speech. Moreover, the words are often presented in a creative nonlinear fashion which allows expression of seemingly unrelated thoughts and emotions. Evidence indicates a relation between words that are high in emotion or imagery and the right hemisphere [54]. Many therapists, including Freud and Jung, ask the patient to think of images to circumvent verbal, or left hemisphere, resistance to threatening material. There is also thought to be a link between free association, pictorial images and primary process thinking. Previously we related primary process thinking, which is oriented toward hedonism and gratification, to right hemisphere, emotional functions.

The association between hemispheric activation, affect, imagery, and performance may give some insight into the therapeutic process. Prochaska postulates catharsis as one of five change processes in therapy [55]. Emotional imagery may facilitate right hemisphere activation which in turn qualitatively alters cognition and affect. In some cases this increased activation may trigger a spontaneous expression of emotion or catharsis which may be therapeutically beneficial. The engagement of the right hemisphere can also be theoretically linked to primary process thinking which would be congruent with the clinical observations of regressive behavior that often accompanies a cathartic emotional release.

Further, Tucker and Williamson propose that anxiety and obsessive, repetitive behavior may result from the redundancy bias of the left hemisphere [17]. Systematic desensitization is one commonly employed method to reduce phobic anxiety. The technique involves two types of imagery. The first is relaxation imagery. After the subject obtains a relaxed state he or she then images the feared stimuli in closer and closer approximations. Since the repeated imaging is unpairing the stimuli (e.g., snakes) with the usual elicited response (anxiety, fear, running away) this may be an example of the bilateral function of imagery. In this case the imagery may be engaging the motor system to create new responses to a learned situation.

Imagery has also been used to reduce depression [56]. Two types of imagery have been successful in alleviating depressed affect. For some individuals angry or aggressive imagery is beneficial. Schultz links the effectiveness of aggressive imagery to Freud's conceptualization of depression as hostility directed inward. For these individuals, the imagery facilitates a cathartic release of suppressed affect which leads to a reduction in conflict and a corresponding decrease in depression. For a second group, the depression was alleviated by engaging the subjects in socially gratifying imagery. For these individuals, the depressed mood seemed to be linked to a dependency state where they suffered from a lack of self-esteem. The socially gratifying imagery might function to reframe the world, distract the individual from the depressed state, or provide a partial fulfillment of a basic, unfulfilled need that underlies the emotional state.

In conclusion, psychologically healthy individuals may engage in a variety of types of imagery for a variety of different functions. Imagery may be one way to enhance a particular mood, such as elation, anger, or depression. It may provide an individual with a way to access childhood memories that are relatively inaccessible to verbal modes of thought. Imagery can be used to inhibit a particular mood, to alleviate depression, or to maintain a neutral state despite experiencing unpleasant or upsetting events. Imagery can facilitate sexual arousal and can be used to increase the feeling of emotional closeness to individuals with whom one is not currently interacting. Imagery may be effective in helping people deal with pain and unescapable discomfort. It is a useful therapeutic device.

Further research in neuropsychology promises to clarify specific brain mechanisms that generate and manipulate imagery, and to clarify the relation of these mechanisms to emotional processes. This research holds the promise of new insight into the potential for more effective self-control through imagination.

REFERENCES

1. C. A. Garfield, *Peak Performance: Mental Training Techniques of the World's Greatest Athletes*, Warner Books, Los Angeles, 1984.
2. E. Hall and C. Hardy, Using the Right Brain in Sports, *New Path to Sport Learning*, (transcript of a symposium), Coaching Association of Canada, Ottawa, Canada, 1982.
3. K. Porter and J. Foster, *The Mental Athlete: Inner Training for Peak Performance*, Wm. C. Brown, Publishers, 1986.
4. M. J. Farah, The Neurological Basis of Mental Imagery: A Componential Analysis, *Cognition, 18*, pp. 245-269, 1984.
5. S. M. Kosslyn, Seeing and Imagery in the Cerebral Hemispheres: A Computational Approach, *Psychological Review, 94*, pp. 148-175, 1987.
6. D. M. Bear, Hemispheric Specialization and the Neurology of Emotion, *Neurological Review, 40*, pp. 195-202, 1983.

7. E. K. Silberman and H. Weingartner, Hemispheric Lateralization of Functions Related to Emotion, *Brain and Cognition, 5*, pp. 322–353, 1986.
8. D. M. Tucker, Lateral Brain Function, Emotion, and Conceptualization, *Psychological Bulletin, 89*, pp. 19–46, 1981.
9. D. M. Tucker and S. L. Frederick, Emotion and Brain Lateralization (Chapter 2), in *Handbook of Psychophysiology: Emotion and Social Behavior*, H. Wagner and T. Manstead (eds.), John Wiley, New York, in press.
10. H. A. Sackeim, M. S. Greenberg, A. L. Weiman, R. C. Gur, J. P. Hungerbuhler, and M. Geschwind, Hemispheric Asymmetry in the Expression of Positive and Negative Emotions: Neurologic Evidence, *Archives of Neurology, 39*, pp. 210–218, 1982.
11. G. Gainotti, Studies on the Functional Organization of the Minor Hemisphere, *International Journal of Mental Health, 1*:3, pp. 78–82, 1972.
12. H. Terzian, Behavioral and EEG Effects of Interacarotid Sodium Amytal Injection, *Acta Neurochirgia, 12*, pp. 230–239, 1964.
13. J. C. Borod, E. Koff, and R. Buck, The Neuropsychology of Facial Expression: Data from Normal and Brain-damaged Adults, in *Nonverbal Communication in the Clinical Context*, R. Blanck, R. Buck, and R. Rosen (eds.), 1986.
14. M. A. Safer, Sex and Hemisphere Differences in Access to Codes for Processing Emotional Expressions and Faces, *Journal of Experimental Psychology: General, 110*, pp. 86–100, 1981.
15. W. G. Dopson, B. E. Beckwith, D. M. Tucker, and P. C. Bullard-Bates, Asymmetry of Facial Expression in Spontaneous Emotion, *Cortex, 20*, pp. 243–251, 1985.
16. K. H. Pribram and D. McGuiness, Arousal, Activation, and Effort in the Control of Attention, *Psychological Review, 82*:2, pp. 116–149, 1975.
17. D. M. Tucker and P. A. Williamson, Asymmetric Neural Control Systems in Human Self-regulation, *Psychological Review, 91*, pp. 185–215, 1984.
18. D. M. Tucker, K. Vannatta, and J. Rothlind, Arousal and Activation Systems and the Adaptive Control of Cognitive Priming, in press.
19. A. M. Isen, Toward Understanding the Role of Affect in Cognition, in *Handbook of Social Cognition*, Vol. 3, R. S. Wyer, Jr., and T. K. Srull (eds.), Lawrence Erlbaum, Hillsdale, New Jersey, 1984.
20. J. A. Easterbrook, The Effect of Emotion on Cue Utilization and the Organization of Behavior, *Psychological Review, 66*, pp. 183–201, 1959.
21. K. W. Spence, A Theory of Emotionally Based Drive (D) and Its Relation to Performance in Simple Learning Situations, *American Psychologist, 13*, pp. 131–141, 1958.
22. H. Ehrlichman and J. Barrett, Right Hemisphere Specialization for Mental Imagery: A Review of the Evidence, *Brain and Cognition, 2*, pp. 55–76, 1983.
23. J. Levy, Cerebral Asymmetry and the Psychology of Man, in *The Brain and Psychology*, M. Wittrock (ed.), Academic Press, New York, 1980.
24. S. P. Springer and G. Deutsch, *Left Brain, Right Brain*, Freeman, San Francisco, 1981.

25. J. C. Bradshaw and N. C. Nettleton, The Nature of Hemispheric Specialization in Man, *Behavioral and Brain Science, 4*, pp. 51-63, 1981.
26. D. M. Tucker, C. E. Stenslie, R. S. Roth and S. L. Shearer, Right Frontal Lobe Activation and Right Hemisphere Performance, *Archives of General Psychiatry, 38*, pp. 169-174, 1981.
27. E. Bisiach, E. Capitani, H. Luzzo and D. Perani, Brain and Conscious Representation of Outside Reality, *Neuropsycholgia, 19*, pp. 543-551, 1981.
28. D. Galin, Implications for Psychiatry for Left and Right Cerebral Specialization, *Archives of General Psychiatry, 31*, pp. 572-583, 1974.
29. J. T. McLaughlin, Primary and Secondary Process in the Context of Cerebral Hemispheric Specialization. Paper Presented at New Orleans Psychological Society, February, 1977.
30. K. I. Robbins and D. W. McAdams, Interhemispheric Alpha Asymmetry and Imagery Mode, *Brain and Language, 1*, pp. 189-193, 1974.
31. R. G. Ley, Cerebral Asymmetries, Emotional Experience, and Imagery: Implications for Psychotherapy, in *The Potential of Fantasy and Imagination*, A. A. Sheikh and L. T. Shaffer (eds.), Random House, New York, 1979.
32. D. Kimura, Dual Functional Asymmetry of the Brain in Visual Perception, *Neuropsychologia, 4*, pp. 275-285, 1966.
33. M. P. Bryden, *Laterality: Functional Asymmetry in the Intact Brain*, Academic Press, New York, 1982.
34. Seamon and Gazzangia, Coding Strategies and Cerebral Laboratory Effects, *Cognitive Psychology, 5*, pp. 249-256, 1973.
35. Davidson and G. Schwartz, Patterns of Cerebral Lateralization during Cardiac Biofeedback versus the Self-regulation of Emotion: Sex Differences, *Psychophysiology, 13*, pp. 62-74, 1976.
36. D. M. Tucker, R. S. Roth, B. A. Arneson and V. Buckingham, Right Hemisphere Activation during Stress, *Neuropsychologia, 15*, 697-700, 1977.
37. P. Bakan, Hypnotizability, Laterality of Eye Movement and Functional Brain Asymmetry, *Perceptual and Motor Skills, 28*, pp. 927-932, 1969.
38. M. Hiscock, Eye Movement Asymmetry and Hemispheric Function: An Examination of Individual Differences, *Journal of Psychology, 97*, pp. 49-52, 1977.
39. H. Ehrlichman and A. Weinberger, Lateral Eye Movements and Hemispheric Asymmetry: A Critical Review, *Psychological Bulletin, 85*, pp. 1080-1101, 1978.
40. R. J. Davidson and H. Ehrlichman, Lateralized Cognitive Processes and the Electroencephalogram, *Science, 207*, pp. 1005-1007, 1980.
41. H. Ehrlichman and M. S. Weiner, EEG Asymmetry during Covert Mental Activity, *Psychophysiology, 17*, pp. 228-235, 1980.
42. W. O. Haynes, Task Effect and EEG Alpha Asymmetry: An Analysis of Linguistic Processing in Two Response Modes, *Cortex, 16*, pp. 95-102, 1980.
43. R. G. Robinson, Differential Behavioral and Biochemical Effects of Right and Left Hemispheric Cerebral Infarction in the Rat, *Science, 205*, pp. 707-710, 1979.

44. P. W. Sheehan, Hypnosis and the Process of Imagination, in *Hypnosis: Developments in Research and New Perspectives* (2nd ed.), E. Fromm and R. E. Shorr (eds.), Aline, Chicago, 1979.
45. J. J. Horan, F. C. Laying and C. H. Purcell, Preliminary Study of Effects of "in vivo" Emotive Imagery in Dental Discomfort, *Reports, 32*, p. 1328, 1976.
46. F. F. Flach, *The Secret Strength of Depression*, Bantam Books, New York, 1986.
47. E. Hall, *Beyond Culture*, Anchor, Garden City, New York, 1977.
48. R. Gordon, A Very Private World, in *The Function and Nature of Mental Imagery*, P. W. Sheehan (ed.), Academic Books, New York, 1972.
49. D. M. Tucker, Neural Control of Emotional Communication, in *Nonverbal Communication in the Clinical Context*, P. Blanck, R. Buck and R. Rosenthal (eds.), Cambridge University Press, Cambridge, England, 1986.
50. C. Whittaker, The Learning Tree, in *The Naked Therapist*, S. B. Knoop (ed.), Edits, San Diego, 1976.
51. D. Giannitrapani, Developing Concepts of Lateralization of Cerebral Functions, *Cortex, 3*, pp. 353–370, 1967.
52. P. Fedio, Behavioral Characteristics of Patients with Temporal Lobe Epilepsy, *Psychiatric Clinics of North America, 9*, pp. 267–281, 1986.
53. G. S. Klein, *Psychoanalytic Theory: An Exploration of Essentials*, International Universities Press, New York, 1976.
54. J. H. Day, Right Hemisphere Language Processing in Normal Right Handers, *Journal of Experimental Psychology: Human Perception and Performance, 3*, pp. 518–528, 1977.
55. J. Prochaska, Systems of Psychotherapy: A Transtheoretical Analysis, The Dorsey Press, Chicago, Illinois, 1984.

CHAPTER 9
Imaging, Image-Monitoring, and Health

ROBERT G. KUNZENDORF AND ANEES A. SHEIKH

'Good physical health' belongs not to the person who is temporarily free from disease, but to the person who is psychophysiologically equipped to fight off disease [1]. As the current chapter will show, part of the psychophysiological equipment for sustaining good physical health is the mental image and its neural underpinnings.

The evidence connecting vivid mental imagery with good physical health raises questions, however, about the relationship between fantasy and mental health. This evidence indicates that, at one extreme, immune responsiveness and good physical health tend to be experienced not only by people who generate vivid images and who know *that they are generating images*, but also by people who generate hallucinatory images. At the other extreme, immune deficiency and poor physical health tend to be experienced by people with depressive affect and with deficient fantasy.

In order to clarify the relationship between vivid imagery and good health, both physical and mental, the current chapter examines the effect of 'image-monitoring' (knowing *that one is fantasizing*) on imagery and health. This examination will show that many unipolar depressives with poor physical health are people who try not to fantasize, because they cannot escape the knowledge *that distressing fantasies come from 'within themselves,'* and *that pleasant fantasies are 'only imaginary.'* In contrast, many hallucinators are bipolar depressives who, temporarily, stop monitoring the fact *that they are imaging* and who, thereby, resume their fantasies and restore their health.

IMAGING, HALLUCINATING, AND GOOD HEALTH

The vivid image and the vivid hallucination are nearly identical sensations yet qualitatively different cognitions, both of which are associated with immune responsiveness and good physical health. This association is explained by the fact that vivid imagers and hallucinators can centrally innervate the neural locations underlying sensations and, consequently, can activate any neuroimmune functions that are regulated in the same locations or innervated in the same manner [2, 3].

Qualitative Difference between Imaging and Hallucinating

Given that vivid images and hallucinations are similar sensations with similar psychosomatic effects, many psychologists associate not only hallucinations, but also images, with the denial of reality and the suppression of reality-testing [4-8]. However, Kunzendorf has shown that there is a qualitative difference between mentally imaged sensations and reality-obscuring hallucinations [9, 10]. Specifically, Kunzendorf has found that more vividly imaged sensations are more quickly discriminated from perceptual sensations, whereas more vividly hallucinated sensations are less quickly discriminated from perceptual sensations [9]. According to Kunzendorf's interpretation of this finding, the greater amount of 'effort' that it takes to image vividly is 'monitored' by the nonhallucinating brain and is used to distinguish vividly imaged sensations from similar perceptual sensations [10].

Thus, contrary to the assumptions of many psychologists [e.g., 11-17], an image of perceptual vividness is neither necessary nor sufficient for an hallucination to occur. Indeed, Hilgard has described the "diaphanous" hypnotic hallucination which, like a "ghost or wraith," "still has perceptual reality" [18, p. 14]. Moreover, Spanos and Radtke have reviewed evidence showing that the images of unhypnotized persons are as vivid as the hallucinations of hypnotized persons [19]. Similarly, Starker has reviewed evidence showing that the images of nonhallucinators are as vivid as, or more vivid than, the images of schizophrenic hallucinators [20]. In hypnosis and schizophrenia, imaged sensations become hallucinated sensations regardless of their vividness, only because the *self-conscious* process of *image-monitoring* is attenuated.

Imaging, Hallucinating, and Good Physical Health

Even though imaging and hallucinating do not reflect the same level of 'image monitoring,' vivid imaging and vivid hallucinating do innervate the same sensations at the same neural locations. Accordingly, vivid imagers and hallucinators, unlike imageless thinkers, can imaginally control any autonomic processes that are connected with the locations of imaged sensations or with the processes of imaging. Specific theories as to the nature of this neural connection—associative theories, structural theories, and disregulatory theories—have been reviewed by Sheikh and Kunzendorf [2]. Furthermore, extensive evidence that vivid imagers have voluntary control of autonomic defenses against disease has been reviewed by Sheikh and Kunzendorf [2], and extensive evidence that imageless thinkers (alexithymics) have poor defenses and poor health has been reviewed by Kruck and Sheikh [21]. The present review focuses on evidence that vivid imagers *and hallucinators*, when attacked by a debilitating disease, can imaginally anticipate their recovery and can thereby control their neuroimmune defenses.

Recent findings indicate that normal imagers, especially vivid imagers, do have imaginal control of neuroimmune defenses against cancer. Simonton, Matthews-Simonton, and Creighton found that, when terminal cancer patients imaged their immune systems fighting off cancer, their likelihood of recovery increased [22]. Achterberg, Lawlis, Simonton, and Matthews-Simonton found that terminal cancer patients with more vivid images of the immune system's fight against cancer were more likely to recover [23]. Moreover, Hall found that, when people without cancer imaged their immune systems fighting off potential disease, people with vivid imagery—and only those with vivid imagery—actually increased the number of cancer-fighting lymphocytes in their blood streams [24].

At the same time, recent findings indicate that schizophrenic hallucinators, much like vivid imagers, have a healthy resistance to cancer. Rassidakis, Kelepouris, Goulis, and Karaiossefidis found that the proportion of schizophrenics who die from malignant tumors is one third of the proportion for normal people and one third of the proportion for other psychotics [25]. More recently, Modrzewska and Book confirmed that the proportion of deaths which are cancer-related is significantly less for schizophrenics than for normal people [26]. Even Baldwin's recent review of earlier research, showing a low cancer rate in some studies of schizophrenic health and a normal cancer rate in other studies, is consistent with the thesis that schizophrenic hallucinations help the immune system fight off cancer [27]. As Cohen, Baker, Cohen, Fromm-Reichmann, and Weigert note [28], "it is particularly difficult to make a differentiation between schizophrenia and manic-depressive psychosis," and as research yet to be reviewed shows, depression is associated with a high cancer rate. Thus, those early studies showing that schizophrenics have a normal cancer rate, rather than a low rate, may have failed to tease apart the schizophrenic cancer rate and the depressive cancer rate.

Imaging, Hallucinating, and Immune Sensitivity

Good physical health, such as that experienced by vivid imagers and hallucinators, requires an immune system that is sensitive to "invasion by foreign agents and germs" [29, p. 13] and responsive to "internal threats such as neoplastic cells" [30, p. 7]. Recent research indicates that imaging is associated with immune sensitivity and responsiveness, whereas hallucinating is associated not only with immune sensitivity but also with allergic responding or "ultra-sensitive reaction to invasion . . . [by] things which are harmless" [29, pp. 14-15].

Friedman, Cohen, and Iker have shown that immune sensitivity to harmful antigens is associated with schizophrenic tendencies like hallucinating [31]. They injected antigenic stimuli (cholera vaccines) into schizophrenic, normal, and depressed subjects. Both one week and two weeks following the injection, schizophrenic subjects had significantly higher antibody levels than normal subjects, and normal subjects had marginally higher antibody levels than depressed subjects. Although earlier researchers did not find that antigenic stimulation elevates antibody levels in schizophrenics [32, 33], they also, unlike Friedman *et al.*, did not tease apart the elevating effects of schizophrenia and the potentially confounded effects of depression.

Three groups of researchers have found that immune hypersensitivity to "harmless" allergens is also associated with schizophrenic tendencies like hallucinating. One group—Kunzendorf and Butler [34]—administered the MMPI-168 [35] to 181 college students and confirmed that the simple correlation between schizophrenic tendencies ([36], scale *Sc*) and depressive tendencies [36, scale *D*] is high ($r = .55$). In addition, Kunzendorf and Butler found that, controlling for depression, the partial correlation between schizophrenia and allergy ([37], scale 30) is high ($r = .35$), whereas the partial correlation between schizophrenia and poor physical health [37, scale 19] is insignificant ($r = -.04$). (Controlling for schizophrenia, the partial correlation between depression and allergy is insignificant, $r = -.05$, whereas the partial correlation between depression and poor physical health is high, $r = .49$.) In accord with these findings, research by a second group of behavioral scientists—Strahilevitz and Davis [38], Strahilevitz, Fleischman, Fischer, Harris, and Narasimhachari [39], and Torrey, Peterson, Brannon, Carpenter, Post, and Van Kammen [40]—showed that schizophrenics have elevated immunoglobulin levels, which are indicative of allergy [41]. The third group—DeLisi, Weinberger, Potkin, Neckers, Shiling, and Wyatt [42], and Ferguson, Schmidtke, and Simmons [43]—reported that these elevated levels of immunoglobulin are reduced by medication which suppresses schizophrenic hallucinations.

Ikemi and Nakagawa showed that not only real allergens, but also hallucinated allergens, can induce allergic reactions in hypersensitive subjects [44]. All of Ikemi and Nakagawa's subjects experienced allergic reactions (itching, redness, swelling, and/or blistering) when they knowingly touched a Japanese plant similar to poison ivy. In addition, all of the subjects experienced allergic reactions when they touched a nonallergenic plant that they hallucinated to be the 'poisonous' plant.

Table 1. Ranges and Correlations

	Ranges		Simple correlations				
	Poss.	Actual	*Sc*	*Ma*	*D*	Al'gy	PPH
Imaging scale							
Vividness	1 -- 5	1.7 -- 5	-.21*	-.04	-.16*	-.21*	-.11
MMPI-168 scales							
Sc	0 -- 28	0 -- 19		.67*	.53*	.77*	.61*
Ma	0 -- 23	5 -- 18			.27*	.66*	.39*
D	0 -- 41	3 -- 27				.56*	.68*
Allergy	0 -- 25	0 -- 19					.71*
PPH	0 -- 15	0 -- 12					

*$p < .05$.

Finally, in a previously unpublished study comparing hallucinations and images, Butler, Kunzendorf, and Sheikh [45] found that allergic reactions are associated with hallucinatory mental states like schizophrenia and mania, but not with normal imaging abilities. These researchers replicated and extended Kunzendorf and Butler's study [34], by administering the Vividness of Visual Imagery Questionnaire [46] and the Vividness of Auditory Imagery Questionnaire [47], as well as the MMPI-168 [35], to 145 college students. Five MMPI scales–Allergy, Poor Physical Health, Schizophrenia (*Sc*), Depression (*D*), and Hypomania (*Ma*)–were scored. The mean of the visual imagery scores and the auditory imagery scores defined a sixth scale–an Imagery Vividness scale with scores ranging from 5 ("as vivid as normal perception") to 1 ("no image at all"). The possible ranges, actual ranges, and simple correlations for these six scales are summarized in Table 1. The partial correlations are summarized in Table 2.

As Table 1 indicates, Butler, Kunzendorf, and Sheikh found, as previous researchers have found, that people with schizophrenic tendencies have less vivid imagery and that people with depressive tendencies have less vivid imagery. Starker has reviewed the past evidence showing that images of schizophrenic hallucinators tend to be less vivid than images of normal persons [20]. In addition, Starker and Singer [48–49], Tucker, Stenslie, Roth, and Shearer [50], and Gold, Jarvinen, and Teague [51] have obtained evidence showing that images of depressed persons tend to be less vivid than images of normal persons. Reasons why the imagery of both schizophrenics and depressives should be less vivid than that of normals will be considered later in this chapter.

Table 2. Partial Correlations (controlling for the four remaining scales)

	Allergy	Poor Physical Health
Imaging scale		
Vividness	-.16*	.12
MMPI-168 scales		
Sc	.33*	.11
Ma	.38*	-.13
D	.07	.46*

*$p < .05$.

As Table 2 indicates, poor physical health was not correlated with schizophrenic tendencies, with manic tendencies, or with vivid images, but was positively correlated with depression. Accordingly, the immune system of the vivid imager, like that of the schizophrenic or manic hallucinator, appears to be sensitive to intrusion by disease. At the same time, the allergy scale was negatively correlated with vivid imagery, was not correlated with depression, and was positively correlated with schizophrenic tendencies and with manic tendencies. Apparently, the immune system of the schizophrenic or manic person fails to differentiate between diseaseful substances and allergenic substances, just as the mind of the schizophrenic or manic hallucinator fails to monitor the difference between perceived sensations and imaged sensations.

DEPRESSION AND POOR HEALTH

As suggested in the above discussion and documented in the following discussion, depression is associated with deficient imagery, with immune deficiency, and with poor physical health. According to the current thesis, the depressive fails to centrally innervate the sensory neurons that are subjectively experienced as images and, as a consequence, fails to centrally regulate the immune functions that are neurally connected with imaging.

Depression, Image-Monitoring, and Deficient Imagery

Whereas vivid imagers tend to generate both anticipatory images [52-54] and satisfying fantasies [55, 56], depressed people tend to generate either escapist images [55] or distressing fantasies [57-60]. Moreover, depressed people cannot avoid the disheartening self-awareness *that positive fantasies of escape are 'only imaginary'* and *that negative images of distress come from 'within themselves,'* so long as they 'monitor' the central origins of their images. However, they can self-consciously try not to fantasize very often or very vividly. Both clinical evidence and experimental research suggest that this is what most depressed people do.

Exemplary cases of depressed people who desire not to image negative distress and not to fantasize positive escape have recently been reported by clinical psychologists. For example, the depressed person who desires not to generate distressing imagery has been described by Horowitz:

> John, a veteran of the Vietnamese war, complained of recurrent frightening and unbidden images of a face contorted by pain. The images were much more intense than his ordinary thought images, but he knew they were not real even during the image experience. . . . The face was that of a Vietnamese woman he had killed during a night patrol. . . . While watching the woman writhe in pain, and her efforts to escape, he felt sexually aroused (a feeling reported occasionally by other combatants such as fighter pilots) [15, pp. 287–288].
>
> John had been forced by circumstances to be involved in an act that he considered horrible. But he and his buddies had committed such acts as killing men and women before, they had rationalized more stressful episodes with such concepts as "they're all gooks," "it's them or us," "the kids and women'll shoot you too". . . . But to be aroused sexually by looking at a woman he had shot was especially horrible to him and he felt intense guilt [15, p. 288].

In Horowitz's clinical study of this distressing imagery, the depressed veteran desires not to image, because he is self-conscious that the sexual component of his distressing memory image comes from 'within' himself. Similarly, in Becker's clinical study of escapist imagery, the depressed person tries not to "imagine . . . a better world than the one that is given him by nature, [because] with him the mechanisms of illusion are known and destroyed by self-consciousness" [61, p. 188].

In accord with these clinical case studies, research studies indicate that depressed people are less imaginative—and more realistic—than normal people. As noted earlier in this chapter, four research studies [48-51] have found that depressed people image less vividly and less frequently than normal people. In addition, the following four studies [62-65] have found that depressed people are more 'in touch with reality' than normal people are. Nelson and Craighead [62] found that depressed students accurately recall the amount of punishment in a laboratory task, whereas normal students underestimate the frequency of punishment. Lewinsohn, Mischel, Chaplin, and Barton found that depressed subjects' self-ratings of social competence are consistent with observers' ratings, whereas normal subjects' self-ratings are higher than observers' ratings [63]. Golin, Terrel, Weitz, and Drost found that depressed subjects' expectations of success at dice throwing reflect statistical reality, whereas normal subjects' expectations of success reflect an 'illusion of control' [64]. Alloy and Abramson found that, when estimating the degree of contingency between responses and reinforcements, depressed subjects make accurate estimates, whereas normal subjects make low estimates for undesired reinforcements and high estimates for desired reinforcements [65]. Presumably, in all four of these studies, the reason why depressed persons are more 'in touch with reality' is because they stop generating escapist imagery.

Depression and Immune Deficiency

According to the present thesis, when depressed people stop imaging, they not only stop innervating the neurons that are subjectively experienced as images, but also stop regulating the immune functions that are neurally connected with imaging. Thus, whereas hallucinators and imagers experience immune hypersensitivity and immune sensitivity, respectively, depressed persons experience both deficient imagery and deficient immunity.

Empirical findings confirm that depression is associated with immune deficiency. In the pioneering studies of this association, Bartrop, Luckhurst, Lazarus, Kiloh, and Penny [66] and Schleifer, Keller, Camerino, Thornton, and Stein [67] found that antigenic stimulation produces lower antibody levels in bereaved persons than in control subjects. In follow-up studies, Kronfol, Silva, Greden, Dembinski, Gardner, and Carroll [68], Linn, Linn, and Jensen [69], Schleifer, Keller, Meyerson, Raskin, Davis, and Stein [70], and Kiecolt-Glaser, Ricker, George, Messick, Speicher, Garner, and Glaser [71] found that antigenic stimulation also produces lower antibody levels in depressives than in normals. In additional, Kiecolt-Glaser *et al.* [71] and Locke, Kraus, Leserman, Hurst, Heisel, and Williams [72] found lower levels of natural killer cell activity in depressives than in normals.

Depression and Poor Physical Health

Depression is associated not only with immune deficiency *per se*, but also with the unhealthy and diseaseful consequences of immune deficiency. This latter association with poor physical health is manifested most dramatically in depressed people's inability to 'fight off' and recover from cancer. Numerous studies connecting depression with cancer susceptibility and cancer mortality have been reviewed by LeShan [73], Perrin and Pierce [74], Bahnson and Kissen [75], Hurst, Jenkins, and Rose [76], Jacobs and Ostfeld [77], Levitan, Levitan, and Levitan [78], and Shekelle, Raynor, Ostfeld, Garron, Bieliauskas, Liv, Maliza, and Paul [79]. Of course, some of the reviewed studies do not empirically connect depression with higher susceptibility or higher mortality. However, the depressives in some studies may have cancerous tendencies that are immunologically offset by manic or schizophrenic hallucinations.

Indeed, in four recent studies, the immune deficiency and poor physical health that are associated with depression appear to have been counteracted by the immune hypersensitivity that is associated with manic and schizophrenic tendencies. In a prospective study of depressed persons, Whitlock and Siskind

[80] reported that those depressives who exhibit no reality-denying hallucinations and no mood swings are more at risk of developing cancer. Likewise, in a prospective study of cancer patients, Greer, Morris, and Pettingale [81] reported that those patients who hopelessly accept the reality of cancer are more likely to die, whereas those patients who actively deny reality are more likely to survive with no recurrences of cancer. Furthermore, in two studies that have already been described in more detail, Kunzendorf and Butler [34] and Butler, Kunzendorf, and Sheikh [45] found 1) that depressive tendencies are positively correlated with schizophrenic tendencies and with manic tendencies, 2) that, controlling for schizophrenia and mania, depression is positively correlated with poor physical health but uncorrelated with immune hypersensitivity, and 3) that, controlling for depression, schizophrenia and mania are positively correlated with immune hypersensitivity but uncorrelated with poor physical health. This pattern of correlations suggests that manic tendencies and schizophrenic tendencies not only promote immune hypersensitivity, but also defend against depression and immune deficiency.

IMAGE-MONITORING, DEPRESSED IMAGING, AND 'HEALTHY' HALLUCINATING

The unimaginative and unhealthy depressive, as described above, is disheartened by his self-awareness *that distressing images are 'internally generated'* and *that escapist fantasies are 'only imaginary.'* The physically healthy hallucinator avoids such disheartening self-awareness, by monitoring neither the internal source of distressing hallucinations nor the imaginary nature of escapist hallucinations. The dynamic interplay between image-monitoring, depressed imaging, and 'healthy' hallucinating is illustrated in the following case studies of distressing and escapist imagery.

Distressing Imagery, Depression, and Hallucination

One group of clinical studies indicates that *distressing imagery*—in particular, sexually conflicted fantasy—can promote both depression and *paranoid hallucination*. In examining the relationship between depression and latent homosexuality, O'Connor found that half of the depressives under his observation exhibited homosexual conflict [82]. Also, in studying paranoid hallucinating and latent homosexuality, Planansky and Johnston found that half of the paranoid schizophrenics in their hospital hallucinated either voices accusing them of being homosexual or individuals coercing them into perverse behavior [83].

According to the present interpretation of such studies, latent homosexuals *imagine* voices accusing themselves of being perverse, simply because "most of our planned activity is represented subjectively as listening to ourselves talk"

[52, pp. 104–105]. Moreover, latent homosexuals become depressed by such imaginary accusation, if they are resisting self-discovery yet are self-consciously monitoring the 'internal' source of their accusatory imagery. However, latent homosexuals avoid both self-discovery and depression, if they stop 'monitoring' the internal source of their accusatory images and begin hallucinating 'external' voices and 'false' accusations. Indeed, Bliss describes many sexual deviants who, in coping with perverse desires and coercive images, spontaneously experience self-hypnosis and hallucination [84].

Even Freud's classic case study of latent homosexuality and paranoia conforms to the above interpretation [85]. Freud's paranoid subject reported that "relief from the pressure caused by the presence of the faeces in the intestines produces a sense of intense well-being in the nerves of voluptuousness" [85, p. 407]. However, he imaged voices accusing him of being a "sexual disgrace" and "jeering at him" [85, p. 399], and he became depressed. Finally, he escaped depression, when he began hallucinating not only the accusatory voices, but also God compelling him to seek anal pleasure and to become a woman.

Escapist Imagery, Depression, and Hallucination

Another group of clinical studies indicates that escapist images, particularly religious fantasies of escape from death, can promote both depression and schizophrenic hallucination. In clinical cases of psychological depression, Farr and Howe [86] and Gallenmore, Wilson and Rhoads [87] found that attention to religion and concern over an after-life are very prevalent, more so than in other psychological conditions. In cases of schizophrenia, Searles found that the denial of death is a motivating force behind many hallucinations, especially religious ones [88]. Moreover, depression oftentimes precedes an initial episode of religious hallucinating [89] and sometimes follows a final episode of acute schizophrenia [90].

A case illustrating the interplay between escapist imagery, depression, and religious hallucinating has been observed by the first author of this chapter. One of the author's students, a lapsed Catholic, sought comfort from religion when his grandmother died. However, he could not convince himself that heaven and God really exist. He became depressed and eventually became an alcoholic. His depression and alcoholism were brought to an end by an hallucinatory experience, in which he 'saw' Jesus and 'conversed' with him about the meaning of life. The student is presently convinced that his belief-strengthening experience was not hallucinatory. He has become deeply involved in a fundamentalist religious group, and has not 'seen' or 'heard' Jesus again.

Like the religious hallucination of this student, "the whole of mythical thought may be interpreted as a constant and obstinate negation of the phenomenon of death" [91, p. 84]. Mythical images of an after-life might even correspond to reality, but a person has no way of *knowing* whether they do so. A normal person simply *knows* that his images of an after-life are 'self-generated.'

Such self-knowledge, however, can prove depressing—particularly, if a person is trying to quell death-related distress by imaging an after-life. The 'religious' schizophrenic avoids both self-knowledge and death-related distress, when he stops 'monitoring' his escapist images of immortality and starts hallucinating them.

Conclusions: Physical Health and Depression, Hallucination, Imagination

As the above discussion indicates, depression and schizophrenic hallucination are two different responses to the disturbing self-awareness which results from 'monitoring' certain images. Some depressed people start feeling melancholy and stop generating imagery, in response to their self-awareness *that threatening images come 'from within.'* Other depressed people stop imaging better worlds and start feeling melancholy, in response to their self-awareness *that escapist images are 'only imaginary.'* In either case, when depressed people stop vividly imaging, they not only stop innervating the sensory neurons that are subjectively experienced as images, but also stop activating the immune functions that are neurally connected with imaging. Consequently, depression is associated with immune deficiency and poor physical health, as this chapter has documented.

In contrast, schizophrenic hallucinating is associated with the resumption of vivid imaging and the restoration of physical health. Some hallucinators, rather than be depressed by the self-awareness *that threatening images come 'from within,'* stop monitoring stressful images and start experiencing paranoid hallucinations. Other hallucinators, rather than be depressed by the self-awareness *that hopeful fantasies are 'only imaginary,'* stop monitoring vivid images of better worlds and start experiencing vivid hallucinations of them. Schizophrenics who generate such 'unmonitored' hallucinations during psychotic episodes do not, during their normal states of self-consciousness, image as vividly or as frequently as normal people [10, 20, 49, 92-98]. Nevertheless, the vivid hallucinations of schizophrenics—just like the vivid images of normal people [99]—innervate sensory nerves, activate immune functions, and counteract poor physical health. However, unlike normal imagers, schizophrenic hallucinators have 1) minds that fail to monitor the difference between imaged sensations and perceived sensations and 2) immune systems that fail to differentiate between diseaseful substances and allergenic substances. Accordingly, schizophrenia is associated with immune hypersensitivity.

Because schizophrenic hallucinating and depressive affect are frequently found in the same person [28, 34, 45, 89, 100, *and Table 1*], immune hypersensitivity and poor physical health are often found in the same person also [34, 45, *and Table 1*]. According to the theory and evidence presented in this chapter, the 'unmonitored' hallucinations of such a person take the place of a healthy imagination and, in doing so, serve both to counteract depression and to counterbalance immune deficiency [34, 45, 80].

From a practical perspective on mental health, the question arising from this theory and evidence is whether short-term hallucinations should be tolerated, for the sake of long-term physical health. The psychotherapist Jung suggests that, unlike current conceptualizations of mental health, primitive conceptualizations favored such tolerance [101, p. 31]:

> I have more than once been consulted by well-educated and intelligent people who have had . . . visions, which have shocked them deeply. They have assumed that . . . anyone who actually sees a vision must be pathologically disturbed. A theologian once told me that Ezekial's visions were nothing more than morbid symptoms, and that, when Moses and other prophets heard "voices" speaking to them, they were suffering from hallucinations. You can imagine the panic he felt when something of this kind "spontaneously" happened to him. . . . The primitive man confronted by a shock of this kind would not doubt his sanity; he would think of fetishes, spirits, or gods.

Although modern psychological ideology does not countenance the curative effects of hallucinating in *faith healing* and other 'primitive rituals' [102-104]), the anthropological "literature on 488 societies [reveals] that 62 percent of [this] worldwide sample have ritualized patterns involving hallucinations" [105, p. 187]. Indeed, psychological ideology itself accepts the curative effects of hallucinating in *hypnotic healing* and similar 'psychophysiological rituals' [103-104, 106-109]. Furthermore, according to Rossi's recent book on hypnotic healing, the general process of hypnosis includes the specific "process of falling into a spontaneous state of hypnosis under circumstances of traumatic stress" [109, p. 53]. Perhaps then, modern psychology can and should tolerate all short-term hallucinating—not only hypnotic hallucinating, but also ritualized hallucinating and spontaneous hallucinating in stressful circumstances which would otherwise be psychologically depressing and physically unhealthy.

REFERENCES

1. G. E. Schwartz, Psychobiology of Health: A New Synthesis, in *Psychology and Health*, B. L. Hammonds and C. J. Sheirer (eds.), American Psychological Association, Washington, DC, pp. 149-193, 1983.
2. A. A. Sheikh and R. G. Kunzendorf, Imagery, Physiology, and Psychosomatic Illness, *International Review of Mental Imagery, 1*, pp. 95-138, 1984.
3. R. G. Kunzendorf, Mind-Brain Identity Theory: A Materialistic Foundation for the Psychophysiology of Mental Imagery, in *The Psychophysiology of Mental Imagery: Theory, Research, and Application*, R. G. Kunzendorf and A. A. Sheikh (eds.), Baywood, Amityville, New York, pp. 9-36, 1990.
4. S. Freud, 'The Relation of the Poet to Day-Dreaming, in *On Creativity and the Unconscious*, B. Nelson (ed.), Harper and Row, New York, pp. 44-54, 1958.

5. A. Freud, *The Ego and the Mechanisms of Defense*, Hogarth, London, 1937.
6. D. Rapaport, Consciousness: A Psychopathological and Psychodynamic View, *Problems of Consciousness*, Josiah Macy Foundation, New York, pp. 18-57, 1951.
7. M. M. Gill and M. Brenman, *Hypnosis and Related States: Psychoanalytic Studies in Regression*, International Universities Press, New York, 1959.
8. P. Bakan, Dreaming, REM Sleep, and the Right Hemisphere: A Theoretical Integration, *Journal of Altered States of Consciousness, 3*, pp. 285-307, 1977-78.
9. R. G. Kunzendorf, Hypnotic Hallucinations as "Unmonitored" Images: An Empirical Study, *Imagination, Cognition, and Personality, 5*, pp. 255-270, 1985-86.
10. R. G. Kunzendorf, Self-Consciousness as the Monitoring of Cognitive States: A Theoretical Perspective, *Imagination, Cognition, and Personality, 7*, pp. 3-22, 1987-88.
11. A. Binet and C. Féré, *Animal Magnetism*, D. Appleton, New York, 1888.
12. W. Wundt, *Lectures on Human and Animal Psychology*, J. E. Creighton and E. B. Titchener, (trans.), Swan Sonnenschein, London, 1896.
13. D. O. Hebb, Concerning Imagery, *Psychological Review, 75*, pp. 466-477, 1968.
14. R. R. Holt, On the Nature and Generality of Mental Imagery, in *The Function and Nature of Imagery*, P. W. Sheehan (ed.), Academic Press, New York, pp. 3-33, 1972.
15. M. J. Horowitz, Image Formation: Clinical Observations and a Cognitive Model, in *The Function and Nature of Imagery*, P. W. Sheehan (ed.), Academic Press, New York, pp. 281-309, 1972.
16. S. C. Wilson and T. X. Barber, The Fantasy-Prone Personality: Implications for Understanding Imagery, Hypnosis, and Parapsychological Phenomena, in *Imagery: Current Theory, Research, and Application*, A. A. Sheikh (ed.), Wiley, New York, pp. 340-387, 1983.
17. T. X. Barber, Changing "Unchangeable" Bodily Processes by (Hypnotic) Suggestions: A New Look at Hypnosis, Cognitions, Imagining, and the Mind-Body Problem, in *Imagination and Healing*, A. A. Sheikh (ed.), Baywood, Amityville, New York, pp. 69-127, 1984.
18. E. R. Hilgard, Imagery and Imagination in American Psychology, *Journal of Mental Imagery, 5*, pp. 5-65, 1981.
19. N. P. Spanos and H. L. Radtke, Hypnotic Visual Hallucinations as Imaginings: A Cognitive-Social Psychological Perspective, *Imagination, Cognition, and Personality, 1*, pp. 147-170, 1981-82.
20. S. Starker, From Image to Hallucination: Studies of Mental Imagery in Schizophrenic Patients, *International Review of Mental Imagery, 2*, pp. 192-215, 1986.
21. J. S. Kruck and A. A. Sheikh, Alexithymia: A Critical Review, *International Review of Mental Imagery, 2*, pp. 90-144, 1986.
22. O. C. Simonton, S. Matthews-Simonton, and J. L. Creighton, *Getting Well Again*, Bantam Books, New York, 1978.

23. J. Achterberg, G. F. Lawlis, O. C. Simonton, and S. Matthews-Simonton, Psychological Factors and Blood Chemistries as Disease Outcome Predictors for Cancer Patients, *Multivariate Experimental Clinical Research, 3*, pp. 107–122, 1977.
24. H. Hall, Imagery and Cancer, in *Imagination and Healing,* A. A. Sheikh (ed.), Baywood, Amityville, New York, pp. 159–169, 1984.
25. N. C. Rassidakis, M. Kelepouris, K. Goulis, and K. Karaiossefidis, On the Incidence of Malignancy among Schizophrenic Patients, *Agressologie, 14*, 269–272, 1973.
26. K. Modrzewska and J. A. Book, Schizophrenia and Malignant Neoplasms in a North Swedish Population, *Lancet, 1*, pp. 275–276, 1979.
27. J. A. Baldwin, Schizophrenia and Physical Disease, *Psychological Medicine, 9*, pp. 611–618, 1979.
28. M. B. Cohen, G. Baker, R. Cohen, F. Fromm-Reichmann, and E. V. Weigert, An Intensive Study of Twelve Cases of Manic-Depressive Psychosis, in *Essential Papers on Depression*, J. C. Coyne (ed.), New York University Press, New York, pp. 82–139, 1986.
29. Allergy Foundation of America, *Allergy: Its Mysterious Causes and Modern Treatment*, Grosset and Dunlap, New York, 1967.
30. J. A. Grant, Fundamentals of the Immune System and Hypersensitivity Reactions, in *Allergy: Theory and Practice*, P. E. Korenblat and H. J. Wedner (eds.), Grune and Stratton, New York, pp. 7–23, 1984.
31. S. B. Friedman, J. Cohen, and H. Iker, Antibody Response to Cholera Vaccine: Differences between Depressed, Schizophrenic, and Normal Subjects, *Archives of General Psychiatry, 16*, pp. 312–315, 1967.
32. L. E. DeLisi, J. Ortaldo, A. Maluish, and R. Wyatt, Deficient Natural Killer Cell (NK) Activity and Macrophage Functioning in Schizophrenic Patients, *Journal of Neural Transmissions, 58*, pp. 99–106, 1983.
33. W. T. Vaughan, J. C. Sullivan, and F. Elmadjian, Immunity and Schizophrenia: A Survey of the Ability of Schizophrenia Patients to Develop an Active Immunity following the Injection of Pertussis Vaccine, *Psychosomatic Medicine, 11*, pp. 328–332, 1949.
34. R. G. Kunzendorf and W. Butler, Personality and Immunity: Depressive Tendencies versus Manic and Schizophrenic Tendencies, *Psychological Reports, 59*, p. 622, 1986.
35. J. E. Overall and F. Gomez-Mont, the MMPI-168 for Psychiatric Screening, *Educational and Psychological Measurement, 34*, pp. 315–319, 1974.
36. W. G. Dahlstrom, G. S. Welsh, and L. E. Dahlstrom, *An MMPI Handbook* (vol. 1), University of Minnesota Press, Minneapolis, 1972.
37. W. G. Dahlstrom, G. S. Welsh, and L. E. Dahlstrom, *An MMPI Handbook* (vol. 2), University of Minnesota Press, Minneapolis, 1975.
38. M. Strahilevitz and S. D. Davis, Increased IgA in Schizophrenic Patients, *Lancet, 2*, p. 370, 1970.
39. M. Strahilevitz, J. B. Fleischman, G. W. Fischer, R. Harris, and N. Narasimhachari, Immunoglobulin Levels in Psychiatric Patients, *American Journal of Psychiatry, 133*, pp. 772–777, 1976.

40. E. F. Torrey, M. R. Peterson, W. L. Brannon, W. T. Carpenter, R. M. Post, and D. P. Van Kammen, Immunoglobulins and Viral Antibodies in Psychiatric Patients, *British Journal of Psychiatry, 132*, pp. 342–348, 1978.
41. H. N. Claman and D. Nerrill, Serum Immunoglobulins in Rheumatoid Arthritis, *Journal of Laboratory and Clinical Medicine, 67*, pp. 850–854, 1966.
42. L. E. DeLisi, D. R. Weinberger, S. Potkin, L. M. Neckers, D. Shiling, and R. Wyatt, Quantitative Determination of Immunoglobulins in CSF and Plasma of Chronic Schizophrenic Patients, *British Journal of Psychiatry, 139*, pp. 513–518, 1981.
43. R. M. Ferguson, J. R. Schmidtke, and R. L. Simmons, Effects of Psychoactive Drugs on *in vitro* Lymphocyte Activation, in *Neurochemical and Immunologic Components in Schizophrenia*, D. Bergsma and A. I. Goldstein (eds.), A. R. Liss, New York, pp. 379–402, 1978.
44. Y. Ikemi and S. Nakagawa, A Psychosomatic Study of Contagious Dermatitis, *Kyushu Journal of Medical Science, 13*, pp. 335–350, 1962.
45. W. Butler, R. G. Kunzendorf, and A. A. Sheikh, *Cognition and Immunity: Depression versus Imagery and Hallucination*, unpublished research, 1986.
46. D. P. Marks, Visual Imagery Differences in the Recall of Pictures, *British Journal of Psychology, 64*, pp. 17–24, 1973.
47. R. G. Kunzendorf, Imagery and Consciousness: A Scientific Analysis of the Mind-Body Problem (Doctoral Dissertation, University of Virginia, 1979), *Dissertation Abstracts International, 40*, pp. 3448B–3449B, 1980.
48. S. Starker and J. L. Singer, Daydreaming and Symptom Patterns of Psychiatric Patients: A Factor Analytic Study, *Journal of Abnormal Psychology, 84*, pp. 567–570, 1975.
49. ———, Daydream Patterns and Self-Awareness in Psychiatric Patients, *Journal of Nervous and Mental Disease, 161*, pp. 313–317, 1975.
50. D. M. Tucker, C. E. Stenslie, R. S. Roth, and S. L. Shearer, Right Frontal Lobe Activation and Right Hemisphere Performance Decrement during a Depressed Mood, *Archives of General Psychiatry, 38*, pp. 169–174, 1981.
51. S. R. Gold, P. J. Jarvinen, and R. G. Teague, Imagery Elaboration and Clarity in Modifying College Students' Depression, *Journal of Clinical Psychology, 38*, pp. 312–314, 1982.
52. G. A. Miller, E. Galanter, and K. H. Pribram, *Plans and the Structure of Behavior*, Holt, Rinehart, and Winston, New York, 1960.
53. J. Piaget and B. Inhelder, *Mental Imagery in the Child*, Basic Books, New York, 1971.
54. D. P. J. Przybyla, D. Byrne, and K. Kelley, The Role of Imagery in Sexual Behavior, in *Imagery: Current Theory, Research, and Applications*, A. A. Sheikh (ed.), Wiley, New York, pp. 436–467, 1983.
55. J. L. Singer, *The Inner World of Daydreaming*, Harper and Row, New York, chapters 7–8, 1975.
56. ———, *Mind-Play: The Creative Uses of Fantasy*, Prentice-Hall, Englewood Cliffs, New Jersey, 1980.
57. A. T. Beck, Role of Fantasies in Psychotherapy and Psychopathology, *Journal of Nervous and Mental Disease, 150*, pp. 3–17, 1970.

58. K. D. Schultz, Imagery and the Control of Depression, in *The Power of Human Imagination*, J. L. Singer and K. S. Pope (eds.), Plenum, New York, pp. 281-307, 1978.
59. ————, The Use of Imagery in Alleviating Depression, in *Imagination and Healing*, A. A. Sheikh (ed.), Baywood, Amityville, New York, pp. 129-158, 1984.
60. R. G. Kunzendorf, Confronting Death through Mental and Artistic Images, in *Death Imagery*, A. A. Sheikh (ed.), American Imagery Institute, Milwaukee, Wisconsin, in press.
61. E. Becker, *The Denial of Death*, Free Press, New York, 1973.
62. R. E. Nelson and W. Craighead, Selective Recall of Positive and Negative Feedback, Self-Control, and Depression, *Journal of Abnormal Psychology, 86*, pp. 379-388, 1977.
63. P. M. Lewinsohn, W. Mischel, W. Chaplin, and R. Barton, Social Competence and Depression: The Role of Illusory Self-Perceptions, *Journal of Abnormal Psychology, 89*, pp. 203-212, 1980.
64. S. Golin, F. Terrell, J. Weitz, and P. Drost, The Illusion of Control among Depressed Patients, *Journal of Abnormal Psychology, 88*, pp. 454-457, 1979.
65. L. B. Alloy and L. Abramson, Judgment of Contingency in Depressed and Nondepressed Students, *Journal of Experimental Psychology: General, 108*, pp. 441-485, 1979.
66. R. W. Bartrop, E. Luckhurst, L. Lazarus, K. Kiloh, and R. Penny, Depressed Lymphocyte Function after Bereavement, *Lancet, 1*, pp. 834-836, 1977.
67. S. J. Schleifer, S. Keller, M. Camerino, J. Thornton, and M. Stein, Suppression of Lymphocyte Stimulation following Bereavement, *Journal of the American Medical Association, 250*, pp. 374-377, 1983.
68. Z. Kronfol, J. Silva, J. Greden, S. Dembinski, R. Gardner, and B. Carroll, Impaired Lymphocyte Function in Depressive Illness, *Life Sciences, 33*, pp. 241-247, 1983.
69. M. W. Linn, B. S. Linn, and J. Jensen, Stressful Events, Dysphoric Mood, and Immune Responsiveness, *Psychological Reports, 54*, pp. 219-222, 1984.
70. S. J. Schleifer, S. E. Keller, A. T. Meyerson, M. J. Raskin, K. L. Davis, and M. Stein, Lymphocyte Function in Major Depressive Disorder, *Archives of General Psychiatry, 41*, pp. 484-486, 1984.
71. J. K. Kiecolt-Glaser, D. Ricker, J. George, G. Messick, C. E. Speicher, W. Garner, and R. Glaser, Urinary Cortisol Levels, Cellular Immunocompetency, and Loneliness in Psychiatric Inpatients, *Psychosomatic Medicine, 46*, pp. 15-23, 1984.
72. S. E. Locke, L. Kraus, J. Leserman, M. W. Hurst, J. S. Heisel, and R. M. Williams, Life Change Stress, Psychiatric Symptoms, and Natural Killer Cell Activity, *Psychosomatic Medicine, 46*, pp. 441-453, 1984.
73. L. LeShan, Psychological States and Factors in the Development of Malignant Disease: A Critical Review, *Journal of the National Cancer Institute, 22*, pp. 1-18, 1959.

74. G. M. Perrin and I. R. Pierce, Psychosomatic Aspects of Cancer: A Review, *Journal of the National Cancer Institute, 22*, pp. 397–421, 1959.
75. C. B. Bahnson and D. M. Kissen (eds.), Psychophysiological Aspects of Cancer, *Annals of the New York Academy of Sciences, 125*, pp. 773–1055, 1966.
76. M. W. Hurst, D. Jenkins, and M. Rose, The Relation of Psychological Stress to Onset of Medical Illness, *Annual Review of Medicine, 27*, pp. 301–312, 1976.
77. S. Jacobs and A. Ostfeld, An Epidemiological Review of Bereavement, *Psychosomatic Medicine, 39*, pp. 344–357, 1977.
78. L. J. Levitan, H. Levitan, and M. Levitan, The Incidence of Cancer in Psychiatric Patients—Cancer and the Emotions: A Review, *Mount Sinai Journal of Medicine, 47*, pp. 627–631, 1980.
79. R. B. Shekelle, W. Raynor, A. Ostfeld, D. Garron, L. Bieliauskas, S. Liv, C. Maliza, and O. Paul, Psychological Depression and 17 Year Risk of Death from Cancer, *Psychosomatic Medicine, 43*, pp. 117–125, 1981.
80. F. A. Whitlock and M. Siskind, Depression and Cancer: A Follow-Up Study, *Psychological Medicine, 9*, pp. 747–752, 1979.
81. S. Greer, T. Morris, and K. W. Pettingale, Psychological Response to Breast Cancer: Effect on Outcome, *Lancet*, pp. 785–787, October 13, 1979.
82. W. O'Connor, Some Notes on Suicide, *British Journal of Medical Psychology, 21*, pp. 222–228, 1948.
83. K. Planansky and R. Johnston, The Incidence and Relationship of Homosexual and Paranoid Features in Schizophrenia, *Journal of Mental Science, 108*, pp. 604–615, 1962.
84. E. L. Bliss, *Multiple Personality, Allied Disorders, and Hypnosis*, Oxford University Press, Oxford, 1986.
85. S. Freud, Psycho-Analytic Notes upon an Autobiographical Account of a Case of Paranoia, *Sigmund Freud: Collected Papers* (vol. 3), E. Jones (ed.), Basic Books, New York, pp. 385–470, 1959.
86. C. B. Farr and R. L. Howe, The Influence of Religious Ideas on the Etiology, Symptomatology, and Prognosis of the Psychoses, with Special Reference to Social Factors, *American Journal of Psychiatry, 11*, pp. 845–865, 1932.
87. J. L. Gallenmore, W. P. Wilson, and J. M. Rhoads, The Religious Life of Patients with Affective Disorders, *Diseases of the Nervous System, 30*, pp. 483–487, 1969.
88. H. Searles, Schizophrenia and the Inevitability of Death, *Psychiatric Quarterly, 35*, pp. 632–655, 1961.
89. W. L. Lowe, Psychodynamics in Religious Delusions and Hallucinations, *American Journal of Psychotherapy, 7*, pp. 454–462, 1953.
90. S. Roth, The Seemingly Ubiquitous Depression following Acute Schizophrenic Episodes, A Neglected Area of Clinical Discussion, *American Journal of Psychiatry, 127*, pp. 51–58, 1970.
91. E. Cassirer, *An Essay on Man*, Yale University Press, New Haven, Connecticut, 1944.

92. L. H. Cohen, Imagery and Its Relations to Schizophrenia Symptoms, *Journal of Mental Science, 84*, pp. 284-346, 1938.
93. J. L. Despert, A Comparative Study of Thinking in Schizophrenic Children and in Children of Pre-school Age, *American Journal of Psychiatry, 97*, pp. 189-213, 1940.
94. P. F. D. Seitz and H. B. Molholm, Relation of Mental Imagery to Hallucinations, *Archives of Neurology and Psychiatry, 57*, pp. 469-480, 1947.
95. M. K. Opler and J. L. Singer, Ethnic Differences in Behavior and Psychopathology, *International Journal of Social Psychiatry, 2*, pp. 11-22, 1956.
96. J. L. Singer, *Daydreaming: An Introduction to the Experimental Study of Inner Experience*, Random House, New York, p. 164, 1966.
97. E. A. Brett and S. Starker, Auditory Imagery and Hallucinations, *Journal of Nervous and Mental Disease, 164*, pp. 394-400, 1977.
98. S. Starker and A. Jolin, Imagery and Hallucination in Schizophrenic Patients, *Journal of Nervous and Mental Disease, 170*, pp. 448-451, 1982.
99. A. A. Sheikh, Eidetic Psychotherapy, in *The Power of Human Imagination* (pp. 197-224), J. L. Singer and K. S. Pope (eds.), Plenum, New York, 1978.
100. J. S. Strauss, R. F. Kokes, B. A. Ritzler, D. W. Harder, and A. V. Ord, Patterns of Disorder in First Admission Psychiatric Patients, *Journal of Nervous and Mental Disease, 166*, pp. 611-623, 1978.
101. C. G. Jung, Approaching the Unconscious, in *Man and His Symbols,* C. G. Jung (ed.), Dell, New York, pp. 1-94, 1964.
102. B. Wallace and L. E. Fisher, *Consciousness and Behavior* (1st edition, chapter 9), Allyn and Bacon, Newton, Massachusetts, 1983.
103. H. F. Ellenberger, *The Discovery of the Unconscious: The History and Evolution of Dynamic Psychiatry*, Basic Books, New York, 1970.
104. W. E. Edmonston, *The Induction of Hypnosis*, Wiley, New York, 1986.
105. E. Bourguignon, Hallucination and Trance: An Anthropologist's Perspective, *Origin and Mechanisms of Hallucinations* (pp. 183-190), W. Keup (ed.), Plenum, New York, 1970.
106. T. X. Barber, "Hypnosis," Suggestions, and Psychosomatic Phenomena: A New Look from the Standpoint of Recent Experimental Studies, *American Journal of Clinical Hypnosis, 21*, pp. 13-27, 1978.
107. K. S. Bowers and P. Kelly, Stress, Disease, Psychotherapy, and Hypnosis, *Journal of Abnormal Psychology, 88*, pp. 490-505, 1979.
108. T. X. Barber, Changing "Unchangeable" Bodily Processes by (Hypnotic) Suggestions: A New Look at Hypnosis, Cognitions, Imagining, and the Mind-Body Problem, in *Imagination and Healing* (pp. 69-127), A. A. Sheikh (ed.), Baywood, Amityville, New York, 1984.
109. E. L. Rossi, *The Psychobiology of Mind-Body Healing: New Concepts of Therapeutic Hypnosis*, Norton, New York, 1986.

CHAPTER 10
Imagery, Psychoneuroimmunology, and the Psychology of Healing

HOWARD HALL

PSYCHONEUROIMMUNOLOGY

The emerging field of psychoneuroimmunology (PNI) [1] has provided evidence that psychosocial factors have a ***bidirectional*** influence on a number of immune measures and the immune response [2-4]; that is, these variables have been associated with either a suppression or an enhancement of immune functioning. This influence of psychosocial factors on immunity is consistent with the view that psychological variables may be associated both with physical illness and with the recovery from disease [5], and is complemented by evidence that various autonomic physiologic activities are capable of voluntary self-regulation through such procedures as meditation [6, 7], hypnosis [8], relaxation [9], imagery [10, 11], biofeedback [12], autogenic training [13].

The possibility that psychologic variables may exert a bidirectional influence on immunity has important implications for the self-regulation of biological systems. The most widely researched area in the field of PNI has been the down regulation or immunosuppressive effects of numerous psychosocial factors on the immune system. In this chapter, however, bidirectional immune changes across a number of studies in the area of PNI will be examined. Following that, attempts to produce directional changes in immune functioning with hypnosis-like procedures will be discussed. Finally, a distinction will be made between traditional hypnotic approaches and "The Psychology of Healing" with its implications for psychoneuroimmunology.

CLASSICAL CONDITIONING OF IMMUNE RESPONSES

Some of the strongest laboratory data for the role of the central nervous system in immune functioning comes from work in the area of conditioned immune responses. Until recently the immune system was thought to operate autonomously without central nervous system involvement. Classical conditioning, however, is conceptualized in terms of the learning of relations among events or stimuli via the central nervous system [14, 15]. Furthermore, research is beginning to elucidate the neural correlates of classical conditioning [16]. Thus, given that classical conditioning is a central nervous system based phenomenon and that immune responses can be classically conditioned, there is strong empirical support for CNS involvement in immunoregulation. Furthermore, there is experimental evidence for the bidirectional conditioning of immune responses.

Employing the taste aversion learning paradigm, Ader and Cohen [17] demonstrated conditioned immunosuppression in rats. In this study the taste of a novel saccharin drinking solution (the conditioned stimulus–CS), was paired with the injection of an immunosuppressive drug cyclophosphamide (the unconditioned stimulus–US). Following the CS-US pairing, when the saccharin solution (the CS) was presented to the animal alone without the immunosuppressive drug, blood measures indicated conditioned immunosuppression to the stimulus. This finding has been replicated in their lab as well as by other researchers [18].

Bidirectionally, there is evidence for the classical conditioning of immunoenhancement. Recently Spector [19] paired the odor of camphor (the CS) with a drug that increases interferon and natural killer cell activity polyinosinic-polycytidylic acid (PolyI:C) (the US). After such conditioning, mice demonstrated a sizable immunoenhancement effect to the odor of camphor alone.

Researchers in the area of classical conditioning of immune responses have replicated these earlier findings and extended work in this area to 1) the regulation of tumors by conditioning [20], 2) the conditioning of immune responses to sham skin grafts in mice [21], and 3) the conditioned secretion of protease II from mast cells in rats [22]. There is much evidence that a stimulus that elicits an unconditional immune response can be paired with an initially neutral stimulus (the conditioned stimulus-CS) so that CS will come to elicit a conditioned immune response of either immunosuppression or immunoenhancement.

Contemporary learning perspectives, however, view the simple pairing of two stimuli as an insufficient condition for demonstrating Pavlovian conditioning. It would be of interest to observe if more sophisticated conditioning designs, such as Kamin's [23] blocking paradigm, could be replicated with the conditioning of immune responses. In the blocking study a group of rats (Group A) were first presented a light (CS1) paired with a shock, the unconditioned stimulus (US). Next, a second conditioned stimulus, a noise (CS2), was presented with CS1 and paired with the US. A control group (Group B) had no prior experience with CS1 but were presented with CS1, and CS2, paired with the US at the start of the study. When learning was tested to the noise (CS2),

Kamin observed learning in the Control Group B but not in Group A. He argues that the presence of CS2 was redundant in Group A, because subjects had already learned an association between CS1 (the light) and the US (shock). Thus, learning was blocked to the redundant stimulus (CS2). The blocking of a conditioned immune response would be a very powerful demonstration of Pavlovian conditioning of the immune system.

STRESS: ANIMAL STUDIES

A widely researched area in the field of psychoneuroimmunology is the impact of stress on immune functioning. Animal studies are of particular benefit in this area because they afford a high degree of experimental control not possible in research with humans. A wide range of experimental stressors have been employed in animal research. Such stressors have included: electric shock, rotation, crowding, restraint, exposure to a natural predator [2], and biochemically stimulated stress [24].

Experimentally induced stress has been found to have a bidirectional impact on immune responses. Research has shown that various stressors can both increase susceptibility to viral and infectious illnesses as well as provide a protective effect to the host against such infections [2, 4, 25]. A paradigm employed in animal research to assess immunocompetence has been to examine the impact that stressors have on experimentally implanted tumors [24].

One variable that has been found to influence the directional effects of stress on immune responses is the timing of the stressor. Some generalization can be observed about timing effects of stressors. For example, acute stress tends to have an immunosuppressive effect, whereas chronic stress has been associated with immunoenhancement [26].

The timing of the stressor in relationship to the neoplastic process has also been observed to influence the direction of the immune reaction. Administering a stressor before the implantation of an experimental tumor may result in enhanced immunocompetence [27]. If the stressor follows tumor implantation, however, impaired immune functioning has been observed [24]. Additionally, the type of the stressor employed also influences the specific immunological reactions. For example, predator stress, chronic handling and isolation have always been found to have a suppressive impact, and have not been associated with immunoenhancement [26].

STRESS: HUMAN STUDIES

Immunosuppression

There are reports that various stressors may impair immunocompetence in humans and that such lowered resistance may be associated with the increased incidence of a number of immunologically related disorders including herpes simplex viruses, infectious mononucleosis, upper respiratory tract infections, and trenchmouth [2]. The range of psychological variables associated with impairment of the various immune components has included self-reported life stress, bereavement, academic stress from final examinations, loneliness, and sleep deprivation.

Academic Stress

Jemmott et al. investigated the impact of examination stress on first-year dental school students [28]. These researchers took salivary secretory immunoglobulin A measures five times over a one-year period. Three of the time points coincided with major examinations and two were during nonstressful periods. The results of this study indicated that secretory SIgA rates were significantly lower during the three high stress periods compared to the low stress period. Measurements of power motivation were also associated with different SIgA levels. Personality-motivational variables and immunity, however, will be discussed later in this chapter.

Kiecolt-Glaser et al. also examined the impact of final examinations stress on first-year medical students [29]. In this study baseline blood measures were taken one month before the exam period and again on the first day of finals. There was a significant decrease of natural killer cell activity during the examination period compared to baseline. Elevated scores on measurements of loneliness and number of stressful life events were also associated with decreased levels of natural killer cell activity.

Bereavement

The death of a spouse has been rated as the most stressful, commonly occurring, life event [30]. Bartrop, Luckhurst, Lazarus, Kiloh, and Penny examined the impact of the death of a spouse on immune responses at two time points [31]. The first was at around two weeks after bereavement and the second six weeks later. There was a significant depression of immune activity as measured by the ability of lymphocytes to proliferate, at the second time period. The first time period revealed no significant differences.

Schleifer, Keller, Camerino, Thornton, and Stein also observed that conjugal bereavement was associated with a decreased ability of lymphocytes to proliferate in response to a mitogen during the two months following the death of a spouse compared to prebreavement levels [32]. Bereavement, however, was not associated with changes on T or B lymphocyte numbers.

Depression

Impaired immune function has also been associated with depressive mood states. Kronfol et al. examined immune function in a drug-free group of patients diagnosed with a primary depressive illness [33]. When compared to a control group of volunteers, the depressed group demonstrated a marked reduction of the response of lymphocytes to mitogenic stimulation. These authors concluded that depressive illness may be associated with impaired immunological functioning.

Stress and Coping

Locke and Colligan defined "stress" as:

> ". . . the perception of individuals that their life circumstances have exceeded their capacity to cope. In this context, stress occurs within the person in his or her subjective experience" [34, p. 62].

As can be observed from the above definition, stress and coping have been closely associated. In other words it is not just the presence of a stressor that may determine potential detrimental effects on an individual, but how well one copes with the situation or event. Lazarus and Folkman defined "coping" as:

> ". . . the process of managing demands (external or internal) that are appraised as taxing or exceeding the resources of the person" [35, p. 283].

Recent research has suggested an association between coping styles and the prediction or prognosis of illnesses, such as cancer. For example, Greer and Morris observed in a pseudoprospective study of women undergoing a breast biopsy, a significant association between extreme suppression of anger and other emotions with a diagnosis of breast cancer [36]. Coping was also predictive of follow-up disease status for the breast cancer patients. At a 5-year follow-up these researchers observed that recurrence-free status was associated with patients who initially coped with their diagnosis of cancer with either a "fighting spirit" or "denial." Patients with the poorest prognosis responded with feelings of helplessness or with stoic acceptance [37].

Research has also revealed an association between the expression of emotion and immunological levels for patients with breast cancer. Pettingale, Greer, and Tee observed significantly higher levels of serum IgA levels in patients who habitually suppressed anger compared to those who were able to express anger [38]. They also pointed out that there is evidence that elevated serum IgA levels may be associated with advancing metastatic disease.

Levy, Herberman, Maluish, Schlein, and Lippman also observed a relationship between coping and immunological status for breast cancer patients [39]. In this study, patients who demonstrated listlessness, apathetic, fatigue-like symptoms along with reported lack of social support and were rated as well-adjusted to having cancer had lower natural killer cell levels than patients who appeared to be more disturbed with having cancer.

Research with rats has also found a relationship between stress, coping, and immune status [40]. Suppressed lymphocyte proliferation was observed in rats given inescapable shock. Rats given identical shock, but who could control the shock with a wheel turn, did not show this immunosuppression [40].

Coping has also been observed to influence the level of natural killer cell-activity in an undergraduate student population. Locke et al. observed that individuals with good coping ability, who had experienced a high number of life stressors but who had few psychological symptoms, had higher natural killer cell activity levels than individuals who reported a high number of symptoms associated with a high number of life change stressors (i.e., poor copers) [41].

Personality and Stress

Research by McClelland, Floor, Davidson, and Saron observed that certain personality patterns may be associated with decreased immunocompetence [42]. These researchers had undergraduate, male college students write a story about Thematic Apperception Test picture stimuli. Subjects' responses were then coded to identify individuals with three stressful characteristics: 1) high need for power over others coupled with an 2) active inhibition of this power need (activity inhibition) and 3) a high number of reported power related stressors. Subjects high on these three variables had lower levels of salivary IgA, higher amounts of urinary epinephrine and more reports of illnesses than other subjects. Thus, certain personality factors and motivational variables combined with life event stressors may be associated with impaired immunocompetence.

IMMUNOENHANCEMENT

Positive Emotions

In this chapter, the detrimental effects of psychological factors on immunocompetence have already been reviewed. Conversely, it has been suggested that positive emotions may be associated with enhanced immunity. As Lazarus and Folkman argued:

> Generally the theme of the bodily costs of stress and coping centers on negative emotions. As the findings regarding challenge suggest, attention might also be fruitfully given to the bodily consequences of positive emotions, such as joy, love, and exhilaration, or to challenge-related emotions as distinguished from threat-related ones. It has been suggested, for example, that just as negative emotions can result in damaging hormonal secretion patterns, positive ones might produce biochemical substances having protective tissue effects, perhaps warding off disease or even facilitating recovery and health [35, p. 314].

Relaxation Training

Peavey, Lawlis, and Goven investigated the effects of biofeedback-assisted relaxation on phagocytic immune functioning [43]. These researchers found that experimental subjects who initially had high levels of self-reported stress, were able to significantly increase phagocytic capacity following relaxation training. It was suggested that relaxation may have contributed to the observed immunoenhancement effect by providing subjects with an increased ability to cope with stressors. Also relaxation may have decreased sympathetic activity and adrenalin production.

In a Geriatric population Kiecolt-Glaser et al. observed significant enhancement of natural killer cell activity and significant decreases in antibody titers to Herpes Simplex virus following relaxation training three times a week for a month [44]. No significant changes were observed for a social-contact condition or the no contact control group, from the baseline measure to the end of intervention and one month follow-up.

Progressive muscle relaxation training with focused breathing and imagery instructions to image enhanced immune function has been associated with increases in Salivary immunoglobulin A [45]. Comparable enhanced immune responses were observed with a second group that received the same relaxation training but were not instructed to engage in imagery. A vigilance task control group failed to demonstrate changes in this measure.

Humor, Love and Hope

Positive emotions such as humor, love, and hope have been associated with changes in secretory immunoglobulin A levels. Dillon, Minchoff, and Baker reported significant increases of salivary IgA concentration following the viewing of a humorous Richard Pryor film [46]. No such increases were observed for college student subjects who watched a didactic videotape which served as a control film.

David McClelland has also found enhancement of salivary IgA after college students watched a film of Mother Teresa caring for the sick and dying in Calcutta. In an interview with Joan Borysenko, McClelland argued that:

> Some kind of tender loving care seems to be a crucial ingredient in healing. So the idea was that this kind of care had a positive effect on the immune system [47].

McClelland also investigated the success of a local healer in treating students with the common cold. In this study, students who felt they were coming down with a cold were taken to a local healer who would given them either an actual folk/psychic healing by saying: "you're healed" or a placebo/sham treatment where the healer told another student, "You heal him. I give my power to you" [34].

The results of this study were that eleven of the thirteen students given actual healing treatment did not come down with colds. For the placebo treated subjects, however, eleven of the thirteen subjects did get colds [47]. Even more interesting, there was an enhancement of salivary IgA in those subjects actually treated compared to the sham healing group. When the physicians at the Harvard University Health Service heard about these results they skeptically said: "... tell them they're better, and they'll get better" [34]. In a subsequent study McClelland did this by taking another group of students who were coming down with colds, and randomly sending half to either the University Health Service or to the local healer. This time, none of the students treated by the healer developed colds, whereas, all of the students who went to the clinic came down with severe colds [34].

Udelman and Udelman reported a relationship between immune responses and the measures of "hope" in a population of patients diagnosed with depressive neurosis [48]. In this study there was a direct correlation between indicators of hope as measured by the Rheumatology Reaction Pattern Survey, with T-cell counts and an inverse correlation with B cells.

Hypnosis

Hypnosis-like procedures have been associated with the inhibition of a number of immunologically based disorders [5, 49]. Studies with adults have demonstrated that hypnosis-like inductions with specific suggestions resulted in suppression of delayed cutaneous hypersensitivity response [50].

In the Foreword to Ader's [51] classic book on psychoneuroimmunology, Robert A. Good reported on an experiment he conducted in 1961 that was never published because a similar observation [50] was presented earlier in a British Journal. Good reported:

> In short, we observed that well-selected hypnotic subjects trained to respond with deep somnolence to hypnotic suggestion could receive signals that influenced greatly their immune responses to simple protein antigens to which they had been made allergic. We used the classical method of Prausnitz-Kustner Reaction. Serum from a highly allergic donor was injected into the skin of each forearm. Twenty-four hours later, under deep hypnosis at the time of challenge, the suggestion was made that the skin of one arm was not to react to the challenge of the sensitizing antigen while the skin of the opposite arm should respond in the usual way. With each of three well-trained hypnotic subjects, the results were the same. Whereas in the skin of the one arm the reaction showed the usual wheal, erythema, itching, burning, and swelling, the opposite arm showed only a wheal and very minimal erythema. There seemed from these experiments little doubt that manifestations of allergic challenge had been influenced significantly by the mind under the influence of hypnosis.
>
> ... we were all convinced that the effector limb of allergic immunity could be influenced by the brain. We had our own clear

> view of poorly understood interactions of brain and immunologic processes [51, p. xviii].

Meditation has also been associated with inhibition of the delayed hypersensitivity reaction to varicella zoster viral antigen and to in vitro measures of lymphocyte stimulation to varicella zoster [52]. In a three-phase study, with each phase consisting of three weekly immune assessments, a single subject design was employed. The subject was a 39-year-old woman with nine years of experience in an Eastern religious practice. During phase one of the study, the subject was asked to respond normally to the antigen. During the second phase she was requested to inhibit her immune responses to the antigen using any strategy she wished. Smith et al. describe her approach as follows:

> First she would dedicate her intention concerning the study for universal good instead of self-advancement. She would also tell her body not to violate its wisdom concerning her defense against infection. Finally, she would visualize the area of erythema and induration getting smaller and smaller. Soon after each phase 2 injection, she would pass her hand over her arm, sending "healing energy" to the injection site [52, p. 2111].

On the final phase of the study, the subject was asked to again allow herself to respond normally to the antigen. When phase 2 immune responses are compared to baseline and follow-up, the results of this study indicate that this subject could voluntarily inhibit both the delayed hypersensitivity response and the in vitro lymphocyte stimulation measures. Also the subject was able to replicate this phenomenon nine months later when the entire sequence was repeated.

There have been very few studies, however, on enhancing immunocompetence with hypnotic-like procedures. In our lab we found some evidence for immunoenhancement one hour following a hypnotic-like procedure [10]. Three immune measures demonstrated a modest increase for some subjects. They were lymphocyte count, white cell count, and lymphocyte proliferation to Pokeweed mitogen. The lymphocyte count increase was a multivariate effect moderated by the subjects' ages, their level of hypnotizability and the interaction of these two variables.

Olness has also found increases in salivary IgA following a hypnotic relaxation-imagery exercise in children between the ages of six and twelve years [53]. This study involved three experimental conditions where subjects either received specific suggestions regarding increasing their immune responses or they were just told to increase their immunity without specific direction. A third control condition just involved talking to the children. The only group demonstrating significant increases in salivary IgA from baseline to post hypnosis was the hypnosis condition with specific suggestions to enhance immunocompetence. There was no effect for hypnotizability, however. Children with high hypnotic ability were no better at increasing immune responses than low hypnotizable subjects.

HYPNOSIS, THE PSYCHOLOGY OF HEALING AND PSYCHONEUROIMMUNOLOGY

The field of experimental hypnosis is closely associated with the subject-characteristic of hypnotic susceptibility. As Sheehan noted:

> Not all subjects exhibit "hypnotic" behavior . . . and it is clear that the explanation for this individual variation in hypnotic response must often be sought in other factors than in the process of induction. One place we may clearly look is to the subject-characteristics that differentiate hypnotizable from nonhypnotizable people [54, p. 382].

Orne also pointed out the importance of the subject-characteristic of hypnotic ability versus the hypnotic procedure when he argued:

> . . . the condition of hypnosis is diagnosed on the basis of subject's response to test suggestions, not the mere fact that he has been exposed to a hypnotic induction procedure [55, p. 190].

Along these lines Bowers and Kelly suggested that high hypnotic susceptibility might be related to an individual's ability to be healed using a psychological procedure [56]. Bowers and Kelly recommended assessing hypnotic levels with standard scales in psychosomatic research, in order to determine the importance of that factor.

High hypnotic ability might be important for altering immune function and other physiological parameters but it might also interfere with such alterations given the unique features of this phenomenon.

Orne outlined some unique characteristics of hypnosis. He stated:

> Hypnosis is said to exist when suggestions from one individual seemingly alter the perceptions and memories of another. In its extreme form hypnosis is easily identified: appropriate suggestions will cause an S to perceive an individual who is not actually there and behave as if he were, or if the S is told to forget certain events that have transpired, he will suddenly seem unable to recall them. In a similar manner, appropriate suggestions will alter any desired aspect of memory and perception, making possible an incredibly wide range of distortions of subjective experience [55, pp. 183-184].

Given this unique aspect of hypnosis it is possible that highly susceptible subjects in a traditional hypnotic paradigm might experience an altered perception of their physiological functioning in the absence of any real physiological changes or voluntary self-regulation. This would be similar to hysteria, as Bowers noted:

> The symptoms of hysteria are very similar to some of the phenomena that can be suggested in hypnosis, such as blindness, deafness, paralysis, and the inability to feel painful sensations [57, p. 6].

Early in his career in biofeedback Neal Miller explored the possibilities of employing hypnosis as a means of volitionally altering physiology [58]. In one study he took highly hypnotizable subjects and instructed them, while under hypnosis, to increase the temperature in one hand and decrease it in the other. Although these subjects were convinced under hypnosis that one hand was hot and the other cold, objective recordings revealed no temperature differences. In other words, these subjects had an altered perception of their physiology in the absence of any real changes. They hallucinated a temperature change or had a hysterical type of experience in the absence of any self-regulation. Thus, hypnosis and high hypnotic ability have been associated with physiological alterations, yet certain unique aspects of hypnosis may also interfere with self-regulation if highly hypnotic subjects hallucinate a physiological alteration in the absence of any objective changes.

Along similar lines White observed that bronchial asthma patients who received hypnotic treatment almost always reported improvement in their condition despite the absence of change or even worsening of objective measures of respiratory function [59]. It should be pointed out, however, that the findings in this study do not rule out the possibility of voluntary regulation of respiratory function, only that hypnosis may interfere with such self-regulation.

A recent study of the use of hypnosis to treat warts failed to find an association between wart regression and high hypnotic ability [60].

In the area of psychoneuroimmunology it is possible that highly hypnotic subjects, given the suggestion to increase or decrease immune reactions while under hypnosis, might hallucinate immunological changes in the absence of any real differences. It is interesting to note that a recent study failed to observe changes of the delayed-type hypersensitivity response with hypnotic suggestions given to highly hypnotizable/untrained subjects [61]. Perhaps these highly hypnotic subjects had hallucinated an immune change in this study. Interestingly, when questioned, these subjects were convinced they had altered their immune responses [62].

Research in the area of voluntary immunomodulation is more complex than hypnotizing subjects and giving them suggestions to alter their immune systems. Ongoing research in this area suggests the importance of such factors as experience, practice in self-regulation, the ability to relax and reduce sympathetic arousal, the nature of the imagery, the moderating effect of individual differences, and the choice of the particular immune measure [63]. Experimentally, hypnotizability has not been found to be associated with the ability of subjects to alter their immune systems [63].

To suggest that a traditional hypnosis paradigm might interfere with phsyiological alterations does not call into question the authenticity of hypnotic phenomenon or even the importance of hypnotic ability or altered perceptions in such areas as the reduction of pain [64]. The area of experimental hypnosis, however, offers very few suggestions regarding how hypnosis might effect immune responses. The ability of highly hypnotizable subjects to alter perceptions, dissociate, or hallucinate, does not easily provide an explanation for psychological healing.

It is now generally accepted that psychosocial factors are associated with immunological responses. This association is probably not restricted to highly hypnotic subjects. Thus the question we are asking in our lab is how can we employ psychological procedures such as imagery, relaxation, suggestions, and hypnosis-like techniques to voluntarily and directionally influence immune responses. Unlike today's emphasis on hypnotic ability, historically hypnosis was developed as a psychological means of treating illnesses [49]. Because I am interested in the impact of psychological procedures on both low and highly hypnotic individuals, I call the area I work in "The Psychology of Healing" [5]. Please note that individuals who score low on standard scales of hypnotizability are theoretically unable to enter into hypnosis [55]. Thus if a hypnotic procedure was employed to alter some physiological parameter and both high and low susceptible subjects demonstrated an effect, it would not, by definition be a hypnotic effect [55]. This would be a psychology of healing effect, however, because it demonstrated the impact of psychological variables on self-regulation.

Recently there have emerged new perspectives to account for psychological factors in healing with hypnotic-like procedures. Barber argued:

> The meaning or ideas embedded in the words that are spoken by one person and deeply accepted by another can be communicated to the cells of the body (and to the chemicals within the cells); the cells then can change their activities in order to conform to the meanings or ideas that have been transmitted to them [8, pp. 115-116].

Even more germane, Rossi's new book on the Psychobiology of Mind-Body Healing integrates concepts from psychology, immunology, endocrinology, and the autonomic nervous system to conceptualize how hypnosis-like procedures might influence healing [65]. Dr. Rossi has also incorporated Candace Pert's exciting work on neuropeptides into his psychobiology of Mind-Body Healing. Pert describes her thinking as follows:

> My argument is that the three classic areas of neuroscience, endocrinology, and immunology, with their various organs—the brain (which is the key organ that the neuroscientists study), the glands,

and the immune system (consisting of the spleen, the bone marrow, the lymph nodes, and of course, the cells circulating through the body)—that these three areas are actually joined to each other in a bidirectional network of communication and that the information carriers are the neuropeptides. These are well-studied physiological substrates showing that communication exists in both directions for every single one of these areas and their organs [66, p. 14].

THE PSYCHOLOGY OF HEALING

Our current work is not in the area of traditional hypnosis but the Psychology of Healing. In this area we attempt to produce directional changes in bodily functioning with hypnotic suggestions and imagery. Our notion is that in a deeply relaxed state with the subject's attention focused, we suggest images which are stimuli that carry information which is employed by the central nervous system to influence biological responses in specific directions.

Our Psychology of Healing research lab is continuing to explore the optimum conditions for altering physiology. High hypnotic ability may facilitate the use of images to communicate bodily changes. That is an empirical issue which requires an assessment of hypnotizability in such research. Direct suggestions for highly hypnotizable subjects, however, may produce altered perceptions or hallucinations in the absence of physiological changes.

Our research interests in the Psychology of Healing are geared toward understanding how shamans and other healers were able to influence disease processes with psychological, hypnotic, and imagery procedures. There is enough evidence that psychosocial factors may influence immune responses in a bidirectional manner. The Psychology of Healing addresses how that might be accomplished in an explicit manner.

Psychology of Healing Protocol

Our protocol, unlike traditional experimental protocols, is geared toward creating a psychological ritual that everyone can experience. Imagery and suggestion can then be employed to alter physiology. It is not geared toward altered perceptions, hysterical reactions, or hallucinations.

This protocol is not one which can just be picked up and read for an experimental or clinical procedure. Substantial preparatory training is necessary before The Psychology of Healing protocol can be effectively employed by researchers. First, our students are required to take a course in the area of traditional experimental hypnosis. Unique hypnotic phenomena are real and students are expected to know that area. The next important experimental component of our training involves learning about the range of responses to hypnotic suggestions. Here students are required to administer about twelve individual hypnotic assessments, Stanford C Scales [67]. The goal here is to give students experience working with extremely high hypnotic and low susceptible subjects. This also provides concrete examples of how some subjects are unable to respond to suggestions such as altered perceptions or hallucinations. Please note that The Psychology of Healing protocol avoids this type of suggestion, since a large number of individuals would be unable to respond to them. Our protocol only involves suggestions that just about everyone can experience. This avoids negative expectations from failure experiences and on the contrary, sets up a positive expectancy set.

Following the work on individual assessment, we next take our students through The Psychology of Healing protocol using them as subjects so that they can experience our procedure.

For their first session, we tell them what they are going to experience. This is a type of role induction. Presented below is a general outline we follow, but it should be noted that this protocol is *never read* verbatim as with experimental hypnosis, but is presented in a clinical manner following the same basic outline. For didactic and research purposes, a transcript is presented. Practice and homework are an important part of our protocol. After this induction, we provide a handout sheet with instructions for self-hypnosis practice.

CONCLUSION

In this chapter, the literature reporting psychosocial factors which had a bidirectional impact on immune functioning was reviewed. Relaxation and imagery based procedures geared toward enhancing immune function were also examined. The success and failure of hypnosis to modulate immune functions were also discussed. Finally, the author's Psychology of Healing perspective was presented and contrasted with traditional hypnotic approaches. The central questions this area addresses is how to employ psychological procedures to voluntarily and directionally alter immune functioning.

APPENDIX

Protocol

Introduction: Initial Session

I'd like to tell you a little bit about hypnosis to clear up any misunderstandings about hypnosis and answer any questions that you may have.

Have you ever been hypnotized before?

What we are going to do today is not hypnosis but is training in self-regulation. Self-regulation training involves a *process of deep relaxation and focused attention*. What I mean by that is that it will help you *reduce outside distractions* as much as possible and help you to *focus* as much as possible *on the things that I am saying to you*. This does not mean that I am going to *take control of your mind*—there is no way that I can do that. *You will be in complete control* of the entire process—you will only become as relaxed and hypnotized as *you allow yourself* to become. I will merely be helping you to do this—to allow yourself to enter an altered state. *With practice*, you'll be *able to do* this completely *on your own*, and you'll become better and better at it the more you practice.

As I said before, self-regulation training is merely *deep relaxation and focused attention*. You'll be *aware of everything that goes on* at all times. In other words, if people are walking around outside—you will still hear them, and you'll be aware of the sounds of the elevator, the sound of my voice, etc. It is not like general anesthesia—you will not be transported to a new world or become some kind of zombie as some people think. After the induction, *you will feel very relaxed*. As a matter of fact, most people are very surprised at how aware they are of everything—how ordinary this experience seems to be—and yet that they are so deeply relaxed and hypnotized. As you *practice this* and become better at it, you will be able to *relax and focus your attention better*, and although you will *still be aware* of outside sounds and distractions, you will *pay less attention* to them, and more attention to the things that I am telling you and your own personal experience.

Sometimes during the induction, some people become *distracted by intrusive thoughts* that enter their heads. They then try to stop these thoughts and force them out. This often distracts them even more—it's like trying to force yourself not to think about pink elephants or to force yourself to relax—you can't do it. The best thing to do is to *gently bring yourself back to the sound of my voice*. Allow the thoughts to come and go without effort—always returning to what I am saying to you. The *hardest thing* for you to do is to *try not to do anything* except listen to the sound of my voice. *Your greatest challenge is to just let happen whatever will happen*—to just sit back and enjoy whatever experience you may have.

Some people worry about whether there are any ill or *bad effects*. On the contrary, this is a very pleasurable, relaxing experience, and is often employed to reduce tension and to make people feel good. *Nothing will ever be done to embarrass you or to make you uncomfortable*. Because you will be the one doing everything—you will be in complete control. You will always be able to come out any time that you want to—*there is no danger whatsoever that you will not "wake up."* The worst thing that has ever happened to someone is that they become so relaxed that they fall asleep. But please don't fall asleep.

Do you have *any questions* about anything I've said so far?

There are *many ways to induce this altered state*. The one that I will be using with you involves helping you to *become completely relaxed* from your feet to your head and then *asking you to imagine various things*.

(Assessing for imagery ability.) *When you think about or imagine something–what is that experience like for you? Do you see pictures or scenes–do you hear things–etc.? How detailed is it? Do you get a clear picture–do you see colors–etc*. or do you just imagine things without seeing them?

Now, I'd like you to close your eyes for just a moment and imagine that you are *somewhere where you feel very calm and relaxed*–totally free of tension and care. Maybe you imagine yourself on a beach or in the mountains. We'll be calling this *your calm scene*, and we'll be using it during the induction. *Tell me about your scene*–what it is like–*in as much detail* as you can imagine it. You should be by yourself–without the distraction of other people–and you shouldn't imagine doing anything in this scene except relaxing and enjoying it.

In addition to asking you to imagine your calm scene during the induction, I'll also be asking you to imagine your immune system. Immunal Imagery Interview Form:

a. There's a subpopulation of white blood cells, or lymphocytes, which become active in the presence of a foreign substance or cancers. This subpopulation of cells directly attack the foreign agent like sharks attacking meat or pac-man eating its foes. Provide your own description of these cells: ________

____

____

b. I next correct any images where lymphocytes are smaller and/or less active than germs or cancers [10].

____

____

____

________________ Do you have any questions? YES ____NO____

If yes, address them: ________________________

____

____

____

How do you feel about doing this induction? ______________________

____

____

____

Do you wear contact lenses? YES_____ NO _____ If subjects' legs are crossed, please have him/her uncross them. OK–we're ready to begin.

Do you have any further questions or concerns?

Now *remember*, the hardest thing for you to do is *not to try*–to just listen to the sound of my voice and the things I am saying to you. Hypnosis is *effortless*–just allow yourself to let go–to *experience whatever happens*. You'll be the one doing it, and you can become *as deeply hypnotized as you allow yourself to be*. Don't analyze what is going on–just experience it. Allow yourself to become absorbed in this process.

Induction

Now, recline the chair and put yourself in as *comfortable a position* as possible. Don't cross your arms or legs. When you feel ready, *close your eyes*. You'll be keeping them closed through the whole session.

The only thing you have to do is *listen to the sound of my voice*. Just allow yourself to experience the pleasant feelings of hypnosis as you let yourself go more and more. I'll *begin by asking you to relax your body*, from your feet to your head. Don't try to force anything–just listen to the sound of my voice–without any effort. Just pay attention to the sound of my voice.

The first thing you may notice is the *feeling of the chair beneath your body*. Feel how it is holding you up–completely supporting you without any effort on your part. The chair is strong and it supports you as you listen to the sound of my voice.

Now gently bring your attention down to your *left foot*, down to the very tips of the left toes. Perhaps you will become aware of the feel of the shoe against your left foot and toes. Now begin relaxing the muscles in your left foot and toes–allow those muscles to begin loosening–relaxing–letting go of tension. If your mind becomes distracted and moves on to something else–that's okay–just gently bring it back, and keep relaxing and letting go as we continue this process. Allow that left foot to loosen more and more, as you sit in the chair and feel the chair supporting you. Good. Just keep gently relaxing.

Allow that feeling of relaxation to flow upward through the foot and the ankle–into the *left calf*. Notice the sensations in the left calf, and as you do, allow those muscles to start loosening–relaxing–letting go of tension–gently. Stay with these feelings, stay with this process. Gently rest your mind, as you continue relaxing your body. Good.

Allow that feeling of relaxation to flow upward–through your left calf and knee into your *left thigh*. Begin allowing the muscles in your left thigh to start loosening–relaxing–letting go of tension–gently. Let those muscles loosen–stay with those feelings. Good. Feel the chair beneath you supporting you and that left leg as you allow yourself to become more relaxed. Allow your mind to rest more and more. You may begin sinking into the chair as you allow your body to relax more and more. Good. Just continue resting and relaxing your left leg.

Now gently bring your attention to your *right foot*, down to the very tips of your right toes. You may feel the shoe against your right foot. Now begin relaxing the muscles in your right foot and toes. Allow those muscles to begin loosening–relaxing–letting go of tension–gently. Good. Notice what sensations may develop as you allow your right foot to relax.

Allow these feelings of relaxation to flow upward through your right foot and ankle into your *right calf*. Begin allowing the muscles in your right calf to begin loosening–relaxing–letting go of tension–gently. Stay with those feelings. Rest your mind as you begin resting your body. Good.

Allow those feelings to flow upward through your right calf and knee into your *right thigh*. Begin allowing the muscles in your right thigh to begin loosening–relaxing–letting go of tension–gently.

Begin relaxing *both hips* along with both legs. Feel the chair beneath both hips as you begin allowing them to loosen–relax–letting go of tension–gently.

Allow the muscles in your *abdomen and stomach* to begin relaxing. Allow them to loosen–relax–letting go of tension–gently. Good. Resting your mind more and more as you're resting your body.

Now the muscles in your *chest and torso*–allow them to loosen–relax–letting go of tension–gently. Allow your breathing to be calm and regular–calm and regular–calm and regular. Continue relaxing your body–gently. Good. Resting your mind. Feel the chair supporting you as you allow yourself to become more and more relaxed. Good.

Now bring your attention down to your *left hand*, down to the very tips of the left fingers. Begin allowing those muscles to start loosening–relaxing–letting go of tension–gently. Feel whatever sensations of relaxation you may be feeling.

Allow the muscles in that left hand to continue relaxing as you allow it to flow through–relaxing the left wrist and forearm–relaxing the muscles through the elbow to the *upper part of the left arm*. Allow the muscles in the entire left arm to begin loosening–relaxing–letting go of tension–gently. Good. Continue resting your mind–just simply listening to the sound of my voice as you relax your body. Good.

Now gently bring your attention over to your *right hand*, down to the very tips of the right fingers. As you do, focus in on those sensations, and begin allowing the muscles in the right hand to start loosening–relaxing–letting go of tension–gently.

Allow those muscles to continue relaxing as you allow the sensations of relaxation to flow through the right hand and wrist into the *right forearm*. Begin relaxing, through the forearm and the elbow to the *upper part of the right arm*–relaxing. Now gently begin allowing the muscles in the entire right arm to begin loosening–relaxing–gently letting go of tension. Good. Continue relaxing the body.

Relax both *shoulders* now along with both arms. Allow your shoulders to begin loosening–relaxing–letting go of tension.

As you are aware of the feeling of the chair beneath your body–let the chair support your *head and neck* muscles so that you don't have to hold any tension in your neck. As the chair supports you, allow the muscles in your neck and throat to begin loosening–relaxing–letting go of tension–gently. Good.

Now the muscles in your lower jaw, mouth and lips. Allow your *jaw muscles* to hang loosely–relax. Now allow your face–your *cheeks, forehead, temples*–up through the top of your head–to relax–letting go of tension–gently. From the top of the head to the bottom of the feet–continue gently relaxing. Good. Very good. Resting your mind as you listen to the sound of my voice.

I want you now to imagine, as vividly as you can (insert *Calm scene*–for example), being out there on a warm sunny beach. You're the only person there. Imagine lying out there. Imagine the emotions that you would feel. Perhaps you imagine being more and more relaxed. Is it possible for you to imagine a warm breeze gently blowing across your face–your arms–your legs? Can you imagine the ocean endlessly moving toward the shore and then back out to sea–rushing toward the shore and then back out to sea–and seeing the ocean extending out into the horizon? Can you imagine what emotions and feelings that would raise inside of you? Can you imagine lying out there and seeing the sand–different shades–darker where it's wet–perhaps brighter and shinier where it's drier. Just lie out there and relax. Look around and enjoy what you might enjoy, look and see what you might imagine and see or experience. And perhaps it might be possible for you to become more relaxed just lying out there–in this peaceful place. Good.

I'm now going to *count from 1 to 20*. As I count, I want you to allow yourself to sink deeper and deeper into relaxation. To assist you in this you might imagine yourself on a cloud up in the sky floating down as I count higher and higher. Or you might imagine yourself in an elevator at the top floor going down into the basement so that when I get to the end you are all the way down. Or sinking down into the chair, or into your own mind, or any image you may wish. Again–do this without any effort–without analyzing how deep you are getting–it's not important. However deep you will go will be fine for our purposes. Let it happen automatically–just allow yourself to go deeper.

Ready–let's begin. 1 start sinking down–deeper and deeper. 2–more and more. 3–gently–down–down–down. 4–deeper–deeper. 5–more–more. 6–down–down–down. 7–deeper–deeper. 8–more–more. 9–deeper–deeper. 10–down–down–down. 11–deeper–deeper. 12–more–more. 13–deeper–deeper. 14–more–more. 15–down–down–down. 16–deeper–deeper. 17–more–more. 18–down–down–down. 19–deeper–deeper–deeper. 20–All the way down–relaxed–listening to the sound of my voice.

I want you to stay in this place for a moment, relaxed, able to hear the sound of my voice. I'm going to ask you to do something from this place. *Extend your right arm*–staying relaxed–I'll help you. Extend your right arm–straight out–good. Now imagine a heavy weight on that right arm–see it, feel it, it's going to begin to push your arm toward the chair. As it does, allow it to push your mind deeper and deeper down into an altered state so that when your hand touches the chair you'll be even more deeply relaxed and hypnotized. Pushing your thoughts deeper so that when your hand and arm touch the chair you can be even more deeply relaxed. Good. All the way down, deeply relaxed. The weight is gone. Your arm is back to normal. Deeply relaxed. And just listening gently to the sound of my voice. Very good. Very good.

Now I want you to imagine your immune system, your white blood cells. Imagine them swimming around increasing in numbers and activity level. Feel them, imagine them, experience them in any way you feel most comfortable. Imagine them attacking and destroying germs/or cancer cells. (Allow about 5 minutes.)

These immune cells will continue to increase in numbers and activity even when you are not thinking about them. When you practice this at home you will also be able to engage these cells more.

I'm now going to *count backwards from 10 to 1*. When I get to 5, I want you to open your eyes. When I get to 1, I want you to be completely awake. Remember, when I get to 5 open your eyes–at 1 be completely awake–out of hypnosis–at 1 be completely awake–feeling refreshed, perhaps relaxed–with a continuation of this feeling of relaxation, but being completely awake and alert. OK–ready–let's go. 10–9–8–7–6–5–open your eyes–4–3–2–1–fully awake.

How do you feel? What was that experience like for you? Was that what you expected? Were you deeply relaxed? Was your attention focused in? How was the imagery–clear? Could you describe what you imagined? Did you always hear my voice? After this I will hand subjects a self-regulation homework sheet with instructions for home practice.

SELF REGULATION HOMEWORK FORM

(Do 2 times a day)

1. Relax your body from feet to head.
2. Imagine being in your calm scene.
3. Count to yourself from 1 to 20 floating down on a cloud becoming deeper and deeper relaxed and hypnotized.
4. Immunal imagery.
5. Count backwards to yourself from 10 to 1. At 5 open your eyes, and at 1 be completely awake.
6. Write down the time and date of each self-hypnosis session (e.g., 7/16/86, 7:00 p.m.) and bring this sheet in with that information at the next session.

REFERENCES

1. R. Adler (ed.), *Psychoneuroimmunology*, Academic Press, New York, 1981.
2. J. B. Jemmott, Psychoneuroimmunology: The New Frontier, *American Behavioral Scientist, 28*:4, pp. 497-509, 1985.
3. J. B. Jemmott and S. E. Locke, Psychosocial Factors, Immunologic Meditation, and Human Susceptibility to Infectious Diseases: How Much Do We Know? *Psychological Bulletin, 95*:1, pp. 78-108, 1984.
4. M. P. Rogers, D. Dubey and P. Reich, The Influence of the Psyche and the Brain or Immunity and Disease Susceptibility: A Critical Review, *Psychosomatic Medicine, 41*:2, pp. 147-164, 1979.
5. H. R. Hall, Hypnosis and the Immune System: A Review with Implications for Cancer and the Psychology of Healing, *American Journal of Clinical Hypnosis, 25*:2-3, pp. 92-103, 1983.
6. H. Benson, *The Relaxation Response*, Avon Books, New York, 1975.
7. ———, *Beyond the Relaxation Response*, Berkley Books, New York, 1985.
8. T. X. Barber, Changing "Unchangeable" Bodily Processes by (Hypnotic) Suggestions: A New Look at Hypnosis, Cognitions, Imagining, and the Mind-Body Problems, in *Imagination and Healing*, A. A. Sheikh (ed.), Baywood Publishing Company, Inc., Amityville, New York, pp. 69-127, 1984.
9. W. S. Agras, The Behavioral Treatment of Somatic Disorders, in *Handbook of Behavioral Medicine*, W. D. Gentry (ed.), The Guilford Press, New York, pp. 479-530, 1984.
10. H. R. Hall, Imagery and Cancer, in *Imagination and Healing*, A. A. Sheikh (ed.), Baywood Publishing Company, Inc., Amityville, New York, pp. 159-169, 1984.
11. A. A. Sheikh and R. G. Kunzendorf, Imagery, Physiology and Psychosomatic Illness, *International Review of Mental Imagery, 1*, pp. 95-138, 1984.
12. National Institute of Mental Health, *Science Reports: Biofeedback–Issues in Treatment Assessment*, U.S. Department of Health and Human Services, Rockville, 1980.

13. W. Luthe and J. H. Schultz, *Autogenic Therapy: Autogenic Methods, Volume 1*, Grune and Stratton, 1969.
14. R. A. Rescorla, Pavlovian Conditioning: It's Not What You Think It Is, *American Psychologist, 43*:3, 151–166, 1988.
15. A. Dickinson, *Contemporary Animal Learning Theory*, Cambridge University Press, London, 1980.
16. E. R. Kandel and L. Tauc, Heterosynaptic Facilitation in Neurones of the Abdominal Ganglion of Aplysia Depilans, *Journal of Physiology, 181*, pp. 1-27, 1965.
17. R. Ader and N. Cohen, Conditioned Immunopharmacologic Responses, in *Psychoneuroimmunology*, R. Ader (ed.), Academic Press, New York, pp. 281-319, 1981.
18. ————, Behavior and the Immune System, in *Handbook of Behavioral Medicine*, W. D. Gentry (ed.), The Guilford Press, New York, 1984.
19. N. H. Spector, Old and New Strategies in the Conditioning of Immune Responses, *Annals of The New York Academy of Sciences, 496*, pp. 522–531, 1987.
20. V. K. Ghanta, T. Miura, N. S. Hiramoto, and R. N. Hiramoto, Augmentation of Natural Immunity and Regulation of Tumor Growth by Conditioning, *Annals of the New York Academy of Sciences, 521*, pp. 29–42, 1988.
21. R. M. Gorczynski, S. Macrae, and M. Kennedy, Conditioned Immune Responses Associated With Allogeneic Skin Grafts in Mice, *The Journal of Immunology, 129*:2, pp. 704–709, 1982.
22. G. MacQueen, J. Marshall, M. Perdue, S. Siegel, and J. Bienenstock, Pavlovian Conditioning of Rat Mucosal Mast Cells to Secrete Rat Mast Cell Protease II, *Science, 243*, pp. 83–85, 1989.
23. L. J. Kamin, Predictability Surprise, Attention and Conditioning, in *Punishment and Aversive Behavior*, B. A. Campbell and R. M. Church (ed.), Appleton-Century-Crofts, New York, 1969.
24. V. Riley, Psychoneuroendocrine Influences on Immunocompetence and Neoplasia, *Science, 212*, pp. 1100–1109, 1981.
25. A. A. Monjan and M. T. Collector, Stress-Induced Modulation of the Immune Response, *Science, 196*, pp. 307–308, 1977.
26. L. S. Sklar and H. Anisman, Contributions of Stress and Coping to Cancer Development and Growth, in *Stress and Cancer*, K. Bammer and B. H. Newberry (eds.), C. J. Hogrefe, Inc., Toronto, pp. 98–136, 1981.
27. S. B. Friedman, R. Ader, and L. J. Grota, Protective Effect of Noxious Stimulation in Mice Infected with Rodent Malaria, *Psychosomatic Medicine, 35*:6, pp. 525-537, 1973.
28. J. B. Jemmott, J. Z. Borysenko, M. Borysenko, D. C. McClelland, R. Chapman, D. Meyer and H. Benson, Academic Stress, Power Motivation and Decrease in Secretion Rate of Salivary Secretory Immunoglobulin A, *Lancet, 25*, pp. 1400–1402, 1983.
29. J. K. Kiecolt-Glaser, R. Glaser, D. Williger, J. Stout, G. Messick, S. Sheppard, D. Ricker, S. C. Romicher, W. Bonnell, and R. Donnerberg, Psychosocial Modifiers of Immuneocompetence in Medical Students, *Psychosomatic Medicine, 46*:1, pp. 7–14, 1984.

30. T. H. Holmes and R. H. Rahe, The Social Readjustment Rating Scale, *Journal of Psychosomatic Research, 11*, pp. 213–218, 1967.
31. R. W. Bartrop, E. Luckhurst, L. Lazarus, L. G. Kiloh, and R. Penny, Depressed Lymphocyte Function After Bereavement, *Lancet*, April 16, pp. 834–836, 1977.
32. S. J. Schleifer, S. E. Keller, M. Camerino, J. C. Thornton, and M. Stein, Suppression of Lymphocyte Stimulation Following Bereavement, *JAMA, 250*: 3, pp. 374–378, 1983.
33. Z. Kronfol, J. Silva, J. Greden, S. Dembinski, R. Gardner and B. Carroll, Impaired Lymphocyte Function in Depressive Illness, *Life Sciences, 33*: 3, pp. 241–247, 1983.
34. S. Locke and D. Colligan, *The Healer Within: The New Medicine of Mind and Body*, E. P. Dutton, New York, p. 62, 1986.
35. R. S. Lazarus and S. Folkman, Coping and Adaptation, in *Handbook of Behavioral Medicine*, W. D. Gentry (ed.), Guilford Press, New York, pp. 282–325, 1984.
36. S. Greer and T. Morris, Psychological Attributes of Women Who Develop Breast Cancer: A Controlled Study, *Journal of Psychosomatic Research, 19*, pp. 147–153, 1975.
37. S. Greer, T. Morris and K. W. Pettingale, Psychological Response to Breast Cancer: Effect on Outcome, *Lancet*, October 13, pp. 785–787, 1979.
38. K. W. Pettingale, S. Greer, and D. E. H. Tee, Serum IgA and Emotional Expression in Breast Cancer Patients, *Journal of Psychosomatic Research, 21*, pp. 395–399, 1977.
39. S. M. Levy, R. B. Herberman, A. M. Maluish, B. Schlien, and M. Lippman, Prognostic Risk Assessment in Primary Breast Cancer by Behavioral and Immunological Parameters, *Health Psychology, 4*, 4, pp. 99–113, 1985.
40. M. L. Laudenslager, S. M. Ryan, R. C. Drugan, R. L. Hyson, S. F. Maier, Coping and Immunosuppression: Inescapable But Not Escapable Shock Suppresses Lymphocyte Proliferation, *Science, 221*, pp. 568–570, 1983.
41. S. E. Locke, L. Kraus, J. Leserman, M. W. Hurst, J. S. Heisel, and R. M. Williams, Life Change Stress, Psychiatric Symptoms and Natural Killer Cell Activity, *Psychosomatic Medicine, 46*:5, pp. 441–453, 1984.
42. D. C. McClelland, E. Floor, R. J. Davidson, and C. Saron, Stressed Power Motivation, Sympathetic Activation, Immune Function, and Illness, *Advances, 2*:2, pp. 42–52, 1985.
43. B. S. Peavey, G. F. Lawlis, and A. Goven, Biofeedback—Assisted Relaxation: Effects on Phagocyte Capacity, *Biofeedback and Self-Regulation, 10*:1, pp. 33–47, 1985.
44. J. K. Kiecolt-Glaser, R. Glaser, D. Williger, J. Stout, G. Messick, S. Sheppard, D. Ricker, S. C. Romisher, W. Briner, G. Bonnell and R. Donnerberg, Psychosocial Enhancement of Immunocompetence in a Geriatric Population, *Health Psychology, 4*: 11, pp. 25–41, 1985.
45. M. L. Jasnoski and J. Kugler, Relaxation, Imagery, and Neuroimmodulation, *Annals of the New York Academy of Sciences, 496*, pp. 722–730, 1987.

46. K. M. Dillon, B. Minchoff, and K. H. Baker, Positive Emotional States and Enhancement of The Immune System, *International Journal of Psychiatry in Medicine, 15*:1, pp. 13–18, 1985–86.
47. J. Z. Borysenko, Healing Motives: An Interview with David C. McClelland, *Advances, 2*:2, pp. 35, 1985.
48. H. D. Udelman and D. L. Udelman, Current Explorations in Psychoimmunology, *American Journal of Psychotherapy, 37*: 2, pp. 210–221, 1983.
49. H. R. Hall, Hypnosis, Suggestions and the Psychology of Healing: A Historical Perspective, *Advances, 3*: 3, pp. 29–37, 1986.
50. S. Black, J. H. Humphrey, and J. S. F. Niven, Inhibition of Mantoux Reaction by Direct Suggestion Under Hypnosis, *British Medical Journal, June 22*, pp. 1649–1652, 1963.
51. R. A. Good, Foreward: Interactions of the Body's Major Networks, in *Psychoneuroimmunology*, R. Ader (ed.), Academic Press, New York, pp. xvii–xix, 1981.
52. G. R. Smith, J. M. McKenzie, D. J. Marmer, and R. W. Steele, Psychologic, Modulation of The Human Immune Response to Varicella Zoster, *Archives of Internal Medicine, 145*, pp. 2110–2112, 1985.
53. K. Olness, T. Culbert, and D. Uden, Self-Regulation of Salivary Immunoglobulin A by Children, *Pediatrics, 83*: 1, pp. 66–71, 1989.
54. P. W. Sheehan, Hypnosis and The Processes of Imagination, in *Hypnosis: Developments in Research and New Perspectives*, E. Fromm and R. E. Shur (eds.), Aldine Publishing Co., New York, pp. 381–411, 1979.
55. M. T. Orne, The Simulation of Hypnosis: Why, How and What it Means, *The International Journal of Clinical and Experimental Hypnosis XIX*, 4, pp. 183–210, 1971.
56. K. S. Bowers and P. Kelly, Stress, Disease, Psychotherapy and Hypnosis, *Journal of Abnormal Psychology, 85*, pp. 490–505, 1979.
57. K. S. Bowers, *Hypnosis for the Seriously Curious*, W. W. Norton and Company, New York, 1976.
58. N. Miller, Personal Communication.
59. H. C. White, Hypnosis in Bronchial Asthma, *Journal of Psychosomatic Research, 5*, pp. 272–279, 1961.
60. N. P. Spanos, R. J. Stenstrom, and J. C. Johnston, Hypnosis, Placebo, and Suggestions in The Treatment of Warts, *Psychosomatic Medicine, 50*, pp. 245–260, 1988.
61. S. E. Locke, B. J. Ransil, N. A. Covino, J. Toczydlowski, C. M. Lohse, H. F. Dvorak, K. A. Arndt, and F. H. Frankel, Failure of Hypnotic Suggestion to Alter Immune Response to Delayed-Type Hypersensitivity Antigens, *Annals of the New York Academy of Sciences, 496*, pp. 745–749, 1987.
62. S. Locke, Personal Communication.
63. H. R. Hall, Research in the Area of Voluntary Immunomodulation: Complexities, Consistencies and Future Research Considerations, *The International Journal of Neuroscience, 47*, pp. 81–89, 1989.
64. E. R. Hilgard and J. R. Hilgard, *Hypnosis in the Relief of Pain*, William Kaufman, Inc., Los Altos, California, 1983.

65. E. L. Rossi, *The Psychobiology of Mind-Body Healing: New Concepts of Therapeutic Hypnosis*, W. W. Norton and Company, New York, 1986.
66. C. B. Pert, The Wisdom of The Receptors: Neuropeptides, the Emotions, and Bodymind, *Advances, 3*: 3, pp. 8-16, 1986.
67. A. M. Weitzenhoffer, *Stanford Hypnotic Susceptibility Scale, Form C*, Consulting Psychologist Press, Palo Alto, 1962.

Index

Contributors

ARREED F. BARABASZ, Ph.D. Dr. Barabasz is Professor in the Department of Counseling Psychology at Washington State University. He is the founding editor of the *Child Study Journal*, a recipient of numerous professional awards, and author of more than 70 publications.

ANNA BERTI, M.D. Dr. Berti, a clinical and experimental neuropsychologist and author of several research papers, is currently on the faculty of Instituto di Clinica Neurologica, Universita di Milano, Italy.

EDOARDO BISIACH, M.D. Dr. Bisiach is Professor of Clinical Neuropsychology at Instituto de Clinica Neurologica, Universita di Milano, Italy. He is widely recognized for his contribution in the field and is currently on the editorial boards of *Brain, Neuropsychologica, and Cortex*.

PIERRE FLOR-HENRY, M.D. Dr. Flor-Henry is the Director of Admissions at the Psychiatric Treatment Centre, Alberta Hospital, Edmonton, Alberta, Canada. He is internationally recognized for his contributions in the field of neuropsychology and is the author of more than 100 scientific publications.

HOWARD HALL, Ph.D. Dr. Hall is Assistant Professor in the Department of Pediatrics at Case Western Reserve University School of Medicine, Cleveland, Ohio. He is highly regarded for his contributions in the field of hypnosis and healing and has published and lectured widely.

MARTHA KOUKKOU, M.D. Dr. Koukkou is on the faculty of the Research Department, Hospital of Psychiatry, Zurich, Switzerland, and the Department of Physiology, University of Athens Medical School. She is a recipient of several awards for her contributions.

ROBERT G. KUNZENDORF, Ph.D. Dr. Kunzendorf is Associate Professor of Psychology at the University of Lowell. He has published extensively in the field of hypnosis and imagery and is President-Elect of the American Association for the Study of Mental Imagery.

JENNIFER LANGHINRICHSEN, Ph.D. Dr. Langhinrichsen recently received her Ph.D. in psychology from the University of Oregon and currently is an intern in the Department of Psychology, Veterans Administration Hospital, Palo Alto, California.

DIETRICH LEHMANN, Ph.D. Dr. Lehmann is Professor of Clinical Neurophysiology and Chief of Brain Mapping Laboratory in the Department of Neurology at University Hospital, Zurich, Switzerland. He is a member of the editorial boards of several journals and co-chairman of the International Society for Brain Electric-Magnetic Topography.

COLIN MARTINDALE, Ph.D. Dr. Martindale, Professor of Clinical Psychology at the University of Maine, is a prolific writer and is internationally known for his contributions in the field of art and creativity. He is the editor of *Empirical Studies of the Arts*.

ANEES A. SHEIKH, Ph.D. Dr. Sheikh, Professor and Chairman of the Department of Psychology at Marquette University, is well known for his contributions in the field of mental imagery. He is past President of the American Association for the Study of Mental Imagery and Editor of the Baywood *Imagery and Human Development Series*.

DAVID SPIEGEL, M.D. Dr. Spiegel is Associate Professor of Psychiatry and Behavioral Sciences, Stanford University School of Medicine. He is the author of numerous papers, book chapters, and books in the field of hypnosis, and he is Associate Editor of *American Journal of Clinical Hypnosis* and Advisory Editor of *International Journal of Clinical and Experimental Hypnosis.*

CHARLES T. TART, Ph.D. Dr. Tart is Professor of Psychology at the University of California at Davis and is internationally known for his research in the area of altered states of consciousness, transpersonal psychology, and parapsychology. His numerous works include his latest book, *Open Mind, Discriminating Mind: Reflections on Human Possibilities.*

DON M. TUCKER, Ph.D. Dr. Tucker is Professor of Psychology at the University of Oregon. He has published and lectured widely and is a member of the Board of Governors of the International Organization of Psychophysiology.